D# 238256

P9-AGV-095

4/11/81 B.S.

DATE D

WORDPLAYS 3

WORDPLAYS 3

© 1984 Copyright by Performing Arts Journal Publications

Taxes: © 1976, 1984 Copyright by Murray Mednick
A Movie Star Has to Star in Black and White: © 1976, 1984 Copyright by Adrienne Kennedy
Right of Way: © 1978, 1984 Copyright by Richard Lees
Hajj . The Performance: © 1984 Copyright by Lee Breuer
Clear Glass Marbles and *Rodeo:* © 1982, 1984 Copyright by Alexander Speer, Trustee for Jane Martin
Native Speech: © 1977, 1984 Copyright by Eric Overmyer

Library of Congress Cataloging in Publication Data
Wordplays 3
Library of Congress Catalog Card No.: 83-62622
ISBN: 0-933826-59-1 (cloth)
ISBN: 0-933826-60-5 (paper)

Design: Gautam Dasgupta
Printed in the United States of America

Publication of this book has been made possible in part by a grant from the National Endowment for the Arts, Washington, D.C., a federal agency, and public funds received from the New York State Council on the Arts.

PAJ Playscripts:
General Editors: Bonnie Marranca and Gautam Dasgupta

WORDPLAYS 3

an anthology of
New American Drama

Performing Arts Journal Publications
New York

THE WORDPLAYS SERIES

We published the first edition of *Wordplays* in 1980, and the book's reception, both in the theatre and in places where theatre is taught, was so positive that we decided to expand the concept into a series. *Wordplays 2* followed, and now we have *Wordplays 3*.

Wordplays is about new approaches to writing for the theatre by American playwrights. We choose plays that we think audiences should know about, hoping that this will give the plays a longer life in the theatre through productions. Sometimes we include writers who have never been published before, others who are not known throughout the country but we feel they should be, and we always want to publish writers who already have a history in the theatre.

For us, the most important thing is that the writing go beyond the cliche into something more provocative, even more difficult at times, to bring us closer to the kind of characters, the feeling of communication, of time, and of space, and the processes of thinking that outline the contemporary experience of living. Our hope is that this ongoing *Wordplays* series embraces the panorama of styles and temperaments reflected in contemporary American plays.

The Publishers

THE PAJ PLAYSCRIPT SERIES

Contents

Taxes

Murray Mednick

Taxes was first performed at New York Theatre Strategy in 1976, with the following cast:

Nickels	*William Hickey*
Fletcher	*Richard Bright*
Lucius	*P. L. Carling*
Mrs. Blickenstaff	*Naomi Riseman*
Flora	*Margaret Harrington*
Mary	*Suzanne Schorr*
Lily	*Romola Robb Allrud*
Jerome	*Patrick McCullough*

Director: Murray Mednick
Sets: William Mikulewitz
Lights: Clarke W. Thornton
Costumes: Kathi Horne

CHARACTERS:

Nickels
Fletcher
Lucius
Mrs. Blickenstaff
Flora (Nickels's wife)
Mary (Flora's younger sister)
Lily
Jerome (Flora and Mary's parents)
Mrs. Smith (Flora's Grandmother, Lily's mother)
2 Young Nurses

SET

The front porch of a California bungalow-style house commonly built around the turn of the century. The porch extends stage left to right then cuts back upstage into darkness from whence Fletcher makes his first entrance. On the porch are several lounges, a table, a rocking chair, an old wheelchair, various plants, and, right, an old, enclosed barbecue equipped with an electric rotisserie. The front walk comes down center.

Scene 1

Dim up to find Nickels rocking slowly, seemingly in agitated observation. A few beats. Enter Fletcher.

NICKELS: Good morning, Fletcher. Not a moment too soon. I was very nearly in a trance there. It's the traffic, Fletcher. It never ceases.

FLETCHER: Yes, an inconvenience being adjacent to the avenue as you are. Quieter in the hills.

NICKELS: Certainly.

FLETCHER: I prefer the hills.

NICKELS: And so do I, Fletcher.

FLETCHER: Less smog, as well.

NICKELS: That depends.

FLETCHER: Oh?

NICKELS: When was the last time you saw them, Fletcher? The hills. They are enshrouded, man, in smog. You can't see the hills for the smog. Look.

FLETCHER: All right.

NICKELS: That means you'd have to go a long way up and out in order to leave the smog behind, Fletcher.

FLETCHER: Still, it would be worth it.

NICKELS: I agree, Fletcher. The smog alone would be insignificant in comparison to this din of motors. (*Pause.*) Listen. Close your eyes and listen. (*They do.*) It's like an endless insect, Fletcher, passing by.

FLETCHER: Hypnotic.

NICKELS: (*Intensely.*) Yes. And it will not be finished going by, Fletcher, in my lifetime. Its body is longer than my lifetime, Fletcher. (*A silence.*)

FLETCHER: How are the women?

NICKELS: Fine.

FLETCHER: The in-laws?

NICKELS: Fine. (*Pause.*) *Whining, voracious beast.*

FLETCHER: (*Opening his eyes.*) One must go on to other things.

NICKELS: I sit here, Fletcher, watching the park. The smog creeping about in the trees. The families picnicking. The joggers jogging. The children swinging. The dogs. And I get a headache, Fletcher. Or I fall asleep.

FLETCHER: Headaches would seem inimical to sleep.

NICKELS: I get a headache when I try to understand it. I fall to dreaming. With my eyes open, staring. It is a singularly dull impression, Fletcher.

FLETCHER: You must try for a greater variety of impression.

NICKELS: That's what I depend on you for, Fletcher. You are my senses. My eyes and ears to the world.

(*Crashing thud of automobiles colliding. A scream. Fletcher leaps to his feet.*)

FLETCHER: What?

NICKELS: An accident, Fletcher. Second today, seventh of the week. Right there at the intersection behind the house. It's a two-way stop, but there ought to be a traffic light. We have petitioned the Chamber of Commerce, the Fire Department, and the Police. But things go on as they have, Fletcher, taking a steady toll of machines, limbs, and blood.

FLETCHER: Look at all the people running.

NICKELS: Yes, they like to see human beings and cars warped and mangled out of shape. They get a charge out of it.

FLETCHER: Perhaps to help—

NICKELS: No, it's the unique impression they're after. Gives them something, to see the mess. Breaks up the illusion of things. Get a boost from it. Like wars and fist-fights.

FLETCHER: Nothing new, I'm afraid.

NICKELS: Not on this planet, Fletcher. Still, tell me what you've seen.

FLETCHER: What I've been through, is more like it.

NICKELS: What you've been through, then.

FLETCHER: The ether.

NICKELS: To the point, Fletcher.

FLETCHER: (*Sigh.*) I went to see the man who sharpens things. Knives, cutters, lawn mowers, blades of every description. (*Sigh.*)

NICKELS: Why, Fletcher! You've lost a hand! What happened?

FLETCHER: I'm coming to that. (*Sigh.*)

NICKELS: Poor fellow.

FLETCHER: I wanted to make an effort to understand him. To learn something from him. The sharpener. He has a lovely little shop. Down on D Street. I brought him my garden tools. Oh, it's a nice place. Machines and instruments for his various manipulations. All shapes and sizes and uses of metal. Motors. A film of soft, black, greasy dust. The smell of oil. Sparks flying. The things of his trade, scattered about as if at random, but each in its proper place, in the manner of craftsmen. I brought him my garden tools. (*Pause.*) Will you help?

NICKELS: Yes, of course.

FLETCHER: Would you—?

NICKELS: I'd be happy to, Fletcher.

FLETCHER: We'll need a sound. A grinder, perhaps. (*Nickels rises, considers.*) Oh, any small electrical engine will do. A suitable whirr, you know.

NICKELS: Yes. (*Goes right, clicks on motor which turns barbecue rotisserie.*) How's that.

FLETCHER: It will do nicely. Thank you.

(*Nickels takes up a position near the barbecue and begins miming the movements of one sharpening a tool.*)

FLETCHER: (*Approaches. Observes.*) I've some things here to be sharpened. Some knives. Garden implements.

NICKELS: Okay. (*Silence.*) I can't do them for you today. If you can come back tomorrow at noon, I'll have them for you then.

FLETCHER: Oh. Well, that would be fine. Perfectly fine.

(*A silence.*)

NICKELS: Just leave them in their bag. Keep them together. Hang the bag on that vise there. I'll know where to find it in the morning.

FLETCHER: All right.

(*A silence.*)

NICKELS: Thank you.

FLETCHER: Well, I'll see you tomorrow then. At noon.

NICKELS: Okay.

FLETCHER: Thank you.

(*He walks uncertainly left, pauses; Nickels turns around and stares out over audience; a beat; Fletcher pulls himself together and reapproaches as Nickels resumes his movements.*)

FLETCHER: Hi.

NICKELS: Hi. (*Pause.*) I haven't done your stuff yet. But I'll get to it in a minute.

FLETCHER: There's no hurry. I don't mind. (*Pause.*) I like to watch a craftsman work. (*A silence.*) I admire people who work with their hands. I can't do anything with my hands. (*A silence.*) I really admire people who are able to earn their living with their hands. I have a lot of respect for it. (*Silence.*) It's good, honest work.

NICKELS: It's okay.

FLETCHER: No, it's more than okay. It's beautiful. Clean, direct, honest. I wish I could do it.

NICKELS: What do you do?

FLETCHER: Me? I'm a philosopher. A teacher of philosophy. I'm in my head all the time.

NICKELS: Sounds like it might be interesting work.

FLETCHER: It's full of lies. I'd rather be a cobbler, or a carpenter, or a plumber. Philosophy is a bunch of bullshit.

NICKELS: You don't say.

FLETCHER: Yeah. I'd just as soon have me a little shop like this one here. Work with my hands. Do a man's job. It has natural integrity, if you know what I mean. I envy you.

NICKELS: Well, it has its good and its bad side, I guess.

FLETCHER: We're not brought up to respect the honest working man, the craftsman, anymore. No, we look up to those who don't have to do an honest day's work for their wages.

NICKELS: You're saying something there.

FLETCHER: There's men in power in this world don't know how to boil an egg.

NICKELS: I'm ready to believe that.

FLETCHER: (*Sigh.*) It's true, I'm afraid. We live in degenerate times. The quality of life is fast diminishing. What's your name?

NICKELS: Randy.

FLETCHER: Glad to meet you, Randy. My name's Fletcher. (*They shake hands.*) Yes, it's all quantity now. The idea of quality's gone down the tubes, Randy. It's a frightening situation. That's why I'm pleased to see a young man who plies an honest craft. (*Silence.*) Who taught you the trade, Randy, if you don't mind my asking.

NICKELS: My grandfather.

FLETCHER: Oh, neat. Passed down in the family. A tradition.

NICKELS: If you'll hand me your bag of things, I'll do them now. (*Pause.*) Yeah, it worked out good for my granddad and good for me. It's only the customers I can't put up with sometimes. Stand silent and steadfast, my granddad used to say. Let them bounce off the walls, let them mire in the grease. You keep your attention to yourself. Sooner or later, they'll go away. (*A silence.*) I never even used to be prejudiced. Always got along with all kinds. The Mex, the blacks, all kinds. I've learnt to be prejudiced now.

FLETCHER: Too bad.

NICKELS: Well, I see how they do. And I don't like it.

FLETCHER: Who?

NICKELS: The Blacks. Stealin' and killin'. Treat each other worse'n pigs. Hostile and mean. Bringin' the property values down. They've just about ruined Pomona.

(*Enter old man Lucius, the gardener.*)

FLETCHER: Don't do no good to hate people. (*Pause.*) Hurts you more'n them. Might blind you to someone you really need to know.

NICKELS: You've got something there.

LUCIUS: I'll tell ya a story.

FLETCHER: Okay.

LUCIUS: I'm over in Pomona cuttin' a lady's grass. With my scythe. Comes lunchtime I drop my scythe and go over to my car, eat a cucumber sandwich, drink a cold beer. It was hotter'n hell. I finish my lunch and go back to the field and the scythe's gone. Stolen. What do you think of that?

FLETCHER: I'm sorry to hear it.

LUCIUS: They stole it. But I'm not prejudiced, myself. Lady I work for is black, and she's nice. Whole family is nice. You know whether I can get another scythe like that one? Old style, ya know, with a handle.

FLETCHER: They don't make 'em anymore, probably. Not like they used to.

NICKELS: You'll be able to find one over at the swap meet down in Chino.

LUCIUS: Think so? When's that on, Saturday or Sunday?

NICKELS: Sunday.

LUCIUS: How much you figure it'll cost?

NICKELS: Five bucks, maybe.

LUCIUS: Well, that's all right. (*Walks slowly away from them to the porch steps; Fletcher follows, discomfited.*) Beautiful day.

FLETCHER: Yes, it is.

LUCIUS: First one in a long while.

FLETCHER: I know.

(*Lucius wanders off. A silence, Fletcher growing increasingly anxious.*)

NICKELS: Your things are ready now.

FLETCHER: Good. Thank you. (*Approaches.*)

NICKELS: You have some fine old tools. Excellent metal.

FLETCHER: Yes, they are heirlooms.

NICKELS: This clipper especially. See?

FLETCHER: Yes.

NICKELS: Try it. You'll want to be careful. Very sharp.

FLETCHER: Uh, yes. I see.

NICKELS: Here. Hold this. I'll show you. (*He gives Fletcher "something" to hold. Fletcher is frightened, distracted. As Nickels is about to demonstrate the clippers, Fletcher inadvertently moves his arm, and Nickels slices his "hand" off.*)

FLETCHER: My hand. My right hand. Oh, my God. (*Runs off, howling.*)

(*Nickels stands a moment in shock, then turns off the barbecue, returns to his chair. Sits. A silence.*)

NICKELS: (*Frantic.*) One bump and you're dead. Be watchful. Be alert. One bump.

(*Mrs. Blickenstaff enters on the sidewalk down left. She makes her way center and turns up towards the house. Nickels leaps to his feet. Mrs. Blickenstaff stops. Nickels sits down again. Mrs. Blickenstaff, using a cane, resumes slowly and with great difficulty up the walk. Nickels shrinks into his chair. Mrs. Blickenstaff works her way laboriously up the porch steps, climbing them one at a time. Stands above Nickels. She is nearly blind.*)

MRS. BLICKENSTAFF: Hello, Mrs. Smith. I haven't seen you in such a long time. How are you, dear?

NICKELS: I'm not Mrs. Smith.

MRS. BLICKENSTAFF: Oh! I'm sorry! I couldn't see you very well from the sidewalk. You looked like Mrs. Smith.

NICKELS: I'm a male person and I'm not that old.

MRS. BLICKENSTAFF: No. I apologize. I am old. Mrs. Smith is very old. Things happen to you when you get old. My vision is not what it once was. I thought you were . . . Where is Mrs. Smith?

NICKELS: She's inside, asleep. She's not well. She lives in a convalescent home.

MRS. BLICKENSTAFF: Oh. Which one? Is it nearby?

NICKELS: It's up the road here in San Dimas. She's incontinent, and she doesn't recognize people. But they let her come home sometimes.

MRS. BLICKENSTAFF: I see. Well, I hope she likes it there. I live up at Hillcrest Manor. It's a home. The food there is wonderful, just wonderful. And we have a little bus, you know, that runs about. But I prefer the exercise of walking. (*Pause.*) Are you a relation?

NICKELS: Mrs. Smith is my wife's grandmother.

MRS. BLICKENSTAFF: Oh. Married, yes. Good. Do you know that American women are bringing up their children now without husbands, alone? It's the trend. They have done with the difficulties of a mate, with no regard for the consequences. What's your name?

NICKELS: Nickels.

MRS. BLICKENSTAFF: Multiply this by millions, Mr. Nickels, and you have an alarming situation. Millions of children growing up without a father. They will be a new breed of creature, Mr. Nickels, a breed to be reckoned with. They will affect everything. Very bad for the country, very bad. I don't know what it can all be leading to. I won't be here to see it . . . but it makes me sad. I fear for the future of this country.

NICKELS: The falcon cannot hear the falconer.

MRS. BLICKENSTAFF: *There* was a writer. A man interested in his past. I used to teach Faulkner, you know. In my high school classes. Bonita High School. I taught American literature. Beginning, intermediary, and advanced. What is your profession?

NICKELS: I'm a philosopher, an observer.

MRS. BLICKENSTAFF: Yes . . . Well . . . Writers are no longer objective, mister. Don't you think? It's their own personal development they're interested in . . . I get tired so easily these days.

(*She begins slowly to descend the steps. Nickels rises and goes inside. Mrs. Blickenstaff turns to him as if he were still there.*)

MRS. BLICKENSTFF: Oh. Will you tell your grandmother that Mrs. Blickenstaff asked for her? Mrs. Blickenstaff.

NICKELS: (*Coming back out.*) Yes?

MRS. BLICKENSTAFF: Oh. Will you mention to your grandmother that Mrs. Blickenstaff called? Perhaps she'll remember me. Mrs. Blickenstaff.

NICKELS: Yes, of course. Thank you for stopping by.

(*He watches her as she makes her way off left. Enter Flora from inside.*)

NICKELS: That was Mrs. Blickenstaff.

FLORA: What did she want?

NICKELS: Greetings to Grandma.

MRS. SMITH: (*Screaming from inside.*) Who was that? Who was that woman?

FLORA: (*To Nickels.*) That's the lady who likes persimmons. It's the persimmons she's after.

NICKELS: Oh?

MRS. SMITH: (*Within.*) Where is she? I want her! Take me outside!

MARY: (*Within.*) All right, Grandma. Take it easy. (*Appears in the screen door holding up Mrs. Smith.*) Flora! (*Flora brings the wheelchair to the door. They put Mrs. Smith in it and wheel her out.*)

MRS. SMITH: Am I a prisoner in my own house?

NICKELS: Christ. (*Goes off in disgust.*)

MRS. SMITH: Where the hell is my visitor? Where'd she go?

(*Mary goes back in, shaking her head.*)

FLORA: She's right here, Grandma.

MRS. SMITH: Well, where? Damn you!

FLORA: (*Voice of an old woman.*) Coming . . .

(*She hobbles down the porch steps, assuming the posture and demeanor of Mrs. Blickenstaff. She goes a little way down the walk until she's completely into it, and turns back.*)

FLORA: (*Approaching.*) Well, Mrs. Smith. Hello, my dear.

MRS. SMITH: I don't know you. I wouldn't know you if you were in my shithouse.

FLORA: (*Indulgently.*) Yes . . . Oh, the time, the time. Where does the time go, Mrs. Smith? All the effort put into time. The losses, the failures, the opportunities missed. Where do our lives go, Mrs. Smith, when we die?

MRS. SMITH: (*After a pause.*) What's that?

FLORA: Time, Mrs. Smith. (*Gazing heavenward.*) Is it up there? In a higher space?

MRS. SMITH: It's up your ass.

FLORA: Is it alive? Suppose that time was a living thing, Mrs. Smith, that history, the body of time, was breathing. What would its breathing mean? (*Taking deep breaths.*) In and out. In and out.

MRS. SMITH: What did you say your name was?

FLORA: Mrs. Blickenstaff, dear.

MRS. SMITH: Where's your horse? Didn't you bring your horse?

FLORA: It could mean that all our sins are truly recorded, Mrs. Smith. Like little tumors in the belly of the worm of time . . .

MRS. SMITH: I was never sick a day in my life, Blickenstein. Are you Jewish? My doctor's a Jew. He owns the hospital, of course. He took me for a ride on his horse and tried to take my clothes off. He got cancer and died. Too much smoking. Too much smog.

FLORA: I see you've got a good crop of persimmons, Mrs. Smith.

MRS. SMITH: They wash me down, wash me down. Always washing me down in soft, warm, downy water. Like tiny feathers tickling. And they put their fingers in. It's fun. That's why I . . . They moved me out of the dining room because of the smell. Stuff just comes out of me. I don't know why. Then they wash me down. I'm glad to get away from all the shits in that shithouse. Noisy fertilizer, not a minute's rest. If your horse and buggy are parked outside, I'd like to go for a ride.

FLORA: May I have some? They're ripe now, and falling.

MRS. SMITH: You look like a spinster. Are you one? Don't like spinsters, never have. They get dried up down there. And they try to steal other people's children from them.

FLORA: No point in letting them go to waste, Mrs. Smith.

MRS. SMITH: You'll have to pay me for them. A nickel apiece. An unfruitful woman's a blot on Nature. Useless. *My* children come to see me all the time. But they're shits. They steal my candy.

FLORA: I don't want many. I haven't time. Don't you understand, you old bitch?

MRS. SMITH: We had horses when I was a girl. We let the manure dry in the barn and used it for our garden. Winters it was so cold we had to ride in the wagon covered with rugs. Icicles hanging from the horse's nose. (*Flora picks up the cane and begins swinging it at the "tree" overhead. Ripe persimmons begin falling one at a time but she can't catch any.*) My Bill will be coming by in his handsome new carriage driving that bay mare of his . . . (*Plop.*) . . . We'll go on to church through the cornfields. Oh, so much corn, you wonder where it goes to! Feeds the nation, I suppose . . . (*Plop.*) . . . He'll let me hold the reins as I'm better with horses than he is. He'll have his hand on my knee. Very gently. Sends a squirrely wiggle up my thigh . . . (*Plop.*) . . . Mary! Mary!

MARY: (*From inside.*) Yes? What do you want?

MRS. SMITH: Come on out here!

MARY: (*Coming out.*) You need something?

MRS. SMITH: Yeah, get some of them persimmons for Mrs. Blickenstein here, will ya?

MARY: All right. (*Climbs a chair and gathers some.*) Here you are.

FLORA: Thank you, my dear. My aim is random, I'm afraid, my fingers palsied, my reflexes . . . unpredictable. Timing's off.

MARY: Don't mention it.

MRS. SMITH: That'll be thirty cents.

(*A beat, then Flora squashes the ripe persimmon in her hands. Two nurses enter wheeling a portable hospital bed.*)

NURSE 1: Hello, Mrs. Smith.

NURSE 2: Hello, Mrs. Smith.

MRS. SMITH: No!

NURSE 2: Time to go, Mrs. Smith.

MRS. SMITH: I want to stay here! This is my house!

NURSE 1: Now, now, Mrs. Smith.

NURSE 2: You know that's not possible. Don't you, Mrs. Smith?

MRS. SMITH: I don't know you! Go back to that shithole you came from!

(*They move her forcibly from the wheelchair to the bed.*)

NURSE 2: We've a lovely party waiting for you, Mrs. Smith.

NURSE 1: With lots of candy.

MRS. SMITH: Candy?

NURSE 1: Yes, dear. You'll have a wonderful time.

(*They wheel her off. Dim out as Nickels reappears and van doors slam, off.*)

Scene 2

Lights up to reveal Fletcher in the wheelchair. One of his legs has been amputated at the knee. A beat. Enter Nickels from inside.

NICKELS: Ah, Fletcher. Fletcher!

FLETCHER: Nickels.

NICKELS: You've lost a limb!

FLETCHER: Yes.

NICKELS: (*After a pause.*) Can you feel it?

FLETCHER: What?

NICKELS: The missing leg.

FLETCHER: Oh, yes. Very much as if it were still there. Invisible, is all.

NICKELS: Does it touch the ground?

FLETCHER: Touch the ground?

NICKELS: The voided foot.

FLETCHER: Oh. Good question. No.

NICKELS: No?

FLETCHER: No. (*Pause.*) It is a bit like reaching for the unreachable. Something of a strain. Never quite touches, you see. Cannot.

NICKELS: Passes through?

FLETCHER: Through?

NICKELS: Like x-rays.

FLETCHER: No. Not that sort of matter. Another order, entirely. (*Pause.*) It is an idea. It exists as an idea.

NICKELS: I see.

(*Enter Flora from inside. She moves very slowly, self-consciously, gracefully, as if performing an inner ballet. She holds her head erect, trying to keep it aligned directly with her spine. Nickels watches her intently. She waters some plants, snips flowers, rearranges, slips a cigarette from Nickels's pack, retires slowly through the door. Nickels sighs heavily.*)

NICKELS: Strange woman. (*Sighs.*) I can't make her out. Is she sad? Purposefully silent? Sick? Is she exercising some secret faculty? I don't know what's going on in there, Fletcher.

FLETCHER: An inward pirouette, surely.

NICKELS: (*Shouting.*) Flora! Flora! (*No response.*)

FLETCHER: She didn't hear you.

NICKELS: She heard me, all right. Not listening. She's feeding her damn fish, is what she's doing. Feeding her fish. She may have drowned for all I know.

FLETCHER: Drowned?

NICKELS: In the fishpond . . . in her thoughts! Anything can happen, Fletcher. We're skating on thin ice.

(*A pause, then the loud crash of automobiles colliding, as before.*)

FLETCHER: *My God.*

NICKELS: An accident, Fletcher. First today. Right there at the intersection behind the house. It's a two way stop, but there ought to be a traffic light. We have petitioned the Chamber of Commerce, the Fire Department, and the Police. But things go on as they have, Fletcher, taking a steady toll . . . Oh, the retracted appendage, Fletcher.

FLETCHER: Consumed.

NICKELS: Consumed?

FLETCHER: Combustion.

NICKELS: Good Grief, man.

FLETCHER: I went to see the neighborhood welder. His name is Mr. Gregory. He doesn't pay his taxes. (*Rises, on crutches, goes to the barbecue and turns it on. Nickels also rises, puts a baseball cap on backwards, puts a football helmet over that, "becomes" the welder.*)

NICKELS: Good morning, sir.

FLETCHER: Good morning, Mr. Gregory. This is the drive shaft on my power mower. It has need of welding.

NICKELS: Can you pay me in cash or kind?

FLETCHER: Not cash, certainly.

NICKELS: Well, what can you barter then?

FLETCHER: I am a professor of philosophy.

NICKELS: Verbiage is of no use to me whatever.

FLETCHER: I understand.

NICKELS: You see, sir, I can have no seizable liquidity. They will garnishee all attachable assets.

FLETCHER: They?

NICKELS: The Internal Revenue Service, sir. The extortion branch of the federal mafia, if you don't mind my saying so.

FLETCHER: Not at all. I am myself a constitutionalist.

NICKELS: Be that as it may, I do not recommend nonpayment of taxes as a course of action for redress of grievance. Unless it is done by one and all. Great lengths are employed, sir, to collect. Deprivation of liberty, strong arm, grand theft. The entire machinery of government is used against you. Legions of bureaucrats are planning ingenious methods for the siphoning of one's resources. So you see, I can have no bank account, cash no checks, own no automobile, nor any other form of readily transformable property.

FLETCHER: Are you a member of the New Left?

NICKELS: I am an anarchist-socialist, sir. I hate assholes right and left. In truth, I am a member of my community who works honestly with his hands. I used to be a speechwriter for the conservatives. Though I agree with much in their philosophy, I am no longer a member of that camp. They think that people are inherently lazy good-for-nothings and that measures must be taken to get them to lead useful lives. The liberals are worse. They are the sons of the rich appointed as suzerains over the poor.

FLETCHER: I have chickens. Will you take three in payment?

NICKELS: Make it five.

FLETCHER: Done.

NICKELS: They believe that the poor need governing by benevolent patricians such as themselves. Let power reside in the neighborhoods, sir, in the towns. Leave us to run our own affairs.

FLETCHER: That is my own political philosophy in a nutshell.

NICKELS: (*Staring at him.*) Oh?

FLETCHER: Yes, succinctly.

NICKELS: Well, what are you doing about it?

FLETCHER: Doing?

NICKELS: Doing, sir.

FLETCHER: (*Pause.*) I shall write an article.

NICKELS: (*Sarcastic.*) Wonderful. Here, hold this a moment, will you? While I inspect your drive shaft. (*Hands the "blowtorch" to Fletcher, who has difficulty holding it because of his missing hand.*)

FLETCHER: (*With mounting panic.*) I—? Uh . . . shouldn't the torch be extinguished?

NICKELS: It'll only be a moment, sir. Then I'll get right to your drive shaft.

(*Lucius wanders on.*)

FLETCHER: Uh . . . my chief concern is with education . . . reversing the trend toward mindless barbarism in our youth . . . a study of mechanics . . . technology . . . Plato says . . .

NICKELS: Plato speaks of a community led by conscious men.

LUCIUS: I'll tell you a story about that.

FLETCHER: (*Wheeling, startled.*) What? (*He lets the blowtorch drop too far, burns his leg, runs off howling.*)

LUCIUS: When I was a youngster, the teachers had no union then. But it was a good job to have. A man was glad to get one of those. Steady, secure. Working for the town. Now it's unionized. Now they're trying to organize your government employees into a union. Be the end of freedom in this country. I am a member of a committee—

NICKELS: (*Sadly.*) Not now, Lucius. Now now.

(*Lucius wanders off, mumbling to himself. Nickels removes his headgear, sits in the wheelchair. Observes, listens to the drone of cars. He is suddenly alarmed. He begins racing frantically up and down the porch in the wheelchair, shouting:*)

NICKELS: Flora! Flora! Flora!

(*Mary appears.*)

MARY: What's the matter?

NICKELS: Flora! Oh, Mary! Look!

MARY: Where?

NICKELS: It's a funeral!

MARY: So it is.

NICKELS: Going right down Bonita Avenue.

MARY: I see.

NICKELS: Must be fifty, a hundred cars in low gear with their lights on. It's the eeriest thing I ever saw. The body in the lead black limousine is a dead one. The dear departed. He is being driven to his everlasting rest by another, living being, wearing a black cap. Other beings follow in their machines slowly, in a decorous line. The machines look like . . . they are wild beasts which have been broken, Mary, tamed! Temporarily. They'll run amok again soon enough, my dear, knocking things about. Uh, huh. Wild electrons, Mary, in temporal orbit round the ritual of internment. No, one cell-ed units, organisms, with oftentimes a double nucleus. Two black dots in the window. Altogether in a line they make the funereal tissue. Yes. When the tissue's function has been exhausted, it disbands, disintegrates, dies. (*Mary begins sucking on a tooth.*) Or becomes cancerous. It forgets its original purpose and goes haywire. It divides and multiplies itself. It's growing geometrically. It enters the San Bernardino Freeway. It needs room to breathe. The line extends from Santa Monica to San Berdoo. It's still grow-ing. It's malignant. It spreads south to the border, north to Frisco. There's no stopping it now. They'd have to cut off California. It's too late—the tumor's in Arizona, Nevada, Utah. It's on its way to the heartland—

MARY: I wonder who it was.

NICKELS: What?

MARY: That died.

NICKELS: Oh. (*Pause.*) Look who's coming.

(*Enter Jerome and Lily, down right.*)

MARY: Hi, Mom. Hi, Dad.

NICKELS: Hi, Jer. Hi, Lil.

LILY: Where's Flora?

NICKELS: God knows. She could be anywhere now.

MARY: She's in the kitchen.

LILY: (*Sigh.*) I've got to go and see Mother later.

MARY: She was here yesterday afternoon for a little while.

JEROME: Thank God I missed that.

LILY: How was she, honey?

MARY: Oh, the same.

LILY: I don't know if it's such a good idea, letting her come home. Just makes it harder on everyone.

MARY: She insists, Ma. She won't eat.

NICKELS: How are you, Lil?

MARY: I'm fine. How are you, Nickels?

(*Lily and Mary go in.*)

NICKELS: Dandy. How ya doin', Jer? (*Jerome does not seem to have heard.*) *How ya*

doin', Jer?
JEROME: Great. How you doin'?
NICKELS: Okay.

(*A long silence. Nickels pretends to be busy with some papers.*)

JEROME: You like sitting in that wheelchair? (*Nickels pretends not to hear. A pause.*) Old Lady Smith used to sit in that wheelchair. You look like her to me sometimes. (*Giggles. A long beat, then Nickels rises and moves to another chair. Pause.*) Don't let me bother you.
NICKELS: Huh?
JEROME: I said, don't let me bother you.
NICKELS: Oh. (*Another silence.*)
JEROME: I haven't seen her since we put her in the rest home. I guess I'm not much of a son-in-law.
NICKELS: Oh, I don't know. What would you do if you saw her?
JEROME: There's no love lost between us, anyway. I never could stand the old bitch.

(*A silence.*)

NICKELS: (*Putting aside the papers.*) Do you want a drink, Jer?
JEROME: How's it coming?
NICKELS: What?
JEROME: The work.
NICKELS: Swell. It's coming along *swell. It's only the first half hour that's rough. I don't know why that is. The first half hour is an agony. Always will be. An agony. But once I get my rhythm going then I get some momentum. Rhythm, momentum.*
JEROME: (*Feigning comprehension.*) I see what you mean.
NICKELS: *Would you like a drink, Jerome?*
JEROME: Yeah, okay.
NICKELS: *I know I want one.* (*Goes inside, talking to himself. Jerome rocks in his chair. Re-enter Lucius.*)
LUCIUS: As I was saying to Nickels earlier. Forty percent of your county tax bill goes to support Welfare. I suppose you know that.
JEROME: Sure, I know it. And I don't like it.
LUCIUS: Forty percent. I don't even know those people what's getting the money. They ain't friends. They ain't neighbors.
JEROME: And they ain't white.
LUCIUS: Total strangers. Now, I got nothing against charity, mind you. I'm not a tight ass with my money, I'm no Scrooge. There's them that wouldn't help ya if you was dying on their doorstep. Not if it cost them a few bucks, they wouldn't. I'm not one of those. I'll help a body when he's down. I'll offer a helping hand. I'll put a dollar in his pocket. But I like to know who

the man is. I like to know something about him. And I'd like to be able to say no if I want to.

JEROME: That's why they won't give you the opportunity, of course. Because most people would. They'd say no. Around here they would. No bleeding heart liberals in this neck of the woods.

LUCIUS: Well, I don't know what's to be done about it.

JEROME: Don't vote democrat, I'll tell you that. But I often wonder whether it pays to vote at all these days. Can't tell the sheep from the wolves. Jury duty and junk mail are the only results I can see.

(Re-enter Nickels with drinks. Lucius wanders away shaking his head.)

NICKELS: *Here ya go, Jer.*

JEROME: Oh, thank you . . . *(Pause.)* I don't think he's worth thirty dollars a month. Do you?

NICKELS: *Who?*

JEROME: Lucius. The old man. Is he worth it? I don't think he's worth it. What does he do?

NICKELS: He mows the lawn, he trims, he cuts back, he cultivates the roses.

JEROME: Huh?

NICKELS: *Mows lawn, trims, cuts back, cultivates roses.*

JEROME: Oh. Is it worth thirty dollars a month?

NICKELS: I don't know, Jer. *(A silence.)*

JEROME: Jesus Christ, will you look at that.

NICKELS: What's that, Jer?

JEROME: Huh?

NICKELS: I said, *what's that?*

JEROME: My God, it's disgusting. Look at that guy, he's got his wife out peddling a bicycle. She must weigh three hundred pounds if she weighs a minute. My God, how can a person let themselves go like that. It's pathetic. Look at that. He's got her out riding in the park. Jesus Christ. He ought to lock her up and starve her for a week. Must've gone out and bought himself a couple bicycles and made her get up on one. I don't know how he did it. Sure, he went out and invested in bicycles so she'd lose weight.

NICKELS: No way of knowing. *No way of knowing.*

JEROME: Sure, that's what he'd done. Went out and bought bicycles. Told her to ride or else. I'll bet you that's what happened. Christ, I'd be ashamed to be seen in public with her.

NICKELS: He ain't such a bargain, either. *He ain't no bargain either.*

JEROME: No. *(Laughs.)* My God, I don't know how he puts up with it. Can you imagine that? Being married to it? The bicycle can't hardly keep her in the air.

NICKELS: Look at him, though. *He's ugly.* They deserve each other. *They de-*

serve each other.

JEROME: Yeah. (*Laughs.*) But can you imagine screwing that? Can you imagine walking it to the store? Can you imagine *feeding* it? Can you imagine the *feed* bill?

NICKELS: What's eating her is the question, Jer.

JEROME: Huh?

NICKELS: *Who eats the fat lady?*

JEROME: What do you mean?

NICKELS: *What* eats the fat lady?

JEROME: Nothing, I guess.

NICKELS: *Something eats her, Jer. Everything is eating something. Everything is being eaten. Something wants all that fat to eat.*

JEROME: You don't say.

NICKELS: Yeah.

JEROME: What, then?

NICKELS: I don't know, Jer. *I don't know, Jer. Something.* It's an interesting question. *Question.*

JEROME: Oh.

NICKELS: Are you really hard of hearing, or are you just pretending?

JEROME: Eh?

NICKELS: *Never mind.* (*Moves closer to him.*) See, nothing's wasted in Nature, Jer. If Nature didn't have no use for fat people then there wouldn't be no fat people. Everything is used, everything has a function. It's a food chain, Jer, a food chain. We eat stuff, stuff eats us.

JEROME: Well, I don't feel that's true. Obesity is a disgusting disease and I hate to see it.

NICKELS: Right. Yeah, I understand. Sure. I know how you feel.

(*Enter Flora and Lily.*)

FLORA: Have you seen the garden, Dad?

JEROME: The garden? Yes, I looked at it.

FLORA: Isn't it wonderful?

JEROME: Wonderful? Oh, sure. It's great. (*Nickels exits for fresh drinks.*) You got a lot more zucchini than you'll need. And what are you going to do with all the beets? Too many beets. The tomatoes are falling down. Don't you believe in weeding?

FLORA: Of course, I do.

JEROME: Doesn't look like it. Looks like a jungle out there. Lucky there's all that old chicken shit in the ground or nothing would've come up.

FLORA: Thanks a lot, Dad.

JEROME: Well, I don't see why you can't be like other people and keep your kitchen garden in neat, cultivated rows. You always have to do things different. Why?

LILY: You haven't set an honest working foot in a garden since day one of your existence, Jerome.

JEROME: Don't snap at me, Lil. She asked me about her garden.

LILY: Well, she won't again.

JEROME: Do you think he's worth thirty dollars a month, Lil? I don't think so. I don't think he's worth even half that. What does he do? He doesn't do anything.

LILY: Who?

JEROME: Lucius! Who the hell did you think I meant?

FLORA: He does a lot, Dad.

LILY: Forget it, Jerome. We've been all through this.

JEROME: Well, what's *he* do, then?

FLORA: Lucius?

JEROME: No, Nickels! What's he do?

FLORA: He's a philosopher, Dad.

JEROME: But what's he do? I don't understand him. I don't know what he's doing.

FLORA: Epistemology is his first love.

JEROME: I don't know what that means.

(*Re-enter Nickels with the drinks.*)

NICKELS: Here ya are, Jer. *Here ya are, Jer.* Lil? Sure you don't want one, Lil?

LILY: Positive.

NICKELS: Jeez, I got a case of nerves all of a sudden. Don't know why that happened.

JEROME: Why be so intense? Take it easy, you'll live longer.

NICKELS: There are planets up there, Jer, and we don't know nothing about 'em. *Planets. Don't know*

JEROME: Bunch of rocks. Floating in the sky.

NICKELS: Right, must be the moon.

FLORA: Right, blame it on the moon.

MARY: (*From inside.*) Dinner's ready!

JEROME: About time.

(*Dim out.*)

Scene 3

In the black: sounds of a badminton game. Lights up to reveal Flora about to serve to Mary, Nickels observing. A badminton net interferes with the front walk making a badminton court to scale.

MARY: Score?

FLORA: Eleven.
MARY: You have eleven?
FLORA: Yup.
MARY: You do not.
FLORA: Do.
MARY: Don't!
FLORA: Nickels?
NICKELS: No idea. Haven't been counting. Sorry.
FLORA: Well, I have eleven.
MARY: Oh, all right! Serve. (*Flora serves, wins point, cackles.*)
NICKELS: Advantage, Flora!
FLORA: Twelve! (*Serves again, slammed by Mary.*)
NICKELS: A killer! Bravo!

(*Mary prepares to serve.*)

FLORA: How many you got?
MARY: Ten.
FLORA: I don't believe it, but go ahead and serve.
MARY: What do you mean, you don't believe it?
FLORA: Never mind. Serve.

(*An intense rally, Flora wins back the serve, cackles.*)

NICKELS: Excellent rally! Well played!

(*Flora, cackling and exaggerating her movements for comic effect, wins two more points.*)

FLORA: Point!
MARY: Just serve, will you.

(*Flora serves, Mary slams her with the birdie.*)

NICKELS: Marvelous retort! (*Mary serves, Flora slams her, hard, with the birdie.*)
    Sweet revenge!

(*Flora serves, wins, cackles.*)

FLORA: Game!

(*Nickels applauds.*)

MARY: I quit.

FLORA: (*Bouncily.*) Come on, Nickels.

NICKELS: No.

FLORA: Come on!

NICKELS: I can't, Flora.

FLORA: Why not?

NICKELS: Nervous. Too nervous.

FLORA: Oh, what are you so nervous about, shithead. Get out here and play.

NICKELS: *I'm nervous because I'm nervous and I don't want to play.*

MARY: I'm going to see Grandma.

FLORA: I'll go with you.

NICKELS: *What the hell do you think is going on anyway.* (*They ignore him and leave.*) People cruising around in the smog and blowing folks' brains out with shotguns. *Be careful.* (*A silence. Enter Fletcher, a black patch over one eye.*) Ah, Fletcher. Good to see you.

FLETCHER: (*Wearily.*) My God, man, the noise. The clamor. It is difficult to find peace in these days, even for a moment.

NICKELS: Sit down, sir. Rest yourself.

FLETCHER: Rest? I cannot bear, subjectively, the ominous disquiet. Nor the unrelieved onslaught upon my senses, most especially the grinding of machines. (*Pause.*) I would like to sit in a silent place. But there are none. (*Pause.*) Fear, the anxious beating of wings . . .

NICKELS: Can you not be still?

FLETCHER: I hear voices. So many madly insistent, I fear for my sanity.

NICKELS: But whose voices?

FLETCHER: Mine, man. They are all mine. They take turns to devil me. The recording is in desperate need of an Editor, sir. (*Laughs nervously.*)

NICKELS: It is not hopeless.

FLETCHER: No. There is an instant or two, briefly held, of nothing, of simply being there. (*Bitterly.*) Snatched away in the mouths of demons. Thoughts for my future . . . the genitalia of women . . .

NICKELS: Fletcher?

FLETCHER: Yes?

NICKELS: You are losing organs of perception.

FLETCHER: One eye. An accident.

NICKELS: Self-inflicted?

FLETCHER: No.

NICKELS: I meant to ask you . . . During the moments of being simply, what?

FLETCHER: I am an amateur, man.

NICKELS: Yes, but the whatness of it.

FLETCHER: Oneself.

NICKELS: All right, then.

FLETCHER: A sensation.

NICKELS: Of?

FLETCHER: One's skin. Incipient flotation. . . ? The certainty of loss of concentration to follow.

NICKELS: Oh. (*Another auto crash, as before. Again, Fletcher is startled.*) Second today. Right there at the intersection behind the house. It's a two-way stop, but there ought to be a traffic light. We have petitioned.

FLETCHER: My vision being halved, sound has doubled. (*Sigh.*) You know the saying, "hell is in the senses."

NICKELS: No, never heard that one.

(*A pause. They listen. Nickels rises ceremoniously and turns on the barbecue, waits.*)

FLETCHER: (*With foreboding.*) And so I arranged a consultation with our family physician. A Doctor Seymour.

(*Nickels "becomes" Doctor Seymour, while Fletcher anxiously looks at a magazine.*)

NICKELS: Well, Mr. Fletcher. How nice to see you. Come in, come in.

FLETCHER: Thank you.

NICKELS: And how is everything? Family healthy?

FLETCHER: Yes, they're all well.

NICKELS: Good, good. Any ill effects from the amputation?

FLETCHER: No, no.

NICKELS: Still feeling pain there, are you?

FLETCHER: A little.

NICKELS: Strange, that. As if the foot were still attached.

FLETCHER: Yes, I know.

NICKELS: Unfortunate thing. Terrible burn. Had to be done. Better a partial extremity than the whole man, eh?

FLETCHER: Of course.

(*Pause.*)

NICKELS: I saw that nice old Buick of yours down to Bill's Texaco station the other day. What year is it?

FLETCHER: It's a thirty-nine.

NICKELS: Thirty-nine. Straight eight, standard shift?

FLETCHER: Yes.

NICKELS: Lovely car. Running okay?

FLETCHER: Runs good. I was concerned with the mileage, you know.

NICKELS: Yes. The era of cheap energy is at an end. So is cheap labor, for that matter. The fantasy is over and we're heading for a crack up. A breakdown, if you will.

FLETCHER: That is very much to the point, Doctor.

NICKELS: Oh? What seems to be the trouble, then?

FLETCHER: It's my nerves.

NICKELS: I see. Tension?

FLETCHER: Yes.

NICKELS: Concentrated where?

FLETCHER: (*Demonstrating.*) Here. Sometimes there. Here. There.

NICKELS: Varying, indiscriminate.

FLETCHER: Yes.

NICKELS: Circumstantial?

FLETCHER: Quite.

NICKELS: Insomniac?

FLETCHER: Yes.

NICKELS: What happens?

FLETCHER: Voices. Talking. Old songs. Images. Hateful, repetitious. Visceral tension, as in a coiled spring. Resultant violent impulses.

NICKELS: Expressed?

FLETCHER: Surely not.

NICKELS: Turned inward then.

FLETCHER: Possibly.

NICKELS: You must be tired.

FLETCHER: Exhausted.

NICKELS: A sleeping potion?

FLETCHER: Counter-productive.

NICKELS: Well . . . Other symptoms?

FLETCHER: Unpredictable trembling. Twitch of left eyelid. An occasional stutter. Irritability. Phantasmagoria.

NICKELS: Visions? Hallucinations?

FLETCHER: I can't recall.

NICKELS: I see. Are you religious?

FLETCHER: Are you insured for malpractice? (*Regrets his remark.*)

NICKELS: (*Coldly.*) Any other symptoms?

FLETCHER: Feeling of malaise. General unease. Abject terror.

NICKELS: What are nerves, sir? Be objective.

FLETCHER: In truth, I cannot see them.

NICKELS: Cellular beings, sir.

FLETCHER: Ganglia.

NICKELS: Correct. Ganglia. And their function?

FLETCHER: To wave about in response to stimuli.

NICKELS: Correct. And what is it, sir, animates these sensitive receptors? (*Fletcher is intimidated.*) Electricity, sir. Electricity. I ask you now, once again —are you religious?

FLETCHER: No, nervous.

NICKELS: Let's look at the situation from a fresh angle.

FLETCHER: But the diagnosis.

NICKELS: Patience, sir, the mightiest cure of them all. If that which animates the ganglia is electricity, what then is the nervous system?

FLETCHER: An electric circuit?

NICKELS: A mini transformer, sir. I say mini. Why?

FLETCHER: I don't know, Doctor Seymour.

NICKELS: Because it is but one cell in the Great Body. (*Pause.*) You look frightened. Dispense with your paranoia, sir, and see things as they are. (*Triumphant.*) The Great Body, sir, is Mankind, which is the sensitivity of Planet Earth.

FLETCHER: I get your drift.

NICKELS: Nerves, then, may be considered as a charge of electricity.

FLETCHER: An overcharge?

NICKELS: Perhaps a discharge.

FLETCHER: And the remedy?

NICKELS: Electricity, sir, comes from God. Nerves are therefore sacred.

FLETCHER: I see.

NICKELS: You don't. I can't help you.

FLETCHER: (*Relieved.*) No blame. You did the best you could.

NICKELS: Come to our church, the Holy Brothers of Man. It's on D Street.

FLETCHER: I know it.

NICKELS: Come to services. Sunday at nine. Best thing for you.

FLETCHER: (*Trying to leave.*) I will. Thank you.

NICKELS: You won't regret it. Where are you going?

FLETCHER: Oh, I thought—

NICKELS: No escaping Fate, Fletcher. It's all written down. I must check you up. Sit.

FLETCHER: (*Moaning.*) Oh, no. (*Sits down.*)

NICKELS: This won't take long, Fletcher. Routine. Say, "ah."

FLETCHER: Aaaahhh. (*Gags.*)

NICKELS: Hmm. Low threshold there. (*Fletcher begins to shake.*) You shouldn't smoke so much. Clouds the lungs, stains the teeth. (*Pretends use of stethoscope.*) Ah, very rapid heartbeat. Sound, but overdoing it, sir. Relax. Breathe deeply. Yes. Once again. Heart is sound but intemperately racehorse at the moment, Fletcher. All right, cough. (*Fletcher coughs.*) Again. (*Fletcher coughs and throws up.*) Now, now, Fletcher. Restraint, please. An adult's control, sir. We'll be through in a minute. Must take blood pressure, look in the eyes and ears. (*Mimes proper movements.*) There we are. (*Fletcher moans in agony.*) Hmm. Pain from lack of circulation in non-existent hand, eh? (*Fletcher nods, trembling violently.*) Okay, pressure's off a bit. Nothing alarming. Must calm yourself, boy. (*Produces a pocket flashlight, looks, with difficulty, into Fletcher's ears . . . into his good eye . . . Fletcher wildly resisting—lurches forward in a frenzy—SQUASH.*)

FLETCHER: *No. No. My eye. My eye. I'm blind. Blind.* (*Hobbles off, screaming.*)

(*Nickels bends to pick the ''eye'' up off the floor. Inspects it. Enter Lucius.*)

LUCIUS: Do you want to hear how—
NICKELS: No.

(*Exit Lucius. Enter Flora and Mary.*)

NICKELS: How's Grandma Smith?
FLORA: She's okay.
MARY: God. (*Laughs.*)
NICKELS: What?
FLORA: Oh, she pooped all over herself again.
NICKELS: Jeepers.
MARY: She pretends like it never happened, of course.
FLORA: She just lets go. She forgets.
MARY: The nurses had to clean her up.
FLORA: They're used to it.
NICKELS: Some job, boy.
FLORA: You wouldn't believe them.
NICKELS: How so?
FLORA: The way they talk.
MARY: Oblivious. (*Goes about removing the badminton net.*)
FLORA: Worse. Nothing there. Devoid.
NICKELS: (*Going to the barbecue to turn it off.*) I don't know what I'm doing,
    Flora. I'm at a loss.
FLORA: What is it?
NICKELS: (*Unable to say.*) What?
FLORA: (*Impatiently.*) Nickels. Do something with your hands. Something
    physical. Dig a garden. Build a wall. Work with Lucius. (*Nickels laughs.*)
    Why are you laughing?
NICKELS: Nothing.
FLORA: They're bringing Grandma home in a little while.
NICKELS: What for?
FLORA: (*As she goes inside.*) She wants to see the roses.
NICKELS: Great . . .

(*Dim out.*)

Scene 4

Lights up to find Mrs. Smith asleep in the wheelchair. Flora enters with a bunch of roses.
She pins one to the old woman's dress.

MRS. SMITH: Go away. You're a perfect stranger to me. I want my nurses.

FLORA: All right, Mrs. Smith. Mary! (*Mary comes to the door.*) She wants her nurses. (*Imitating Nurse 1.*) Here we are, Mrs. Smith.

MARY: (*Imitating Nurse 2.*) How are you, my dear?

MRS. SMITH: I don't know you.

MARY: Yes. Well, we know you, Mrs. Smith.

FLORA: We certainly do.

MARY: We certainly do.

FLORA: (*Finding hidden knives and forks and taking them away.*) We can't play with things that don't belong to us, Mrs. Smith.

MARY: Someone might get hurt.

MRS. SMITH: I know what you do. You put your fingers in places you're not supposed to.

FLORA: Now, Mrs. Smith. (*To Mary.*) Did I tell you Margie sold that Dodge Dart of hers?

MARY: Oh, no.

FLORA: Sold it to a guy right here in San Dimas.

MARY: Oh, no.

FLORA: Gave him a good deal on it.

MARY: My Christ.

MRS. SMITH: Where are you taking me?

FLORA: Time to eat, Mrs. Smith.

MRS. SMITH: Take me home. I have company waiting.

FLORA: We can't forget to eat now, can we?

MARY: I wish Margie'd spoke to me about that Dart.

FLORA: I know.

MARY: She knew I wanted to buy that Dart.

FLORA: I know. (*Holding her nose.*) Whoops.

MARY: Oh, dear.

FLORA: You've done it again, haven't you, Mrs. Smith?

MARY: My Christ.

MRS. SMITH: This country is not a big tit. It's the land of opportunity. People thinking they can get something for nothing. Government did that. Roosevelt come along and they started in taking money out of paychecks.

FLORA: All right. We'll have to wash you now, Mrs. Smith.

MRS. SMITH: Dollar was worth something when I was a girl. Ain't fit to wipe your ass with these days. Don't know what all the fuss is about.

FLORA: All right. (*They lift her out of the wheelchair and lay her into the lounge.*)

MRS. SMITH: Might's well burn it all and go back to horses. Horses was a value you could sit on.

MARY: I don't know why Margie did that.

FLORA: I don't either.

MARY: Why didn't she tell me?

FLORA: I don't know.

MRS. SMITH: (*As they "undress" her.*) You keep your horses nearby here? Take me for a ride to see the horses. I can read good horseflesh, ya know. My Bill was a judge of character, but he didn't know horses. Quiet man. I think he painted things.

MARY: I wish she'd of told me.

FLORA: She should have told you.

MARY: I'd have bought that Dart.

FLORA: I know.

MARY: Who'd she sell it to?

FLORA: Dude in San Dimas.

MARY: Far out. I think that's low.

FLORA: It is low.

MRS. SMITH: My daughter, Lily, will be coming by to take me home. I don't like it at this hotel anymore. The food is terrible and they charge you an arm and a leg for it. Jews, I think. And the service is no damn good. Stinking all the time. Filth.

FLORA: We have to turn you over now, dear.

MARY: My Christ.

MRS. SMITH: Do you know that the people here are sex perverted? I don't like to see the goings on. Hear it all night, the groaning and biting. Lily will take me home through the corn field and I'll drive the horses. She'll give them a piece of her mind.

MARY: I was gonna buy it from Margie, wasn't I?

FLORA: I heard you say it to her down at the tacoria.

MARY: That's right on. I did.

FLORA: You did.

MARY: I'd have given her whatever that dude give her.

FLORA: Cash money.

MARY: Cash money. It's a good little car.

(*Mrs. Smith makes a move at some butts in an ashtray. Flora slaps her hand, but she's already got one in her mouth and is chewing it.*)

MARY: My Christ.

FLORA: Mrs. Smith, you can't eat no tobacco. How many times do you have to be told? Now spit it out.

MARY: Spit it out.

FLORA: Spit it out, it's no good for you. (*She spits it all over herself.*)

MARY: My Christ. (*Flora wipes her face and chest while Mary finishes removing her dress.*) Lie still now. My Christ. (*Starts washing her behind.*)

FLORA: It was a good car, too.

MARY: Oh, I think it's the best of them little economy cars.

FLORA: The Dodge Dart.

MARY: The Dodge Dart.

MRS. SMITH: I'm gonna tell my daughter, Lily, what you done. She'll be here any minute. She'll kick you in the knees.

FLORA: What year is it?

MARY: It's a seventy-one.

FLORA: Seventy-one?

MARY: Seventy-one.

(*They finish "wiping" her and wash her down with a cold wet towel as she squirms.*)

FLORA: I think it was really low of her not to have asked you.

MARY: Really low. Especially when I had told her, down to the tacoria, that I did want to buy that Dart.

FLORA: I know.

MARY: My Christ.

FLORA: I guess she was ready to sell it.

MARY: She was.

FLORA: All right, Mrs. Smith.

(*They go inside, talking about the Dart. Dim out on Mrs. Smith.*)

Scene 5

Still in the black.

NICKELS: Who dealt?

FLORA: Mom dealt.

JEROME: Lily, do you intend a bid. (*A silence.*) Lily!

LILY: Just a minute, Jerome.

JEROME: Well, what are you *doing*.

LILY: I'm thinking.

JEROME: Christ, you'd think this was tournament bridge the way she plays.

(*Lights up revealing the bridge game on the lawn as Mary comes through the door with drinks and Lily says:*)

LILY: One diamond.

FLORA: Pass.

NICKELS: Two diamonds. (*A silence.*)

JEROME: What was that?

NICKELS: One diamond, pass, two diamonds . . .

JEROME: What?

NICKELS: *One diamond, pass, two diamonds.*

(*A silence. Lily puts her cards down.*)

LILY: (*To Mary.*) Thank you, honey.
MARY: You're welcome, Mom.

(*Lily picks up her knitting. Knits.*)

JEROME: Two hearts. (*A silence.*) Lil, are you gonna knit or play bridge?
LILY: (*Slowly picks up her hand.*) Four diamonds.
FLORA: Double.

(*Nickels cracks up.*)

JEROME: (*To Flora.*) Why did you do that?
FLORA: I don't know, Dad.
JEROME: Pass.
LILY: Redouble.

(*Nickels cracks up again.*)

JEROME: *What* are you doing? *Why* are you *doing* that?
LILY: I don't know what you mean, Jerome.
JEROME: We're not playing tournament bridge, Lil. We're *playing* with beginners!
LILY: Well, this is a good way to learn then.
JEROME: I don't believe you, Lil.
LILY: You can believe what you want to. (*Goes back to her knitting.*)
JEROME: (*To Flora.*) Do you have four sure tricks in your hand?
FLORA: Huh?
JEROME: Do you have four sure tricks in your hand? To set her you've got to have four sure tricks in your own hand.
FLORA: What about your hand?
JEROME: You don't *double* unless you're sure you can set her in your own hand.
LILY: Don't count on him, honey.
JEROME: You shut up.
FLORA: (*To Jerome.*) No.
JEROME: Then what did you double for?
FLORA: I just had a feeling that she couldn't make it.
JEROME: A feeling?
NICKELS: You can't bid on feelings, Flora.
FLORA: You mind your own business.
NICKELS: Okay. (*Cracks up.*)

FLORA: Plus, I have three aces.
LILY: That's still only three tricks, honey.
NICKELS: Okay, misdeal.
MARY: What happened, Mom?
LILY: Nothing.

(*Mary goes inside.*)

JEROME: (*To Lily.*) I still don't understand why you *re*-doubled.
LILY: It won't be the first or last time.
JEROME: God. A ruthless woman.
NICKELS: You deal, Flora.
FLORA: I'm sorry, Dad. (*Deals.*)
JEROME: It's not you, it's your mother. But don't double anyone unless
   you're sure you can set them in your own hand.
FLORA: I won't, Dad.

(*A pause, then an auto crash, as before.*)

NICKELS: First today, fourth of the week. Right there at the intersection be-
   hind the house. It's a two-way stop, but there ought to be— (*Stops.*)
LILY: There should be a light there.
NICKELS: Absolutely.
FLORA: Pass.
NICKELS: Two clubs.
JEROME: You sure you want to do that?
NICKELS: No.

(*Flora laughs.*)

JEROME: Two means you want to go to game.
NICKELS: Right. Make it one club.
JEROME: You can say three if you want.
NICKELS: Three.
FLORA: Double.
JEROME: Will you wait your turn!

(*Nickels and Flora crack up.*)

JEROME: God. (*Pause.*) Three hearts.
FLORA: Way to go, Dad.
JEROME: This is not a contest to see who gets the bid, Flora.
FLORA: Oh.

(*Nickels laughs.*)

FLORA: What are you laughing at?

NICKELS: Nothing.

(*Lily, knitting, still hasn't looked at her hand.*)

JEROME: Lily! For Chrissakes, woman, we're waiting for your bid. You haven't even looked at your hand!

NICKELS: Come on, Lil.

LILY: (*Slowly picking up her hand.*) What was bid?

JEROME: I can't stand this.

NICKELS: Pass, three clubs, three hearts.

LILY: You bid three clubs?

NICKELS: Yeah.

JEROME: What are you *doing*, Lil?

LILY: I'm looking at my hand, Jerome.

JEROME: Will you *bid*.

LILY: Four spades.

JEROME: *What?*

FLORA: (*Giggling.*) Double.

JEROME: No!

NICKELS: Pass.

JEROME: I don't understand what she's doing at all! Five hearts.

LILY: Double. (*Laughs.*)

JEROME: What the *hell* are you *doing*, Lil?

LILY: I'm doubling.

JEROME: You act like you're playing for blood. You did that on purpose. I won't play this way, Lil. (*Rises.*)

FLORA: Where are you going, Dad?

JEROME: I quit.

(*Lily goes back to her knitting.*)

NICKELS: Come on, Jer. *Come on, Jer.*

JEROME: No, I won't play with that woman anymore. (*Stalks inside.*)

FLORA: A Christless performance on my part. Sorry, Mom.

LILY: Don't pay any attention to him, honey.

FLORA: Looks like a banquet going on in the park.

LILY: Maybe it's a Little League convention.

NICKELS: No, they're all Mexican. It's an extended Mexican family. Maybe three generations of 'em. You can see how proud they are to be Americans. Staunch patriots.

LILY: They're the best workers down at the plant, I can tell you that. Honest and hard working.

NICKELS: All of 'em?

LILY: All of 'em.

NICKELS: They really seem to appreciate the good middle-class life here.

LILY: Well, they should.

NICKELS: What?

LILY: Appreciate it.

NICKELS: I know. And they do, boy, they do. All those nice looking kids will provide a groundswell of grassroots conservatism in years to come.

LILY: I certainly hope so.

NICKELS: These people are happy to pay taxes and vote in municipal elections. They are, in short, model citizens.

LILY: I wish some of the white trash around here would follow their example.

NICKELS: And so do I, Lil, so do I.

FLORA: Why don't you go check on the lamb.

NICKELS: I don't know why you're acting so mean.

FLORA: I'm sorry. Please look at the lamb.

(*Nickels starts up right toward the barbecue, where a haunch of lamb is turning on the spit, and Flora goes inside. Lily continues to knit. When Nickels arrives on the porch, Fletcher is revealed behind the screen door in considerable distress: his left arm is gone, he wears dark glasses to conceal his blindness and thick white bandaging around his head.*)

NICKELS: Fletcher! My dear fellow.

FLETCHER: (*Coming out.*) Greetings, Nickels.

NICKELS: Good grief, Fletcher.

FLETCHER: My life, as you know, has been devoted to education. Both in theory and practice.

NICKELS: Yes, but—?

FLETCHER: My efforts shall continue in that direction, regardless of cost.

NICKELS: Fletcher!

FLETCHER: Our educational system is the backbone of this nation.

NICKELS: True, Fletcher. True.

FLETCHER: But the spine of this system, sir, is eroding fast. It is turning, sir, to shit.

NICKELS: What happened, Fletcher?

FLETCHER: (*Sobbing.*) I'm sorry.

NICKELS: A blind man's tears. Never saw that before. You should be in the hospital, Fletcher.

FLETCHER: I'm afraid I've learned all there is to know about hospitals, Nickels.

NICKELS: Tell me. Get it off your chest, man.

FLETCHER: You heard the accident?

NICKELS: Recent?

FLETCHER: Right behind the house here. It's a two-way stop, but there ought to be a—

NICKELS: Traffic light.

FLETCHER: Yes.

NICKELS: We have petitioned.

FLETCHER: There is a school there. Did you know?

NICKELS: A schoolish edifice. Like a prison.

FLETCHER: Very like. Of Moorish architecture.

NICKELS: I know the place.

FLETCHER: Run by the Brothers. Holy Brothers of Man. They are the founding fathers of this community.

NICKELS: Oh?

FLETCHER: I went there.

(Pause. Fletcher taps his crutch against the floor with his one hooked arm as Nickels wraps an old blanket around him.)

FLETCHER: Brother Michael?

NICKELS: It is I.

FLETCHER: Forgive me, sir.

NICKELS: Whatever for?

FLETCHER: My unsightly appearance. These gruesome infirmities.

NICKELS: They are not obscene, my dear man. Fate's chicanery.

FLETCHER: In your school, is there thought of chance?

NICKELS: Chance?

FLETCHER: The accidental.

NICKELS: We oppose it, sir.

FLETCHER: How?

NICKELS: We mortify it with ignorance. We strangle it with discipline. We suffocate it with diligent labor. We stupefy it with play. We annihilate it with History. We cover it with insurance.

FLETCHER: Are the inner lives of children invisible to us?

NICKELS: The Hasidim, in Brooklyn, New York, when the boy of three is ready to learn to read, they place a drop of honey on the *Aleph*. The boy tastes the honey with his finger. And so learning is sweet to him thereafter. I read about it in *National Geographic*.

FLETCHER: But isn't he learning by rote?

NICKELS: I suppose. But later his mind is sharpened by the Commentaries. Finding his way through the Talmudic maze. A memorization of the six hundred and thirteen laws of Deuteronomy together with the lengthy subsidiaries. The histories of the Prophets as well.

FLETCHER: In Hebrew?

NICKELS: Yes.

FLETCHER: How can they understand ancient Hebrew?

NICKELS: They learn the laws.

FLETCHER: The laws must be also principles.

NICKELS: It was a short photo essay, Fletcher. When the boy is thirteen, he becomes *Bar Mitzvah*, that is, a man of duty. For the rest of his life, daily, he must try to remember how to be a Jew. By the effort to remember alone, the day is sanctified.

FLETCHER: (*After a pause.*) Was not this community inaugurated upon a biblical foundation?

NICKELS: It was. The Brothers began it in 1860. To the West of Eden, as they said at the time.

FLETCHER: (*Procrastinating.*) And your school is an offshoot of the Church?

NICKELS: It is.

FLETCHER: Thank you, Brother Michael. You have been most helpful.

NICKELS: Glad to be of service.

FLETCHER: (*Lingering.*) I am preparing an article tentatively entitled "Property Taxes and the Ontology of Awareness in Public Education on the Primary Level." May I quote you?

NICKELS: Will it be published?

FLETCHER: Yes, in the *California Scholar.*

NICKELS: But of course.

FLETCHER: Much obliged.

NICKELS: My privilege.

FLETCHER: I'll send you a copy, pre-publication.

NICKELS: I shall be happy to receive it.

FLETCHER: You may effect the final draft.

NICKELS: Humbly, I assure you.

FLETCHER: Well, goodbye then.

NICKELS: Goodbye.

(*Fletcher leaves reluctantly. A beat, then a thudding auto crash as before. Fletcher's scream.*)

NICKELS: *My God.*

LILY: (*Startled from her reverie.*) What happened?

NICKELS: (*Sad.*) An accident.

LILY: Was anyone hurt?

NICKELS: Yes. A one-legged blind man was trying to help a child cross the road. He got hit by a two-ton truck. Tore his arm off.

LILY: Oh, how awful!

NICKELS: Yes.

LILY: I'm glad I didn't see it.

NICKELS: It wasn't pretty. Blood everywhere.

LILY: I avoid that intersection. When I see my mother, I take Foothill Boulevard and then come down Canyon Road to the convalescent home.

NICKELS: A wise maneuver. (*Sighs deeply, sheds the blanket, comes downstage.*) Tell me, Lil.

LILY: Yes.

NICKELS: While you knit, what is it you're thinking to yourself?

(*A silence.*)

LILY: (*Staring straight ahead.*) When I was a girl, I went to the Brother's School. It's right back there on Bonita. (*Nickels nods.*) We were supposed to wear uniforms, but I refused. The boys were kept separate, and there was no dancing. I saw *Gone With the Wind,* and it changed my life. My father was a painter. This was in the Depression, before the Government started taking money out of people's paychecks. When he was fifty he started painting in oils. When he was fifty. I though I was growing up in a different America than it turned out to be. Roosevelt ruined this country. Young fellow down at the plant, out for a week, so we give him a call. "My wife died," he said. Young woman, five kids. "My wife died. Went into the hospital for a kidney problem. Operation. Everything's fine. Next morning, she died. They don't know why she died. I still can't get used to it." (*Pause.*) "They're gonna dig her up," he says, "they're gonna dig her up again, find out why she died."

MARY: (*Entering with paraphernalia.*) Time to eat, folks!

(*Dim out.*)

Scene 6

After dinner, Mary, Flora, Nickels, Jerome, Lily, and Lucius.

JEROME: What's going on over there across the street?

NICKELS: Appears to be a local celebration of some kind.

MARY: It's the Department of Recreation.

NICKELS: Biggest to-do I ever seen in these parts.

FLORA: Will there be dancing?

LILY: Oh, Jerome—they're setting up drums.

JEROME: Oh, no.

MARY: They put on a rock concert for the teenagers.

JEROME: Are we going to have to hear that damnable electric twang? I don't think those guys ever listen to music. Do they ever listen to Bach, I wonder.

MARY: Do you?

LILY: I don't like Bach.

FLORA: Let's go dancing!

MARY: They don't allow dancing. The Brothers wouldn't permit it. Listening is all.

LUCIUS: Before electricity came in, we'd take the old narrow gauge up to Battle Creek for a hoedown at Firehouse Number Seventeen. Farmers would come in from the surrounding country. Music was loud enough without it having to be plugged in.

NICKELS: When was this?

LUCUIS: This was in 1898, in Michigan.

JEROME: In 1898 you were only three years old, Pop.

LUCIUS: 1908, then.

(*Sound of drums, the band tuning up.*)

LUCIUS: I was thirteen.

JEROME: God, it scares me.

MARY: What does, Dad?

JEROME: I'm afraid they'll riot. Look, they're starting to mill around.

LILY: Oh, Jerome. Maybe you better go inside where you'll be safe.

NICKELS: I tend to share his apprehension.

(*The band strikes up.*)

JEROME: I don't think I'll be able to stand this.

(*Lily knits.*)

NICKELS: Boy, are they lousy.

JEROME: *What?*

NICKELS: *I said, they're a lousy band.*

JEROME: *How can you tell?*

FLORA: Lucius. *Lucius.*

LUCIUS: Yeah?

FLORA: We going down to Chino for the chicken shit and soil?

LUCIUS: Oh, you've got wonderful soil. The garden's right above where the chicken house used to be.

FLORA: I mean for my tomatoes.

LUCIUS: Oh, yes. It'll be good for your tomatoes.

JEROME: The corn will suck all the nitrogen out of it.

MARY: We've got beans growing in with the corn.

FLORA: Beans are a nitrogen fixer.

JEROME: Are they?

LUCIUS: Oh, yes. I'll tell you a story about beans.

(*The band breaks.*)

JEROME: Now I'm really frightened. They won't know what to do with themselves now.

LUCIUS: When I was a boy, my dad had ten acres in red clover. And he said to me, "If you're willing to do the work, you take that ten acres and make a crop of beans and we'll split the profit, fifty-fifty." Navy beans. So we made a deal. I plowed that ten acres into the ground.

MARY: Oh, red clover makes a terrific mulch.

LUCIUS: Well, yes. And I planted my beans. And they come up beautiful. My dad took the hay machine and did some welding, and when the blades had been altered he took 'em down to the blacksmith shop in town and had 'em sharpened. It cut the beans perfect. When I had 'em all in, I stacked 'em in piles to dry, just like you would with hay.

MARY: Conical stacks? . . . bread loaves? . . . beehives?

LUCIUS: Conical. When the beans was dry and hard, I threshed 'em with a regular hay thresher. They was top-grade beans and we had a bountiful crop.

JEROME: What did you realize from your half?

LUCIUS: Six hundred dollars.

FLORA: Six hundred dollars!

LUCIUS: Oh, it was a heap of money in those days and I was just a boy.

LILY: A family could live well on five hundred dollars for the year in those days.

NICKELS: In all, you saw a profit of twelve hundred dollars from those beans.

LUCIUS: That's correct. I put it in the Farmer's National Bank of Battle Creek, Michigan. And I didn't touch it till a few years later when I used it to get myself established down in Texas, I believe. (*He wanders off.*)

NICKELS: The story of the navy beans.

(*The band strikes up again.*)

JEROME: Oh, God. No.

NICKELS: Look, they all have something in their mouths. Everyone is chewing.

JEROME: We've got to get out of here, Lil.

FLORA: Would you guys cut it out.

LILY: You're safe here, Jerome. Just don't make any false moves.

JEROME: If we don't go now, we might not make it.

NICKELS: They're all eating! They're all eating! What are they eating?

LILY: (*Laconic.*) Hot dogs, popcorn, and soft drinks.

JEROME: That's good, that's good. They can't eat and do violence at the same time.

MARY: I'm going home.

JEROME: What do you mean?

MARY: I'm going home tomorrow morning. I'm taking a plane to San Francisco.

JEROME: Why?

LILY: She's got things to do, Jerome.

JEROME: Don't interpret for her, woman.

MARY: I'll see ya at Christmas.

JEROME: Goodbye.

MARY: Good night. (*Exits with Flora.*)

JEROME: Why does she have to do things like that? I don't know what she's doing. What is she doing?

LILY: Who?

JEROME: Mary!

LILY: She's going home, Jerome.

JEROME: I know that. I don't mean that.

LILY: Then I don't know what you're talking about.

JEROME: Why don't you?

LILY: Just leave it alone.

(*The band stops.*)

JEROME: Oh-oh.

NICKELS: Take it easy, Jer.

JEROME: What?

NICKELS: *Take it easy, Jer.*

JEROME: What are they going to do now?

NICKELS: They're waiting for the next thing to happen.

JEROME: What?

NICKELS: *Nothing.*

JEROME: Let's get out of here, Lil.

LILY: What?

JEROME: Let's get out of here, Lil. Stop your knitting.

LILY: I'm not through yet, Jerome.

JEROME: *Stop your knitting and let's go.*

LILY: All right, Jerome. All right.

(*He drags her off. A siren. Enter Flora.*)

FLORA: What was that?

NICKELS: A signal.

FLORA: Where are my parents?

NICKELS: They left.

FLORA: Why?

NICKELS: Look, the teenies have dispersed. No longer there. An apparition. Jerome was afraid of it.

FLORA: Beautiful sky. Stars coming out. Would you like some coffee?

NICKELS: Why is it he's hard-of-hearing with me and with no one else?

FLORA: I don't know. Coffee?

NICKELS: Yes, please.

(Flora goes inside. Lights dim low. Nickels rocks in his chair. A long beat, then Fletcher appears in the window at Nickels's right. Both legs have been amputated. He rests on the window sill.)

FLETCHER: Nickels.

NICKELS: Fletcher?

FLETCHER: Yes.

NICKELS: *(Looking to his right.)* My dear Fletcher.

FLETCHER: *(Deep sigh.)* Hello.

NICKELS: *(Sadly.)* Good to see you, Fletcher, as always. I mean, good to be with you. What happened?

FLETCHER: I went to Leroys' Boys' Home. It's up on Baseline.

NICKELS: I've passed the place. But why?

FLETCHER: The Leroys' Boys' Home is a prison for criminal juveniles. Many of these boys are homicidal, psychopathic. *(Sigh.)* As they are under-age, they are kept separate from the prison system proper and are not sentenced as convicted felons. Oftentimes, the murderer, the rapist, the sadist, the arsonist is returned to society before very long. They are beyond rehabilitation, beyond the law.

NICKELS: I share your interest and concern.

FLETCHER: There is a particular case of exceptional moment. His name is Charles. He was a professional killer. He is sixteen years old. *(Sigh.)* I obtained permission for an interview. *(Nickels goes to the barbecue and turns it on.)* A guard escorted me to his cell and left me there alone with him. *(A beat.)* Charles?

NICKELS: Yeah?

FLETCHER: My name is Mr. Fletcher, Charles, and I am an educational psychologist.

NICKELS: What's wrong wit' you? Ain't you got no eyes?

FLETCHER: I am blind, Charles.

NICKELS: Mister, you ain't hardly there at all. You all messed up. Somebody gone at you wit' a meat cleaver.

FLETCHER: Would you be willing to answer some questions, Charles?

NICKELS: Sure. 'Cept I don't know why they sent someone 'round here as fucked up as you. I ain't seen much worse, and I seen plenty.

FLETCHER: How old are you, Charles?

NICKELS: I be sixteen sometime soon.

FLETCHER: Are you a killer?

NICKELS: Right.

FLETCHER: For hire?

NICKELS: Right.

FLETCHER: How old were you when you first killed someone?

NICKELS: For a job?

FLETCHER: No, for any reason.

NICKELS: I was eleven, maybe twelve years old.

FLETCHER: Who was it?

NICKELS: Some chump was in the Assassins.

FLETCHER: The Assassins?

NICKELS: That's some mickey mouse gang used to mess wit' us.

FLETCHER: And you killed him?

NICKELS: Right. I stuck him.

FLETCHER: How did it happen?

NICKELS: I dunno. We was fightin' and I stuck him.

FLETCHER: In self-defense?

NICKELS: Nah. I wanted to stick him and I stuck him. He mighta stuck me.

FLETCHER: Did you feel bad about it?

NICKELS: No. I was worried maybe 'cause I figured somethin' might be wantin' revenge.

FLETCHER: Revenge?

NICKELS: Right. I was thinkin' maybe somethin' out there might want to get me for what I done. But nothin' happened.

FLETCHER: Nothing happened to you?

NICKELS: Right. But I got status.

FLETCHER: Status?

NICKELS: Yeah, status. You know, status.

FLETCHER: No.

NICKELS: Respect, man. Respect for a serious dude.

FLETCHER: When did you start doing it for money? Killing people.

NICKELS: I dunno. Couple years later.

FLETCHER: When you were fourteen?

NICKELS: Yeah.

FLETCHER: Why?

NICKELS: I needed the money.

FLETCHER: Why you?

NICKELS: 'Cause they know when they pay me to do it, that I'm gonna do it.

FLETCHER: Who's they?

NICKELS: The ones what want it done.

FLETCHER: Who are they?

NICKELS: They's people, man. Different people.

FLETCHER: How does it work?

NICKELS: They pay me some, and then I go do it.

FLETCHER: How do you know who to kill?

NICKELS: They give me his picture. And his address. What time he goes to work. Where he hangs out. Stuff like that.

FLETCHER: Was there ever a time when you failed?

NICKELS: Not me, man. I don't fail. I do it. I wait my time and I do it.

FLETCHER: Does it bother you, being in here?

NICKELS: In here? No, it don't bother me.

FLETCHER: Why doesn't it bother you?

NICKELS: I ain't gonna be here long, man. You do somethin', you do your time. Next thing you know, you're out in the street. Nobody messes wit' me in here. I got caught once, is all. I be out before long. They lemme alone in here. It ain't too bad.

FLETCHER: How many people have you killed?

NICKELS: Fourteen, fifteen.

FLETCHER: All for money?

NICKELS: No, some I killed just for reasons. You know.

FLETCHER: What does it feel like when you kill someone?

NICKELS: That's the whole thing, when you've stabbed or shot a guy. That's where it's at.

FLETCHER: What does it feel like?

NICKELS: I dunno. He's lookin' at ya, you know. It's a show. You feel like it's a show.

FLETCHER: Like you and he are in a show.

NICKELS: Yeah, it's a show.

(*A long pause.*)

FLETCHER: *Guard! Guard! Get me out of here! Right away! Get me out of here! Guard! Guard!*

(*Dim out on Fletcher. Nickels goes to barbecue, turns it off.*)

NICKELS: (*Slow dim out.*) Guard. . . .

END

A Movie Star Has to Star in Black and White

Adrienne Kennedy

A Movie Star Has to Star in Black and White was done as a work in progress at the New York Shakespeare Festival in New York on November 5, 1976, with the following cast:

Wallace	*Frank Adu*
Marlon Brando	*Ray Barry*
Eddie	*Robert Christian*
Paul Henreid	*Richard Dow*
Hattie	*Gloria Foster*
Montgomery Clift	*C. S. Hayward*
Jean Peters/Columbia Pictures Lady	*Karen Ludwig*
Clara	*Robbie McCauley*
Bette Davis	*Avra Petrides*
Shelley Winters	*Ellin Ruskin*

Director: Joseph Chaikin
Lights: Beverly Emmons
Costumes: Kate Carmel
Music: Peter Golub

NOTES

The movie music throughout is romantic.

The ship, the deck, the railings and the dark boat can all be done with lights and silhouettes.

All the colors are shades of black and white.

These movie stars are romantic and moving, never camp or farcical, and the attitudes of the supporting players to the movie stars is deadly serious.

The movie music sometimes plays at intervals when Clara's thought is still.

CHARACTERS

Clara
"Leading Roles" are played by actors who look exactly like:
  Bette Davis
  Paul Henreid
  Jean Peters
  Marlon Brando
  Montgomery Clift
  Shelley Winters

(they all look exactly like their movie roles)

Supporting Roles by

  the mother
  the father
  the husband

(they all look like photographs Clara keeps of them except when they're in the hospital)

SCENES

I
Hospital lobby and *Now Voyager*

II
Brother's room and *Viva Zapata*

III
Clara's old room and *A Place In The Sun*

Dark stage. From darkness center appears the Columbia Pictures Lady in a bright light.

COLUMBIA PICTURES LADY: (*Speaks.*) Summer, New York, 1955. Summer, Ohio, 1963. The scenes are *Now Voyager, Viva Zapata* and *A Place In The Sun.*

The leading roles are played by Bette Davis, Paul Henreid, Jean Peters, Marlon Brando, Montgomery Clift and Shelley Winters. Supporting roles are played by the mother, the father, the husband. A bit role is played by Clara.

Now Voyager takes place in the hospital lobby.
Viva Zapata takes place in the brother's room.
A Place In The Sun takes place in Clara's old room.

June 1963.

My producer is Joel Steinberg. He looks different from what I once thought, not at all like that picture in *Vogue.* He was in *Vogue* with a group of people who were going to do a musical about Socrates. In the photograph Joel's hair looked dark and his skin smooth. In real life his skin is blotched. Everyone says he drinks a lot.

    Lately I think often of killing myself. Eddie Jr. plays outside in the playground. I'm very lonely. . . . Met Lee Strasberg: the members of the playwrights unit were invited to watch his scene. Geraldine Page, Rip Torn and Norman Mailer were there. . . . I wonder why I lie so much to my mother about how I feel. . . . My father once said his life has been nothing but a life of hypocrisy and that's why his photograph smiled. While Eddie Jr. plays outside I read Edith Wharton, a book on Egypt and Chinua Achebe. Leroi Jones, Ted Joans and Allen Ginsburg are reading in the Village. Eddie comes every evening right before dark. He wants to know if I'll go back to him for the sake of our son.

(She fades. At the back of the stage as in a distance a dim light goes on a large doorway in the hospital. Visible is the foot of the white hospital bed and a figure lying upon it. Movie music. Clara stands at the doorway of the room. She is a Negro woman of thirty-three wearing a maternity dress. She does not enter the room but turns away and stands very still. Movie music.)

CLARA: (*Reflective; very still facing away from the room.*) My brother is the same . . . my father is coming . . . very depressed.

    Before I left New York I got my typewriter from the pawnshop. I'm terribly tired, trying to do a page a day, yet my play is coming together.

    Each day I wonder with what or with whom can I co-exist in a true union?

(*She turns and stares into her brother's room. Scene fades out; then bright lights that convey an ocean liner in motion.*)

SCENE I

Movie music. On the deck of the ocean liner from Now Voyager *are Bette Davis and Paul Henreid. They sit at a table slightly off stage center. Bette Davis has on a large white summer hat and Paul Henreid a dark summer suit. The light is romantic and glamorous. Beyond backstage left are deck chairs. It is bright sunlight on the deck.*

BETTE DAVIS: (*To Paul.*)
June 1955.

When I have the baby I wonder will I turn into a river of blood and die? My mother almost died when I was born. I've always felt sad that I couldn't have been an angel of mercy to my father and mother and saved them from their torment.

I used to hope when I was a little girl that one day I would rise above them, an angel with glowing wings and cover them with peace. But I failed. When I came among them it seems to me I did not bring them peace . . . but made them more disconsolate. The crosses they bore always made me sad.

The one reality I wanted never came true . . . to be their angel of mercy to unite them. I keep remembering the time my mother threatened to kill my father with the shot gun. I keep remembering my father's going away to marry a girl who talked to willow trees.

(*Onto the deck wander the mother, the father, and the husband. They are Negroes. The parents are as they were when young in 1929 in Atlanta, Georgia. The mother is small, pale and very beautiful. She has on a white summer dress and white shoes. The father is small and dark skinned. He has on a Morehouse sweater, knickers and a cap. They both are emotional and nervous. In presence both are romanticized. The husband is twenty-eight and handsome. He is dressed as in the summer of 1955 wearing a seersucker suit from Kleins that cost thirteen dollars.*)

BETTE DAVIS: In the scrapbook that my father left is a picture of my mother in Savannah, Georgia in 1929.
MOTHER: (*Sitting down in a deck chair takes a cigarette out of a beaded purse and smokes nervously. She speaks bitterly in a voice with a strong Georgia accent.*) In our Georgia town the white people lived on one side. It had pavement on the

streets and sidewalks and mail was delivered. The Negroes lived on the other side and the roads were dirt and had no sidewalk and you had to go to the Post Office to pick up your mail. In the center of Main Street was a fountain and white people drank on one side and Negroes drank on the other.

When a Negro bought something in a store he couldn't try it on. A Negro couldn't sit down at the soda fountain in the drug store but had to take his drink out. In the movies at Montefore you had to go in the side and up the stairs and sit in the last four rows.

When you arrived on the train from Cincinnati the first thing you saw was the WHITE AND COLORED signs at the depot. White people had one waiting room and we Negroes had another. We sat in only two cars and white people had the rest of the train.

(*She is facing Paul Henreid and Bette Davis. The father and the husband sit in deck chairs that face the other side of the sea. The father also smokes. He sits hunched over with his head down thinking. The husband takes an old test book out of a battered briefcase and starts to study. He looks exhausted and has dark circles under his eyes. His suit is worn.*)

BETTE DAVIS: My father used to say John Hope Franklin, Du Bois and Benjamin Mays were fine men.

(*Bright sunlight on father sitting on other side of deck. Father gets up and comes toward them . . . to Bette Davis.*)

FATHER: Cleveland is a place for opportunity, leadership, a progressive city, a place for education, a chance to come out of the back woods of Georgia. We Negro leaders dream of leading our people out of the wilderness.

(*He passes her and goes along the deck whistling. Movie music, Bette Davis stands up looking after the father . . . then distractedly to Paul Henreid.*)

BETTE DAVIS: (*Very passionate.*) I'd give anything in the world if I could just once talk to Jesus.
   Sometimes he walks through my room but he doesn't stop long enough for us to talk . . . he has an aureole.
   (*Then to the father who is almost out of sight on the deck whistling.*)
   Why did you marry the girl who talked to willow trees?
   (*To Paul Henreid.*)
   He left us to marry a girl who talked to willow trees.

(*Father is whistling, mother is smoking, then the father vanishes into a door on deck. Bette Davis walks down to railing. Paul Henreid follows her.*)

BETTE DAVIS:
June 1955.
My mother said when she was a girl in the summers she didn't like to go out. She'd sit in the house and help her grandmother iron or shell peas and sometimes she'd sit on the steps.

My father used to come and sit on the steps. He asked her for her first "date." They went for a walk up the road and had an ice cream at Miss Ida's Icecream Parlor and walked back down the road. She was fifteen.

My mother says that my father was one of the most well thought of boys in the town, Negro or white. And he was so friendly. He always had a friendly word for everybody.

He used to tell my mother his dreams how he was going to go up north. There was opportunity for Negroes up north and when he was finished at Morehouse he was going to get a job in someplace like New York.

And she said when she walked down the road with my father people were so friendly.

He organized a colored baseball team in Montefore and he was the Captain. And she used to go and watch him play baseball and everybody called him "Cap."

Seven more months and the baby.

Eddie and I don't talk too much these days.

Very often I try to be in bed by the time he comes home.

Most nights I'm wide awake until at least four. I wake up about eight and then I have a headache.

When I'm wide awake I see Jesus a lot.

My mother is giving us the money for the doctor bill. Eddie told her he will pay it back.

Also got a letter from her; it said I hope things work out for you both. And pray, pray sometimes. Love Mother.

We also got a letter form Eddie's mother. Eddie's brother had told her that Eddie and I were having some problems. In her letter which was enclosed in a card she said when Eddie's sister had visited us she noticed that Eddie and I don't go to church. She said we mustn't forget the Lord, because God takes care of everything . . . God gives us peace and no matter what problems Eddie and I were having if we trusted in Him God would help us. It was the only letter from Eddie's mother that I ever saved.

Even though the card was Hallmark.

July 1955.
Eddie doesn't seem like the same person since he came back from Korea. And now I'm pregnant again. When I lost the baby he was thousands of miles away. All that bleeding. I'll never forgive him. The Red Cross let him send me a telegram to say he was sorry. I can't believe we used to be so

in love on the campus and park the car and kiss and kiss. Yet I was a virgin when we married. A virgin who was to bleed and bleed . . . when I was in the hospital all I had was a photograph of Eddie in GI clothes standing in a woods in Korea. (*Pause.*) Eddie and I went to the Thalia on 95th and Broadway. There's a film festival this summer. We saw *Double Indemnity*, *The Red Shoes* and *A Place In The Sun*. Next week *Viva Zapata* is coming. Afterwards we went to Reinzis on Macdougal Street and had Viennese coffee. We forced an enthusiasm we didn't feel. We took the subway back up to 116th Street and walked to Bencroft Hall. In the middle of the night I woke up and wrote in my diary.

(*A bright light at hospital doorway. Clara younger, fragile, anxious. Movie music. She leaves hospital doorway and comes onto the deck from the door her father entered. She wears maternity dress, white wedgies, her hair is straightened as in the fifties. She has a passive beauty and is totally preoccupied. She pays no attention to anyone, only writing in a notebook. Her movie stars speak for her. Clara lets her movie stars star in her life. Bette Davis and Paul Henreid are at the railing. The mother is smoking. The husband gets up and comes across the deck carrying his battered briefcase. He speaks to Clara who looks away. Paul Henreid goes on staring at the sea.*)

HUSBAND: Clara, please tell me everything the doctor said about the delivery and how many days you'll be in the hospital.

(*Instead of Clara, Bette Davis replies. Paul Henreid is oblivious of him.*)

BETTE DAVIS: (*Very remote.*) I get very jealous of you Eddie. You're doing something with your life.

(*He tries to kiss Clara. She moves away and walks along the deck and writes in notebook.*)

BETTE DAVIS: (*To Eddie.*) Eddie, do you think I have floating anxiety? You said everyone in Korea had floating anxiety. I think I might have it. (*Pause.*) Do you think I'm catatonic?
EDDIE: (*Staring at Clara.*) I'm late to class now. We'll talk when I come home. (*He leaves.*) When I get paid I'm going to take you to Birdland. Dizzy's coming back.

(*Movie music.*)

CLARA:
July.
I can't sleep. My head always full of thoughts night and day. I feel so nervous. Sometimes I hardly hear what people are saying. I'm writing a lot of

my play, I don't want to show it to anyone though. Suppose it's no good. (*Reads her play.*)
They are dragging his body across the green his white hair hanging down. They are taking off his shoes and he is stiff. I must get into the chapel to see him. I must. He is my blood father. God, let me in to his burial. (He grabs her down center. She, kneeling.) I call God and the Owl answers. (Softer.) It haunts my Tower calling, its feathers are blowing against the cell wall, speckled in the garden on the fig tree, it comes, feathered, great hollow-eyed with yellow skin and yellow eyes, the flying bastard. From my Tower I keep calling and the only answer is the Owl, God. (Pause. Stands.) I am only yearning for our kingdom, God.

(*Movie music.*)

BETTE DAVIS: (*At railing.*) My father tried to commit suicide once when I was in High School. It was the afternoon he was presented an award by the Mayor of Cleveland at a banquet celebrating the completion of the New Settlement building. It had taken my father seven years to raise money for the New Settlement which was the center of Negro life in our community. He was given credit for being the one without whom it couldn't have been done. It was his biggest achievement.

I went upstairs and found him whistling in his room. I asked him what was wrong. I want to see my dead mama and papa he said, that's all I really live for is to see my mama and papa. I stared at him. As I was about to leave the room he said I've been waiting to jump off the roof of the Settlement for a long time. I just had to wait until it was completed . . . and he went on whistling.

He had tried to jump off the roof but had fallen on a scaffold.

(*Movie music. The deck has grown dark except for the light on Bette Davis and Paul Henreid and Clara.*)

CLARA: I loved the wedding night scene from *Viva Zapata* and the scene where the peasants met Zapata on the road and forced the soldiers to take the rope from his neck . . . when they shot Zapata at the end I cried.

(*Deck darker. She walks along the deck and into door, leaving Paul Henreid and Bette Davis at railing. She arrives at the hospital doorway, then enters her brother's room, standing at the foot of his bed. Her brother is in a coma.*)

CLARA: (*To her brother.*) Once I asked you romantically when you came back to the United States on a short leave, how do you like Europe Wally? You were silent. Finally you said, I get into a lot of fights with the Germans. You stared at me. And got up and went into the dining room to the dark sideboard and got a drink.

(*Darkness. Movie music.*)

SCENE II

Hospital room and Viva Zapata. *The hospital bed is now totally visible. In it lies Wally in a white gown. The light of the room is twilight on a summer evening. Clara's brother is handsome and in his late twenties. Beyond the bed is steel hospital apparatus. Clara stands by her brother's bedside. There is no real separation from the hospital room and* Viva Zapata *and the ship lights as there should have been none in* Now Voyager. *Simultaneously brighter lights come up stage center. Wedding night scene in* Viva Zapata. *Yet it is still the stateroom within the ship. Movie music. Marlon Brando and Jean Peters are sitting on the bed. They are both dressed as in* Viva Zapata.

JEAN PETERS: (*To Brando.*)
   July 11.
   I saw my father today. He's come from Georgia to see my brother. He lives in Savannah with his second wife. He seemed smaller and hunched over. When I was young he seemed energetic, speaking before civic groups and rallying people to give money to the Negro Settlement.
   In the last years he seems introspective, petty and angry. Today he was wearing a white nylon sports shirt that looked slightly too big . . . his dark arms thin. He had on a little straw sport hat cocked slightly to the side.
   We stood together in my brother's room. My father touched my brother's bare foot with his hand. My brother is in a coma.
   (*Silent.*)
   Eddie and I were married downstairs in this house. My brother was best man. We went to Colorado, but soon after Eddie was sent to Korea. My mother has always said that she felt if she and my father hadn't been fighting so much maybe I wouldn't have lost the baby. After I lost the baby I stopped writing to Eddie and decided I wanted to get a divorce when he came back from Korea. He hadn't been at Columbia long before I got pregnant again with Eddie Jr.

(*Marlon Brando listens. They kiss tenderly. She stands up. She is bleeding. She falls back on her bed. Brando pulls a sheet out from under her. The sheets are black. Movie music.*)

JEAN PETERS: The doctor says I have to stay in bed when I'm not at the hospital.

(*From now until the end Marlon Brando continuously helps Jean Peters change sheets. He puts the black sheets on the floor around them.*)

CLARA: (*To her brother, at the same time.*) Wally, you just have to get well. I know you will, even though you do not move or speak.

(*Sits down by his bedside watching him. Her mother enters. She is wearing a rose colored summer dress and small hat. The mother is in her fifties now. She sits down by her son's bedside and holds his hand. Silence in the room. The light of the room is constant twilight. They are in the constant dim twilight while Brando and Peters star in a dazzling wedding night light. Mexican peasant wedding music, Zapata remains throughout compassionate, heroic, tender. While Clara and her mother talk Brando and Peters sit on the bed, then enact the Zapata teach-me-to-read scene in which Brando asks Peters to get him a book and teach him to read.*)

MOTHER: What did I do? What did I do?
CLARA: What do you mean?
MOTHER: I don't know what I did to make my children so unhappy.

(*Jean Peters gets book for Brando.*)

CLARA: I'm not unhappy mother.
MOTHER: Yes you are.
CLARA: I'm not unhappy. I'm very happy. I just want to be a writer. Please don't think I'm unhappy.
MOTHER: Your family's not together and you don't seem happy. (*They sit and read.*)
CLARA: I'm very happy mother. Very. I've just won an award and I'm going to have a play produced. I'm very happy. (*Silence. The mother straightens the sheet on her son's bed.*)
MOTHER: When you grow up in boarding school like I did, the thing you dream of most is to see your children together with their families.
CLARA: Mother you mustn't think I'm unhappy because I am, I really am, very happy.
MOTHER: I just pray you'll soon get yourself together and make some decisions about your life. I pray for you every night. Shouldn't you go back to Eddie especially since you're pregnant?

(*There are shadows of the ship's lights as if* Now Voyager *is still in motion.*)

CLARA: Mother, Eddie doesn't understand me.

(*Silence. Twilight dimmer, mother holds Wally's hand. Movie light bright on Jean Peters and Marlon Brando.*)

JEAN PETERS: My brother Wally's still alive.
CLARA: (*To her diary.*) Wally was in an accident. A telegram from my mother. Your brother was in an automobile accident . . . has been unconscious since last night in St. Luke's hospital. Love, Mother.
JEAN PETERS: Depressed.
CLARA: Came to Cleveland. Eddie came to La Guardia to bring me money for my plane ticket and to say he was sorry about Wally who was best man at our wedding. Eddie looks at me with such sadness. It fills me with hatred for him and myself.

(*Brando is at the window looking down on the peasants. Mexican wedding music.*)

JEAN PETERS: Very depressed, and afraid at night since Eddie and I separated. I try to write a page a day on another play. It's going to be called a Lesson In Dead Language. The main image is a girl in a white organdy dress covered with menstrual blood.

(*Clara is writing in her diary. Her mother sits holding Wally's hand, Brando stares out the window, Jean Peters sits on the bed.* Now Voyager *ship, shadows and light.*)

CLARA: It is twilight outside and very warm. The window faces a lawn, very green, with a fountain beyond. Wally does not speak or move. He is in a coma. (*Twilight dims.*)
   It bothers me that Eddie had to give me money for the ticket to come home. I don't have any money of my own: the option from my play is gone and I don't know how I will be able to work and take care of Eddie Jr. Maybe Eddie and I should go back together.

(*Father enters the room, stands at the foot of his son's bed. He is in his fifties now and wears a white nylon sports shirt a little too big, his dark arms thin, baggy pants and a little straw sports hat cocked to the side. He has been drinking. The moment he enters the room the mother takes out a cigarette and starts to nervously smoke. They do not look at each other. He speaks to Clara, then glances in the direction of the mother. He then touches his son's bare feet. Wally is lying on his back, his hands to his sides. Clara gets up and goes to the window. Brando comes back and sits on the bed next to Jean Peters. They all remain for a long while silent. Suddenly the mother goes and throws herself into her daughter's arms and cries.*)

MOTHER: The doctor said he doesn't see how Wally has much of a chance of surviving: his brain is damaged.

(*She clings to her daughter and cries. Simultaneously:*)

JEAN PETERS: (*To Brando.*) I'm writing on my play. It's about a girl who turns into an Owl. Ow. (*Recites from her writings.*) He came to me in the outhouse, in the fig tree. He told me, "You are an owl, I am your beginning." I call God and the Owl answers. It haunts my tower, calling.

(*Silence. Father slightly drunk goes toward his former wife and his daughter. The mother runs out of the room into the lobby.*)

MOTHER: I did everything to make you happy and still you left me for another woman.

(*Clara stares out of the window. Father follows the mother into the lobby and stares at her. Jean Peters stands up. She is bleeding. She falls back on the bed. Marlon Brando pulls a sheet out from under her. The sheets are black. Movie music.*)

JEAN PETERS: The doctor says I have to stay in bed when I'm not at the hospital.

(*From now until the end Marlon Brando continuously helps Jean Peters change sheets. He puts the black sheets on the floor around them.*)

JEAN PETERS: This reminds me of when Eddie was in Korea and I had the miscarriage. For days there was blood on the sheets. Eddie's letters from Korea were about a green hill. He sent me photographs of himself. The Red Cross, the letter said, says I cannot call you and I cannot come.
 For a soldier to come home there has to be a death in the family.

MOTHER: (*In the hallway the mother breaks down further.*) I have never wanted to go back to the south to live. I hate it. I suffered nothing but humiliation and why should I have gone back there?

FATHER: You ought to have gone back with me. It's what I wanted to do.

MOTHER: I never wanted to go back.

FATHER: You yellow bastard. You're a yellow bastard. That's why you didn't want to go back.

MOTHER: You black nigger.

JEAN PETERS: (*Reciting her play.*) I call God and the Owl answers, it haunts my tower, calling, its feathers are blowing against the cell wall, it comes feathered, great hollow-eyes . . . with yellow skin and yellow eyes, the flying bastard. From my tower I keep calling and the only answer is the Owl.
 July 8 I got a telegram from my mother. It said your brother has been in an accident and has been unconscious since last night in St. Luke's hospital. Love, Mother. I came home.
 My brother is in a white gown on white sheets.

(*The mother and the father walk away from one another. A sudden bright light on the*

Hospital Lobby and on Wally's room. Clara has come to the doorway and watches her parents.)

MOTHER: (*To both her former husband and her daughter.*) I was asleep and the police called and told me Wally didn't feel well and would I please come down to the police station and pick him up. When I arrived at the police station they told me they had just taken him to the hospital because he felt worse and they would drive to the hospital. When I arrived here the doctor told me the truth: Wally's car had crashed into another car at an intersection and Wally had been thrown from the car, his body hitting a mail box and he was close to death.

(*Darkness.*)

SCENE III

Jean Peters and Brando are still sitting in Viva Zapata *but now there are photographs above the bed of Clara's parents when they were young, as they were in* Now Voyager. *Wally's room is dark. Lights of the ship from* Now Voyager.

JEAN PETERS: Wally is not expected to live. (*She tries to stand.*) He does not move. He is in a coma. (*Pause.*) There are so many memories in this house. The rooms besiege me.

My brother has been living here in his old room with my mother. He is separated from his wife and every night has been driving his car crazily around the street where she now lives. On one of these nights was when he had the accident.

(*Jean Peters and Brando stare at each other. A small dark boat from side opposite Wally's room. In it are Shelley Winters and Montgomery Clift. Clara sits behind Shelley Winters writing in her notebook. Montgomery Clift is rowing. It is* A Place In The Sun. *Movie music. Brando and Jean Peters continue to change sheets.*)

CLARA: I am bleeding. When I'm not at the hospital I have to stay in bed. I am writing my poems. Eddie's come from New York to see my brother. My brother does not speak or move.

(*Montgomery Clift silently rows dark boat across. Clara has on a nightgown and looks as if she has been very sick, and heartbroken by her brother's accident. Montgomery Clift, as was Henreid and Brando, is mute. If they did speak they would speak lines from their actual movies. As the boat comes across Brando and Peters are still. Movie music. Eddie comes in room with Jean Peters and Brando. He still has his text book and briefcase. Shelley Winters sits opposite Montgomery Clift as in* A Place In The Sun. *Clara is writing in her notebook.*)

EDDIE: (*To Jean Peters; simultaneously Clara is writing in her diary.*) Are you sure you want to go on with this?

JEAN PETERS: This?

EDDIE: You know what I mean, this obsession of yours?

JEAN PETERS: Obsession?

EDDIE: Yes, this obsession to be a writer?

JEAN PETERS: Of course I'm sure.

(*Brando is reading. Clara from the boat.*)

CLARA: I think the Steinbergs have lost interest in my play. I got a letter from them that said they have to go to Italy and would be in touch when they came back.

EDDIE: I have enough money for us to live well with my teaching. We could all be so happy.

CLARA: (*From boat.*) Ever since I was twelve I have secretly dreamed of being a writer. Everyone says it's unrealistic for a Negro to want to write.

Eddie says I've become shy and secretive and I can't accept the passage of time, and that my diaries consume me and that my diaries make me a spectator watching my life like watching a black and white movie.

He thinks sometimes . . . to me my life is one of my black and white movies that I love so . . . with me playing a bit part.

EDDIE: (*To Jean Peters looking up at the photographs.*) I wonder about your obsession to write about your parents when they were young. You didn't know them. Your mother's not young, your father's not young and we are not that young couple who came to New York in 1955, yet all you ever say to me is Eddie you don't seem the same since you came back from Korea.

(*Eddie leaves. Montgomery Clift rows as Shelley Winters speaks to him. Lights on Brando and Peters start slowly to dim.*)

SHELLEY WINTERS: (*To Montgomery Clift.*) A Sunday Rain . . . our next door neighbor drove me through the empty Sunday streets to see my brother. He's the same. My father came by the house last night for the first time since he left Cleveland and he and my mother got into a fight and my mother started laughing. She just kept saying see I can laugh ha ha nothing can hurt me anymore. Nothing you can ever do, Wallace, will ever hurt me again, no one can hurt me since my baby is lying out there in that Hospital and nobody knows whether he's going to live or die. And very loudly again she said ha ha and started walking in circles in her white shoes. My father said how goddamn crazy she was and they started pushing each other. I begged them to stop. My father looked about crazily.

I hate this house. But it was my money that helped make a down payment on it and I can come here anytime I want. I can come here and see my daughter and you can't stop me, he said.

CLARA: (*To diary.*) The last week in March I called up my mother and I told her that Eddie and I were getting a divorce and I wanted to come to Cleveland right away.

She said I'm coming up there.

When, I said. When?

It was four o'clock in the afternoon.

When can you come I said.

I'll take the train tonight. I'll call you from the station.

Should I come and meet you?

No, I'll call you from the station.

She called at 10:35 that morning. She said she would take a taxi. I went down to the courtyard and waited. When she got out of the taxi I will never forget the expression on her face. Her face had a hundred lines in it. I'd never seen her look so sad.

CLARA: (*Reciting her play.*) They said: I had lost my mind, read so much, buried myself in my books. They said I should stay and teach summer school. But I went. All the way to London. Out there in the black taxi my cold hands were colder than ever. No sooner than I left the taxi and passed down a gray walk through a dark gate and into a garden where there were black ravens on the grass, when I broke down. Oow . . . oww.

SHELLEY WINTERS: This morning my father came by again. He said Clara I want to talk to you. I want you to know my side. Now, your mother has always thought she was better than me. You know Mr. Harrison raised her like a white girl, and your mother, mark my word, thinks she's better than me. (It was then I could smell the whiskey on his breath . . . he had already taken a drink from the bottle in his suitcase.)

(*She looks anxiously at Montgomery Clift trying to get him to listen.*)

CLARA: (*Reading from her notebook.*) He came to me in the outhouse, in the garden, in the fig tree. He told me you are an owl, ow, oww, I am your beginning, ow. You belong here with us owls in the fig tree, not to somebody that cooks for your Goddamn Father, oww, and I ran to the outhouse in the night crying oww. Bastard they say, the people in the town all say Bastard, but I—I belong to God and the owls, ow, and I sat in the fig tree. My Goddamn Father is the Richest White Man in the Town, but I belong to the owls.

(*Putting down her notebook. Lights shift back to Peters and Brando on the bed.*)

JEAN PETERS: When my brother was in the army in Germany, he was involved in a crime and was court-martialled. He won't talk about it. I went to visit him in the stockade.

It was in a Quonset hut in New Jersey.

His head was shaven and he didn't have on any shoes. He has a vein that runs down his forehead and large brown eyes. When he was in high school he was in All City track in the two-twenty dash. We all thought he was going to be a great athlete. His dream was the Olympics. After high school he went to several colleges and left them; Morehouse (where my father went), Ohio State (where I went), and Western Reserve. I'm a failure he said. I can't make it in those schools. I'm tired. He suddenly joined the army.

After Wally left the army he worked nights as an orderly in hospitals; he liked the mental wards. For a few years every fall he started to school but dropped out after a few months. He and his wife married right before he was sent to Germany. He met her at Western Reserve and she graduated cum laude while he was a prisoner in the stockade.

(Movie music. Dark boat with Montgomery Clift and Shelley Winters reappears from opposite side. Montgomery Clift rows. Clara is crying.)

SHELLEY WINTERS AND CLARA: Eddie's come from New York because my brother might die. He did not speak again today and did not move. We don't really know his condition. All we know is that his brain is possibly badly damaged. He doesn't speak or move.

JEAN PETERS: I am bleeding.

(Lights suddenly dim on Marlon Brando and Jean Peters. Quite suddenly Shelley Winters stands up and falls "into the water." She is in the water, only her head is visible, calling silently. Montgomery Clift stares at her. She continues to call silently as for help, but Montgomery Clift only stares at her. Movie music. Clara starts to speak as Shelley Winters continues to cry silently for help.)

CLARA: The doctor said today that my brother will live; he will be brain damaged and paralyzed.

After he told us, my mother cried in my arms outside the hospital. We were standing on the steps, and she shook so that I thought both of us were going to fall headlong down the steps.

(Shelley Winters drowns. Light goes down on Montgomery Clift as he stares at Shelley Winters drowning. Lights on Clara. Movie music. Darkness. Brief dazzling image of Columbia Pictures Lady.)

END

Right of Way

Richard Lees

for Carol

Right of Way was first performed at The Guthrie Theatre in Minneapolis on June 2, 1979, with the following cast:

Teddy Dwyer	*Fred Stuthman*
Mini Dwyer	*Anne Pitoniak*
Ruda Dwyer	*Timothy Knear*
Mrs. Finter	*Tara Loewenstern*
Hahn	*Oliver Cliff*
Hahn's Assistant	*Peter Harrer*
S. Fishman	*Jon Cranney*
Newsman	*Tom Hegg*
Cameraman	*Ken Risch*
Policeman	*Richard Grusin*
Doctor	*Gerry Bamman*

Director: Steven Robman
Sets: Marjorie B. Kellogg
Lights: Duane Schuler
Costumes: Jennifer von Mayrhauser

Right of Way was later aired in November 1983 on Home Box Office as an HBO Premiere Films Presentation, starring Bette Davis, James Stewart, and Melinda Dillon in the main roles.

'Teddy and I were born a day apart in April at the turn of the century and I don't care what year it is on the calendar, more than a century has passed since.'

—Miniature Dwyer

The Dwyers
    Teddy and *Mini*, in their seventies
    Ruda, their daughter, middle-aged
Mrs. Finter, a social worker
Hahn, a County Health Inspector
Hahn's *Assistant*
S. Fishman, an attorney
a *Television Newsman*
a *Cameraman*
a *Doctor*
a *Policeman*
the Dwyers' cats

The Dwyer home. Santa Monica, California. A back room just off the garage. And the garage next to it. The room is not a den, not a living room. Clutter everywhere. Piles of books, magazines, and newspapers on furniture and on the floor. Clothes, paper bags, glasses, cups, and dishes with hardened food scattered about on tables and window sills. Two worn chairs and a comfortable old couch covered with a wrinkled print bedspread.

Dishes with catfood and milk on the floor near by. Also a long, narrow table. Windows upstage and stage left with bamboo roll blinds. Plants everywhere—hanging and in clay pots. A large wooden chest in a corner. Next to it piles of books with a piece of wood on top of them—almost resembling a desk. On top of the wood papers and a cactus plant. A doorway to the rest of the house up right. A door leading to the garage stage left. The garage sits just on the other side of the stage left wall in sharp contrast to the realistic clutter of the room. In it is the Dwyers' car, a '61 Pontiac Bonneville, cream color. It might be angled off up left but downstage in full view of the audience is the car's wide, threatening American grille. Also in the garage a small four-pane window which allows light on the car to change through the course of the play and at times appear at odds with light in the room.

Act I

SCENE 1

*(Lights up on the room. The Dwyers and their daughter Ruda. Also one of the Dwyers'
cats curled up in a ball, sleeping.)*

TEDDY: (*Holding a book in hand.*)
'I remember no more than a day
which, who knows, was never destined for me,
an interminable day
which had never begun. Thursday.
I was a man put there by chance
meeting a woman by some vague arrangement.
We undressed
as if to die, or swim, or to grow old
and we put ourselves one into another,
she circling me like a pit,
I banging at her like a man
who would strike a bell
since she was the sound that wounded me
and the hard dome set on its own vibration.

. . .This is a story of ports
where one arrives by chance and climbs the hills
and so many things come to pass.'
RUDA: Lovely, Daddy, but you didn't have me drive all the way down here to
listen to you read from your poetry books, I hope.
TEDDY: Not books, my dear—your namesake, Pablo Neruda.

RUDA: (*Looking at Teddy and Mini.*) Christ, I've driven ten hours for poetry. You said it was something important.

TEDDY: And it is.

MINI: You didn't have to take the coast route, dear.

RUDA: I wanted to take the coast route, Mother. Ten hours of toil—the scenery might as well be pretty.

MINI: Northern Californians suffer so in traffic . . . What did you do with your shop?

RUDA: I left it.

TEDDY: With your hired help?

RUDA: Yes. I trust my people. Unlike—

MINI: We would have closed up. Strictly family in our operation. And in my mother's before it. Do these people make your pots for you, too?

RUDA: They help.

MINI: Cute. Ruda's of Carmel. Pots made with hired help. Cute, huh, Teddy?

(*Teddy chuckles.*)

MINI: Everything's cute up there . . . You could at least have the family name on your store. Like your mother and her mother before her.

RUDA: Not everyone has a name as exploitable as Miniature.

MINI: A life's history in that name. A name that grew out of work—my mother's—and then became a person with her own work, me. Miniature Dwyer's. People still remember the store. 'That place with those hand-made dolls down in Santa Monica.' They come looking for it even today when it's long gone.

TEDDY: Nevertheless, Ruda's pots sell.

RUDA: Pottery, Daddy. Pots are for cooking.

TEDDY: Pottery, snottery—they sell. What do you think it is, Mini, that makes people driving German cars stuffed with money stop in a tiny town halfway between nothing and nowhere and reach into leather pouches to pay cash for something like a pot?

MINI: Sex. Of course pots make good souvenirs, too. But most of these people have just had sex somewhere in the vicinity—the sea encourages it—and pots are good after sex. Don't ask me why. And then you have your other thing, too.

RUDA: What other thing is that, Mother?

MINI: It's cute. Buying a pot is cute. Especially in such a cute place. All those little walkways and shoppes—spelled with two p's and an e—and the fireplaces and cafes and spruce trees. And, as I said, the sea.

TEDDY: Well, whatever it is it works. Ruda makes more off her pots than we ever did off your dolls.

RUDA: Is it me we're going to talk about then? Because if it is I'm going to do some cleaning up here.

TEDDY: (*Looking around the room.*) We have let the place go a little.

RUDA: A little . . . Even the cats must be uncomfortable in here. Do you ever clean their bowls?

MINI: They clean themselves. With their tongues. Clean as a squeak.

RUDA: They smell, Mother. And it's probably unhealthy.

MINI: Ha, they're cleaner than we are. (*Laughs.*)

RUDA: I won't argue with that. (*Going toward one of the cats.*) And where did this one come from?

MINI: That's Bobby DeNiro. And I wouldn't touch him if I were you. He can be dangerous.

TEDDY: (*Stopping Ruda.*) We have had some trouble with him.

RUDA: What kind of trouble?

TEDDY: The Nelkins, next door. They claim he sits on their window sill and hisses at them while they're eating. I guess he jumps the fence out back.

RUDA: Speaking of which—

TEDDY: I know. It's a mess out there, too.

MINI: Also the last thing we need to worry about.

RUDA: Mother, when was the last time you were out there? The weeds are up to the windows. It's like a jungle.

MINI: That's what the hiss people call it—a jungle.

RUDA: That's what it is. If you can't take care of it you should get someone. You're going to have complaints.

TEDDY: Already have. Someone from the city came by. An eyesore complaint, he called it.

RUDA: And you haven't done anything? They can fine you, Daddy. Or worse.

MINI: Let them. It makes no difference to us.

RUDA: It could, Mother. People lose their homes nowadays if they can't take care of them.

MINI: We're not going to lose our home. . . . Sit down, Ruda.

RUDA: But—

MINI: Sit down. We have something to tell you.

(*Ruda looks at them, finds a place to sit.*)

RUDA: What.

MINI: We aren't worried about the house and the lawn these days. Or the cats' bowls and weeds. We aren't worried about any of it.

RUDA: But you have to, Mother, you—

MINI: Well, I'm sorry, we aren't. Isn't that so, Teddy?

TEDDY: It's so, yes. (*To Ruda.*) Now be quiet and listen to your mother. We got you down here from Candytown for a reason.

MINI: Thank you, Teddy.

TEDDY: You're welcome.

MINI: You see, dear, we have something to tell you. We know we haven't been attending to these things lately. We aren't blind and we haven't forgotten. In fact, it's just the opposite. We've chosen not to.

RUDA: You have no choice in some things, Mother. You simply—

MINI: Shut up and listen to me. Please . . . I said we have something to tell you.

RUDA: All right, Mother, I'm sorry.

MINI: That's better. As I was saying, we've chosen not to worry about these things. They're silly and there are more important tasks at hand. We wish to do exactly as we please now and it's our opinion that we're entitled to. After all, there isn't much time.

RUDA: Oh, Mother, you've been saying that for years.

MINI: But now it's the truth.

RUDA: It's always been the truth.

MINI: Not like this time. Am I right, Teddy?

TEDDY: She's right, Ruda.

MINI: You see, dear, your father and I will soon be . . . finished. We've had a good life and we've lived it together. But our time has come. I think you'll agree our lives have been one. Now our death is going to be the same. It's our right and we intend to exercise it. We've made . . . plans.

RUDA: What?

TEDDY: We've lived together. Now we're going to die together.

RUDA: What do you mean? What are you saying?

MINI: I believe we're being clear. Your father and I are going to kill ourselves. We wanted you to know.

(*Ruda looks at them for a moment. Then she smiles, starts to laugh.*)

RUDA: Very funny, Daddy. I'm sure this was your idea. You still think you can get me to move back down here, don't you?

TEDDY: We don't want you to move back, Ruda.

MINI: No, in fact that's the last thing we want. I guarantee you'd get in the way and screw the whole thing up.

TEDDY: We just wanted you to know. We decided it was only fair. And there are some arrangements to be made.

RUDA: You're serious? Both of you are serious?

MINI: Yes, dear.

TEDDY: We are.

RUDA: You actually think you're going to kill yourselves.

TEDDY: Yes, dear.

MINI: We are.

RUDA: What—separately? Together? What?

TEDDY: Oh, together.

MINI: Of course. That's the whole point.

RUDA: And how are you going to accomplish this? I suppose you have it all worked out.

MINI: Yes, dear.

TEDDY: We do.

RUDA: I don't believe what I'm hearing. You've both lost your minds.

TEDDY: On the contrary. We're being sensible. In fact, that's really all we want to do: act sensibly. From our point of view it's reasonable, nothing more.

RUDA: You're sitting here telling me you're going to kill yourselves and you think . . . you want me to believe you're being reasonable?

TEDDY: Yes.

MINI: Exactly. You see, we've made up our minds. It's for real, all right. I've been to see Finnerman and he's certified it. I'm a dead woman right now, in fact.

RUDA: What do you mean, Mother?

MINI: It's just a matter of a short time. I'll know when, he says, it'll be plain, even simple, when it starts. That's when we'll . . . do it.

RUDA: When what starts? What are you talking about?

TEDDY: Your mother's allergic to herself, to her own blood. I couldn't pronounce the name if I tried. But she's got it. Something-something-a-cemia. Or something.

RUDA: What?

MINI: My own blood has turned against me. If my mother was alive she would die.

RUDA: Your doctor told you this?

MINI: Yes. Can't you hear, girl? I just told you he certified it. With a paper.

RUDA: Well, he must be wrong. You look fine to me. We'll go see someone else.

MINI: I don't think so.

TEDDY: We already have, Ruda. Your mother's telling you the truth.

MINI: Finnerman was right. We shouldn't have doubted him in the first place. He has wonderful hands. Softer than Teddy's.

RUDA: But when did all this happen? Why didn't you tell me?

MINI: You're here, aren't you?

(*Ruda looks at her mother for a moment.*)

RUDA: I just don't believe it. There must be something we can do.

MINI: I'm going to die. Face up to it, girl. If your father and I can, then you certainly can.

RUDA: But what is this thing? How can it be killing you when you don't even look—

MINI: What's the difference what it is? It just is.

RUDA: But there's nothing that can be done? I can't believe that.

TEDDY: Well . . .

RUDA: What, Daddy?

(*Teddy doesn't answer.*)

RUDA: What. Tell me.

TEDDY: Well, there was something. Finnerman couldn't guarantee it would work and even if it did it wouldn't be for long.

RUDA: What though?

MINI: They could freeze me and change my blood. Like an automobile engine. Drain me, flush me out, and fill me back up.

RUDA: And that would do it?

TEDDY: Maybe.

MINI: If the cold didn't kill me then the new blood probably would. Finnerman said so.

RUDA: But it would be a chance?

MINI: I haven't seen freezing cold in forty years. Not since we went east to visit Teddy's brother for Easter nineteen thirty-something. Easter bonnets, they were talking about—I had to wear someone's rubber boots to church. At any rate, I have no intention of dying now in an ice-bucket up in Westwood. And as for filling me full of someone else's blood, well . . .

RUDA: Well what?

MINI: Well it's out of the question. Dwyer blood is Dwyer blood. My mother would—

RUDA: (*Interrupting.*) Do it if she was in your position.

MINI: For what—an extra month or two? Even a year? I'm not interested in such a year. Neither of us is.

RUDA: But you can't just turn around and kill yourself, Mother. Is that the answer?

MINI: To us it is, yes.

RUDA: Us? This is you talking, too, Daddy?

TEDDY: I have no intention of living alone at this point. Your mother and I have lived as one; we'll die as one.

MINI: Would you like to know what it is we want to spare ourselves, Ruda? Finnerman describes it as a kind of starvation death. Except every cell in my body is a stomach. The pain will be immense. I'll lose all sense of who I am to it, what I am. I'll lose my insides and I'll lose my outsides. I'll be half my size and weight. Or smaller. A tiny figure like one of my dolls lying there on a rubber sheet in some hideous cinder block building they'll call a hospital. The final Miniature Dwyer—nothing but pain and awareness of pain. I will be a figure you won't recognize. But also one you'll never forget. And inside that figure somewhere will be me. Knowing that this 'civilized' death will be the last anyone sees of me. The Miniature Dwyer that will be remembered will be the one she never dreamt of. Or knew. Or cared to know. Or would let herself know. No, I tell you. Our answer is no.

(*Silence. Ruda looks at her mother. Then after a moment:*)

RUDA: You're asking me to help kill my parents.
TEDDY: No, Ruda. We don't want your help. We don't need it.
RUDA: Just my consent.
TEDDY: Yes. So we know what we leave behind. So we control it.
RUDA: You won't control that, Daddy. No matter what you do.
MINI: (*To Teddy.*) I told you she wouldn't understand. She doesn't have it in her.
RUDA: What would you have me say, Mother—'all right, it's fine with me, just fill me in on the arrangements?'
MINI: Yes.
RUDA: Well, I'm sorry, I can't say that because I don't think it and I don't feel it.
MINI: And what will you feel in the hospital room when I break your hand and bite clear through my tongue from pain?
RUDA: I'll feel sorry.
MINI: Well, feel sorry now and spare us the scene later.
TEDDY: Understand, Ruda, it's not that we want this.
RUDA: What do you mean? What do you want then?
TEDDY: Something we can't have. Not to be what we are: old.
RUDA: That's not you talking, Daddy. I can't believe—I won't believe—this is either of you. I want you both to see someone. I'll arrange it.
MINI: No more doctors.
RUDA: Not a doctor. A counselor. There are people who specialize in this type of thing now. Death counselors, they're called.
MINI: I'm my own specialist. It's me who's dying.
RUDA: And Daddy. Or doesn't he count?
MINI: That's not what I meant. Now look what you're making me say. Tell her, Teddy, that's not what I meant.
TEDDY: Of course it isn't.
MINI: Your father makes up his own mind. Why this . . . was his idea.

(*Ruda looks at Teddy.*)

RUDA: Daddy?

TEDDY: We don't want hospitals. And homes. And all that goes with them. And I don't want to be alone.

RUDA: I'll make some calls in the morning. I'm staying.

MINI: Not in this house you're not.

RUDA: (*Collecting her things.*) Then I'll go to a motel.

MINI: You won't stop us, Ruda.

RUDA: I just want you to talk to someone. What do you have to lose?

TEDDY: We just want to be together. I thought if we told you . . .

MINI: That was our first mistake. But we won't make another. You get out of here, Ruda. Leave us to do as we please. We've got a right. Now let us alone.

RUDA: I can't, Mother.

MINI: Go home and make a pot. Do something constructive. And don't you call any damn death counselor. We don't need it. Do you understand? We'll tell him you're crazy, that you're from Carmelcorn up north. He'll understand. We won't let him in. Do you hear me? We won't let him in.

TEDDY: We just want to be together.

RUDA: (*Exiting up right.*) I'm sorry, Daddy.

MINI: We won't see him. Do you hear me? We won't see any damn death counselor.

(*Lights down.*)

SCENE 2

Lights up. Teddy, Mini, and Mrs. Finter, a social worker.

MRS. FINTER: (*With a clipboard in front of her.*) Your first name, Mr. Dwyer?

TEDDY: Teddy.

MRS. FINTER: Theodore?

TEDDY: Teddy.

MRS. FINTER: All right . . . (*Writes.*) And your age, Ted?

MINI: (*Interrupting.*) Where are you from?

MRS. FINTER: We'll get back to you in a moment, Mrs. Dwyer. (*Turning back.*) Your age, Ted?

MINI: Don't you call him Ted.

MRS. FINTER: I was under the impression that was his name. Is that your name, Mr. Dwyer?

MINI: Not to you it isn't. And I asked you a question.

TEDDY: Easy, Mini.

MRS. FINTER: That's all right, Mr. Dwyer, I understand. Mrs. Dwyer is upset and I don't blame her. The pressure must be great. Mrs. Dwyer, I'm here on behalf of the city and at the request of . . . (*Looks at her board.*) Ruda

Dwyer. Your daughter, I believe. I spoke with her on the phone.

MINI: Where—up in Carmel? That's where she lives, you know.

MRS. FINTER: No, I believe she was here in Los Angeles.

MINI: It's possible. We never know where she is. The flighty type. I'm sure you know what I mean. Northerner.

MRS. FINTER: Yes, of course. But I am here and I'm required to gather certain information. Naturally I have to ask questions but—

MINI: We don't have to answer.

MRS. FINTER: No, you don't. In fact, you can ask me to leave if you like. Of course my report would have to indicate that you were uncommunicative.

TEDDY: Untrue. We can talk.

MRS. FINTER: Thank you, Mr. Dwyer. You won't regret it.

TEDDY: That's not what—

MRS. FINTER: I am here to help after all. Now where were we? Oh yes, your age.

TEDDY: You misunderstand.

MRS. FINTER: Your age, Mr. Dwyer.

TEDDY: (*Looks at Mini.*) What year is it? That's what I am.

MRS. FINTER: Seventy-eight?

TEDDY: If you say so.

MRS. FINTER: And your place of birth?

TEDDY: Chicago.

MRS. FINTER: And how long have you lived in Los Angeles?

TEDDY: I don't know. My father moved his button factory out here in '14, '15, something like that.

MINI: '14 is what you always said. You started high school here.

MRS. FINTER: I see. And you've been here ever since?

TEDDY: Except for trips.

MRS. FINTER: All right. And now you, Mrs. Dwyer, what is your age?

MINI: Teddy and I were born a day apart in April at the turn of the century and I don't care what year it is on the calendar, more than a century has passed since. I'm a good hundred and a half. Minimum.

MRS. FINTER: Also seventy-eight. And your first name is what—Minerva?

MINI: Miniature.

MRS. FINTER: Well, that's an unusual name.

MINI: I'm an unusual person. Like my mother before me. She named me. After her work. She made miniatures. Rooms and tiny houses with one side made of glass. They're collector's items today. Worth a fortune. As are my dolls. I used to have my own store. Miniature Dwyer's. Maybe you heard of it.

MRS. FINTER: No, I'm sorry, I haven't.

MINI: Well, no matter. It's long gone anyway. But I still make my dolls. I've got a trunk full of them right over there. (*Points to the wooden chest in the corner.*) I don't suppose you'd like to see them?

MRS. FINTER: Well yes . . . actually I would.

MINI: (*Getting up.*) Really?

MRS. FINTER: But perhaps next time.

(*Mini stops, looks at her.*)

MINI: What do you mean?

MRS. FINTER: Well, I thought we'd just get to know each other this time, get the preliminaries out of the way.

MINI: I didn't know there would be any next time.

TEDDY: We understood you just needed this information.

MRS. FINTER: Yes, that's right. But for a purpose, of course. So we can talk to each other.

MINI: We don't need any damn information to talk. We don't even like to talk. Teddy has his books; I have my dolls. We keep busy without talk.

MRS. FINTER: (*Looking around.*) Yes . . . Do you read all these books, Mr. Dwyer?

TEDDY: Just the poetry. And not even that so much anymore. There are really only a few I care about now, to tell you the truth.

MRS. FINTER: Then why keep the others . . . around . . . like this?

TEDDY: I like knowing they're here. And they serve other purposes. Practical ones. (*Standing.*) Look at this over here. This is a desk. Supported entirely by poetry. We pay our bills here.

MRS. FINTER: And do you have any trouble in that area?

TEDDY: (*Laughs.*) Once I tried to pull the Collected Frost. Thought the desk could hold without it. I forget who was here but I wanted to prove Frost wasn't just snow on windowpanes and farms in Vermont. It was a real argument. So I thought I'd read the one about the kid whose hand gets lopped off by a buzz saw right in front of his family. I forget the name of it. But anyway I pulled the book and found out I was wrong. The whole desk came down and Mini's cactus here lost two nubs. I thought she was going to kill me.

(*Teddy laughs. Mrs. Finter looks at him. He stops.*)

MINI: She meant the bills.

TEDDY: Hm?

MINI: She meant trouble with the bills. (*To Mrs. Finter.*) Didn't you?

MRS. FINTER: Well, yes, actually I did.

TEDDY: Oh. Well why didn't you say so?

MINI: Teddy still gets his button dividends. And there's the social security. We could live off that if we wanted to. You can see we're modest people. But we also have money from my shop. Even now. We sold it for plenty, you know.

MRS. FINTER: Then the answer is no problems?

MINI: None with the bills.

MRS. FINTER: Then why is it you haven't paid your property taxes this year, Mrs. Dwyer? Or your utilities for the past three months?

TEDDY: What do you mean? We pay our bills. Mini writes the checks right over here at my desk. See for yourself.

MRS. FINTER: Mrs. Dwyer?

(*Mini looks away, doesn't answer.*)

MRS. FINTER: Mrs. Dwyer?

MINI: It's none of your business.

MRS. FINTER: Oh but I'm afraid it is. (*To Teddy.*) I take it you were unaware of this, Mr. Dwyer.

TEDDY: Unaware of what? What's she talking about, Mini?

MRS. FINTER: Apparently Mrs. Dwyer hasn't been mindful of some of her responsibilities. She—

MINI: Nothing wrong with my mind. I pay what's fair. The water's fair and I pay it. Since you're snooping around in our affairs you must know I pay the water.

MRS. FINTER: Yes, I do know that, Mrs. Dwyer. The rationale, however, escapes me.

MINI: Water's fair. They bring it here from God knows where. Without it this city would be a skull baked in sand, so I don't mind paying for it. But I'll be damned if this house costs eighty-five dollars a month electricity to light three bulbs and an ice-box. And I don't see how the place could be worth twice what it was a year ago just because it's tax time all of the sudden. And just because we call up a couple of friends like they tell you you can do for nothing after five o'clock I'm not about to pay half a fortune to the phone company so they can take out their ads and get me to do it all over again for the other half.

MRS. FINTER: Bills are bills, Mrs. Dwyer. We pay for what we use.

MINI: And I say we pay too much. Do you know what it used to cost a month to run this house?

MRS. FINTER: No and it's of no concern to me. My concern is what it costs right now and whether you as occupants of it are able—financially and otherwise—to handle your responsibilities.

MINI: She's a bill collector. Ruda's sicced a bill collector on us.

MRS. FINTER: I am not involved with collection of any kind, Mrs. Dwyer. But I am here to understand the runnings of this household and to offer assistance if I believe it might be useful.

MINI: Well, it wouldn't. We've got everything figured out.

MRS. FINTER: Yes, your daughter explained that to me. It wouldn't be that you were thinking there was no reason to pay these bills, Mrs. Dwyer. That if you were . . . gone . . . then you would be absolved of your debts.

TEDDY: Don't be silly. We pay our bills. There's been some mistake here but we'll straighten it out. Won't we, Mini?

MINI: Maybe if you'd go out and buy me some stamps . . .

MRS. FINTER: I'd be glad to bring you some stamps, Mrs. Dwyer. Next time I come. Would that solve the problem?

MINI: It might.

MRS. FINTER: Do the two of you have trouble getting out for things like stamps?

TEDDY: Oh no, it isn't that. Mini just hates the lines at the post office. They took away the stamp window, you know.

MINI: Still, I go along for the ride. Teddy drives, of course.

MRS. FINTER: Do you, Mr. Dwyer?

TEDDY: Yes.

MINI: I navigate.

MRS. FINTER: And do you still do your own shopping, too? For food, things of that sort?

TEDDY: Oh yes. We have a '61 Bonneville—not a rust spot on it. Out in the garage, right through there. (*Points to the door stage left.*) Care to see it?

MRS. FINTER: Thank you. I'll take your word.

TEDDY: Nice cream color. We go everywhere in it. Still enjoy a good drive. Always did. Yes, we shop. We don't need as much as we used to. But what we want we just go out and get.

MRS. FINTER: Sounds easy enough.

TEDDY: Yes.

MRS. FINTER: And you enjoy your drives?

TEDDY: Oh yes. I said so.

MRS. FINTER: You, too, Mrs. Dwyer?

MINI: Sure.

MRS. FINTER: Then you have no particular troubles which keep you in?

TEDDY: None worth mentioning.

MRS. FINTER: None?

MINI: None.

MRS. FINTER: Then excuse me, why is it you want to kill yourselves?

(*Teddy and Mini look at Mrs. Finter, then at each other.*)

MINI: So someone will come in and clean up here.

MRS. FINTER: (*Smiling.*) Very funny, Mrs. Dwyer. But suicide—multiple suicide, I might add—isn't what I would think of as a laughing matter.

MINI: You've got something going for you then, Mrs. Finter.

MRS. FINTER: Would you like to answer my question, Mrs. Dwyer?

MINI: Not really. Ruda has obviously told you what you want to know.

MRS. FINTER: But I'd like to hear it from you.

MINI: Well, I wouldn't.

MRS. FINTER: I'm afraid I must insist, Mrs. Dwyer.

MINI: You're afraid . . . I'm dying, woman.

MRS. FINTER: That's no reason to kill yourself.

MINI: Isn't it? We're the kind of people who face up to something like this.

MRS. FINTER: I'm sorry but it seems just the opposite to me.

MINI: Well, you're wrong then. We've accepted the death part. We just want it on our own terms. Our own way. We're entitled to that, I think.

MRS. FINTER: Not according to the law, Mrs. Dwyer.

MINI: My mother never saw the inside of a hospital. She went sitting in front of her work. It was business as usual one minute, business as usual the next. Only she was gone.

MRS. FINTER: Your mother was very fortunate.

MINI: Yes she was and if I have anything to say about it I will be, too.

MRS. FINTER: You mean even if you have to arrange it yourself.

MINI: Yes.

MRS. FINTER: And take your husband with you.

MINI: No. Teddy makes his own decisions.

MRS. FINTER: Mr. Dwyer?

TEDDY: I don't want to live alone. Not now.

MRS. FINTER: But Mr. Dwyer, you're talking about suicide. Just because you don't want to be alone—

TEDDY: I know what I'm talking about. Don't you think I've thought about it?

MRS. FINTER: Well, I don't know.

TEDDY: Well, I do. And I have. And it's funny to me that all of the sudden some stranger can just come in here and have something to say about it. Why is it no one wants to talk about death unless it's a matter of whose to stop and when? You don't know . . . what it would mean for me to be without Mini now, to be alone after all this time—a lifetime—together.

MRS. FINTER: But Mr. Dwyer, you have your daughter, your . . . your books, your . . . home . . . and there are certainly places you could go.

TEDDY: I'd rather be dead.

MRS. FINTER: You don't mean that, Mr. Dwyer.

TEDDY: And you don't understand. We just want to be together. Nothing more, nothing less. Just together. Like always.

(*Mrs. Finter looks at both of them for a moment.*)

MRS. FINTER: Who did you say your doctor was, Mrs. Dwyer?

MINI: I didn't.

MRS. FINTER: May I have his name?

MINI: What for?

MRS. FINTER: I'd like to speak with him.

MINI: Why? To check up on me? You don't believe I'm sick?

MRS. FINTER: I'm concerned. And if I'm to help I will have to understand your condition.

MINI: I told you we don't want your help. We don't want anyone's help. We just want to be left to ourselves.

MRS. FINTER: I can always find out from your daughter.

MINI: Well, go ahead then. But neither of you will ever see the inside of this house again. And you won't get any more out of us. We'll take care of ourselves. Do you understand?

MRS. FINTER: I would strongly recommend against it, Mrs. Dwyer.

MINI: I don't give a good goddamn what you would recommend. We never should have let you in in the first place.

MRS. FINTER: I hope I can prevail upon you, Mr. Dwyer, to change your wife's mind in this matter. You're obviously a man of sensibility. Perhaps in one of your books—

TEDDY: (*Smiling.*) 'When I close a book, I open life . . .'

MRS. FINTER: I beg your pardon.

TEDDY: Neruda. He says,
'. . . send books back to their shelves,
I'm going down into the streets.'

MRS. FINTNER: I agree, Mr. Dwyer. But who, may I ask, is Neruda?

(*Teddy laughs.*)

TEDDY: Who is Neruda . . . My daughter's namesake, for one. Also a great poet who had a desk not unlike my own. An army trampled it just before he died. I still travel with him. Daily.

(*Mrs. Finter looks at Teddy now.*)

MRS. FINTER: I see . . . Well, I'll include him in my report.

TEDDY: Good, good, I always like it when I think I've spread the word.

MRS. FINTER: (*Standing.*) And I'm afraid I *will* be back.

MINI: You just try. You'll find out the meaning of the word.

MRS. FINTER: What word is that, Mrs. Dwyer?

MINI: Afraid.

MRS. FINTER: I have a responsibility now in this matter, Mrs. Dwyer.

MINI: We'll sic Bobby DeNiro on you. He happens to be out in our backyard, you know. It's just a question of bringing him in here and telling him what to do.

MRS. FINTER: Yes . . . of course . . . Please think this over, Mr. Dwyer. I assure you I'm operating on your behalf—both yours and your wife's. I would like to be your friend.

MINI: He'll scratch your eyes out.

TEDDY: '. . . the spider book
in which thought
has laid poisonous wires
to trap the juvenile
and circling fly.'

MINI: He protects us.

TEDDY: (*Smiling.*) Neruda . . .

MRS. FINTER: (*Looks at both of them.*) I'll be in touch . . . with you both. For now though, good-bye.

(*Mrs. Finter looks at them: Teddy smiling and rocking on his feet, Mini scowling to herself. Then she turns to leave stage right. Lights down.*)

SCENE 3

Lights up. Mini with several of her dolls sitting upright on the edge of a table. The wooden chest in the corner of the room is open and brimming with more. Mini moves back and forth from the chest to the table selecting dolls, arranging and re-arranging them on the table. After a moment Teddy comes in stage right carrying one of the cats and a few cans of cat food.

TEDDY: (*Off stage.*) Dinner time, ladies and gentlemen. Here we are.

MINI: What do you think?

TEDDY: (*Coming in the room.*) I think some of us are going to go hungry tonight. I've called out back twice so it's not my fault.

(*Teddy puts the cat down.*)

MINI: The faces look different to me every time. (*Taking one of the dolls.*) You I thought were merrier. Why else did I give you green eyes? (*Putting it back and taking another.*) And you—you seem to be blushing. Maybe the sudden light and being stared at. You're used to the box, hm?

TEDDY: (*Opening the cans.*) Now let's see, what do we have here? Oh . . . Bobby's going to be mad tonight. Tuna. And Liver with Bacon. (*Looking at the cat.*) Seen Bobby tonight, my friend? All right, all right, he thinks the same of you.

(*Teddy takes the can, scoops food onto a dish with a fork.*)

MINI: How can I tell what I've accomplished when I never see the same thing in you twice? All of you, always changing on me. How can I know you? On the other hand . . .

TEDDY: (*Still scooping food.*) Oh yes, come and get it . . . oh yes . . .

MINI: It's probably what keeps me going. A face I can never quite make out. The one just behind my head, just out of sight. Can any of you see it? Even when I turn I can't. It stays there, behind me. But I am getting closer. I know that. Anyone agree?

TEDDY: (*To Mini.*) You know, this liver isn't half bad. (*Takes a portion of the cat food, tastes it.*) Really. Try it?

MINI: (*Turning.*) I don't think so. But if there's any tuna left . . .

TEDDY: Sorry. Tuna's reserved for Tatum. You know what a fuss she makes without it. Pacino—he'll eat anything. And Paulie—he looks up at me with those blue eyes cooing.

MINI: And Bobby—where's he?

TEDDY: I don't know. He didn't come in yet either.

MINI: It's still early.

TEDDY: Hope he's not over hissing at the Nelkins.

MINI: I hope he is. All those little cretins crawling all over the neighborhood. Do we call the police when they come tramping through our yard? Bobby hates them as much as we do. They shoot at him with those air pistols. How many of them are there now?

TEDDY: Five capable of movement. Six counting the new one.

MINI: She just churns them out, doesn't she? And she had the nerve to make that crack about my dolls. I was making a peace offering. 'We have our own, thank you,' she says. What does she have of her own? An original Miniature Dwyer? Not on your life. Just that little pack of cretins with their ready-made faces. Disney rejects, all of them.

TEDDY: Still, I don't want any more trouble. You remember what they told us . . .

MINI: Trouble. I want as much of it as possible. I want to pass it out free of charge to anyone who wants it. Let them line up. The police, the social workers, whoever they want to send. I've got an endless supply of trouble and I'll gladly spoon feed it to them all.

TEDDY: Now Mini . . .

MINI: Don't Mini me. I mean it. (*Laughing.*) Ha, did you hear that, Teddy? 'Don't Mini me. I mean it.' You should write that one in your book.

TEDDY: Yes, I should . . . Ah, but will you look at Robby Redford here. (*Going to the cat.*) Preening himself all over. He is fine looking, isn't he?

MINI: Fine looking, yes. But Redford, no.

TEDDY: What do you mean?

MINI: That's not Robby Redford. That's Jimmy Caan.

TEDDY: That's Robby Redford if I'm standing here alive.

MINI: Nope. Jimmy Caan.

TEDDY: Robby Redford.

MINI: Jimmy Caan.

TEDDY: Robby Redford.

MINI: I won't argue. It's Jimmy Caan.

TEDDY: Neither will I. It's Robby Redford.

MINI: It's Jimmy Caan. Look at his left front paw.

TEDDY: That's the one he's been preening.

MINI: That's the one that ripped the Nelkins' dog. That mongrel will think twice before he barks at any of us again. Jimmy was over the fence before the sound was out of the moron mut's mouth. Ha! Did you hear that, Teddy? 'The moron mut's mouth.' Another one. Ha!

TEDDY: Maybe you're right.

MINI: Of course, I'm right. The day I don't know Jimmy Caan from Robby Redford you can put me in my grave. Redford's probably out with Bobby somewhere. (*Looking to the dolls.*) Now leave him alone and come over here for a minute. Tell me what you think.

TEDDY: All right. (*Teddy moves to Mini at the table, looks at the dolls.*) Well . . . I would say . . . just about.

MINI: But not quite. Right?

TEDDY: Right. Not quite.

MINI: How many more, do you think?

TEDDY: Two at most. Maybe just one. If you apply yourself.

MINI: One's what I'm hoping. I get the feeling it may be all I'll have time for. But Teddy?

TEDDY: Hm?

MINI: What if it's not enough? What if one more is all I get and it still isn't enough?

TEDDY: It'll have to be, won't it . . . You can do it. I feel you're very close.

MINI: Do you? I mean, really?

TEDDY: Yes. It's already quite a group. You know it's reached a certain . . . height. One more and—

MINI: I could be over the top.

TEDDY: If you make a true effort, yes, I think it could do it.

MINI: Oh, I hope so. I want so much to be . . . finished. Wouldn't it be nice to feel truly . . . finished?

TEDDY: 'I persist as if in a ruined tunnel,
         at another limit . . .'

MINI: I know what it's going to be. The face I told you about.

TEDDY: ' . . . and everything tells me a day has died.'
How do you know when you're finished?

MINI: The one behind my head. You've seen it, haven't you, Teddy?

TEDDY: Push on. Maybe you'll find out.

MINI: What does it look like to you?

TEDDY: 'Furies and Sufferings.' One of his best.

MINI: Oh, I want so to see it. I'll know it if I do. And then when I make it I'll be done. I know that, too.

TEDDY: You're finished only when you stop. Simple as that . . . Still want to . . . do it?

MINI: What?

TEDDY: You know.

MINI: Oh. Of course. Soon as this is done. And it's time.

TEDDY: All the talk hasn't changed your mind?

MINI: Talk isn't in my blood just now. And you?

TEDDY: I'm ready right now.

MINI: Soon enough then.

TEDDY: What if they come back though?

MINI: Let them.

TEDDY: What do we say?

MINI: Whatever we want. It's none of their concern.

TEDDY: They'll stop us.

MINI: They'll do nothing of the kind.

TEDDY: They'll try.

MINI: Let them. As long as we're here we'll do as we please. We'll tell them what they want to hear. Just enough to get rid of them. Christ, we could even clean up the place. Mow your lawn and they'll leave you alone. Then just as soon as they're out the door—pft—that's it, we're out of here. How much time do we need anyway?

TEDDY: Only an hour or so.

MINI: That we'll have. I guarantee. But when we want it. When we say it's time. They're not going to cheat us out of what we do have left. Agreed?

TEDDY: I suppose.

MINI: What—you're not sure?

TEDDY: Well, if they get their hooks into us, if they get us out of the house—

MINI: They won't get us out of the house.

TEDDY: But if they do, that's it. We won't be able to do a thing about anything. We'll be in one of those places where it'll be against the rules to do anything. We'll be fish in a net waiting for the feel of the deck where we'll flop on our backs til we die. Alone. Do you hear me? Alone.

MINI: (*Going to him.*) We'll do it, Teddy. I promise.

TEDDY: (*Looks at her for a moment.*) Okay. . . (*He moves upstage to the windows, opens one, and turns around to the cat.*) All right, my friend, the party's over. You've had your fill. (*Picking the cat up.*) Now it's back out in the cold, cruel world with everyone else. Good luck to you, little Jimmy—or Robby—whoever you are. (*Throws the cat out the window into the yard.*) Make your way. Make your way. Another day and you make your way.

MINI: (*Gathering her dolls.*) You, too, everybody. Back in your box. The old makes way for the new. We have to move on. Come on. Down you go. There. (*She takes the dolls back to the chest in the corner, sets them inside, and closes the top.*) Now to begin. One of these times . . . for the last time. To the starter box. (*She looks around.*) Where's my starter box? Teddy?

TEDDY: (*Still at the window.*) Hm.

MINI: Where's my starter box?

TEDDY: How should I know? . . . Evening star's out already. Sky's still pale . . . Didn't you have it by the desk the other day?

MINI: Yes, by the desk. (*Sees it.*) Right. Here it is. (*Picking it up.*) I put that gingham and sailcloth inside, didn't I?

TEDDY: Hm?

MINI: The new cloth we bought.

TEDDY: You put it inside.

MINI: (*Opening the box.*) Yes, here we are. Well, the sailcloth is right anyway. (*She takes the box to the table, begins to rummage through it, taking out some things like cloth, yarn, etc.*) We'll need some more stuffing. Or maybe not. Maybe I'll do what I always said.

TEDDY: What?

MINI: I'll stuff it with the insides of our drawers. My oldest seam stockings and your nice patterned socks. And scarves and hankies and both of our underwear.

TEDDY: Not my light blue. I have other plans for them.

MINI: You can keep your light blue. I'll have more than enough without them, I'm sure.

TEDDY: Do you want some help then?

MINI: No, I have to organize here first. We'll go to the drawers later.

TEDDY: All right.

(*Mini continues to remove scraps and various articles from her starter box, laying them out in piles on the table. Teddy looks out the window for another moment. Mini looks under the table for something.*)

MINI: You know, we really *could* do some cleaning. We could pick your books up and put them back on the shelves in the other room. Then we could say they're crazy. Where are these so-called piles of books? On what floor? Where?

TEDDY: (*Turning around at the window.*) What?

MINI: Show me where they are. Is this the room?

TEDDY: Unless I'm seeing things. Or unless . . .

MINI: I don't care what it says in any report. Look for yourself. The woman must be crazy.

TEDDY: (*Looking at Mini.*) . . . it's starting.

MINI: (*Now looking at him.*) What's starting?

TEDDY: Your eyes. Are they . . . ?

MINI: Nothing wrong with my eyes. What are you talking about?

TEDDY: (*Holding up four fingers.*) How many fingers?

MINI: Four. Why?

TEDDY: My books . . .

MINI: Scaling on two of the knuckles. You didn't put your creams on today, did you?

TEDDY: You don't see my books.

MINI: I see them. I was saying we could put them back in the other room. On the shelves.

TEDDY: And why would we want to do that?

MINI: To prove to them they're crazy.

TEDDY: I have a system. Do you know how long it's taken to develop?

MINI: Of course. It's not what I want, silly.

TEDDY: I know where every title is. I know *what* every title is. Do you have any idea of the time and effort involved, the selection, the visualizing necessary to raise that desk on which, among other things, our bills are allegedly paid?

MINI: Allegedly?

TEDDY: Yes.

MINI: The woman, as I was saying, is crazy. And I do know what you put into the desk.

TEDDY: She did her homework, that's all. She had me with my pants down.

MINI: The water's paid.

TEDDY: Imagine what I looked like to her.

MINI: The gas is paid.

TEDDY: A man not in control.

MINI: The electric's paid, too.

TEDDY: Going along with his wife who's in charge. In life.

MINI: They're all paid now.

TEDDY: And in death. Even in death I'm going along. Well, that's not the way it is. Do you understand? I want you to know this was my idea. She resisted, even fought me on it. Do you hear? We fought. You're wrong to say it was any other way. You're wrong even to think it. We know what we're doing. We're doing it out of choice. Both of us. Together. And my books stay where they are. Right here where we are. As long as we are. Here.

MINI: Just the taxes. They'll have to come at me in the next world if they want those.

TEDDY: Hm?

MINI: The woman's crazy if she thinks I'll pay those.

TEDDY: So are you if you think my books are going anywhere.

MINI: It was just a thought.

TEDDY: Well, forget it.

MINI: It's forgotten. (*Going back to the materials she has spread on the table.*) I think neutral might be the answer.

TEDDY: Hm?

MINI: Neutral. A beige or greyish sort of affair. No distinct features. A face that is a face and yet a mirror of the face that looks on.

TEDDY: Then you *have* paid them.

MINI: Maybe a hint of pastel. It can't look sad. Reflective, yes. Sad, no.

TEDDY: The bills.

MINI: A face that neither approves nor disapproves. Just recognizes.

TEDDY: Fine. There'll be no trouble then.

MINI: A knowing face.

TEDDY: We want things to run smoothly now. No interference.

MINI: (*Smiling.*) Yes, neutral.

TEDDY: Then my books can stay?

MINI: (*Still to herself.*) Of course.

TEDDY: Good. I thought maybe there was going to be a fight here.

MINI: Hm?

TEDDY: I said I thought maybe there would be a fight.

MINI: Where?

TEDDY: Here.

MINI: What about?

TEDDY: My books.

MINI: Oh. And I thought it would be the taxes.

TEDDY: No, the books.

MINI: I thought the taxes.

TEDDY: Well, you're wrong. You were talking about moving my books.

MINI: Not me. The crazy woman.

TEDDY: Oh. I thought you.

MINI: Well, you're wrong. I was talking about the taxes.

TEDDY: Then the books can stay.

MINI: Of course.

TEDDY: Good. I thought for a minute there was going to be a fight.

MINI: Well, you were wrong. (*Again going back to her materials on the table.*) Now the clothes—that's another matter. They might have some style. Not necessarily stylish but a style. They must reflect the face, not alter it. They must add without taking away. Be plain but not boring. Bland with intention, you might say. An elegant bland. The sailcloth, for instance, is right. The gingham, I think, is not. What do you say, Teddy?

(*As she has been talking Teddy has gone for his Neruda book near the desk. He flips through it, stops, smiles, then reads:*)

TEDDY: '. . . clothes,
  I make you what you are,
  pushing out your elbows,
  bursting the seams,
  and so your life swells
  the image of my life.
  You billow
  and resound in the wind
  as though you were my soul,
  at bad moments
  you cling
  to my bones
  empty, at night
  the dark, sleep,
  people with their phantoms
  your wings and mine.
  I ask
  whether one day
  a bullet
  from the enemy
  will stain you with my blood
  and then
  you will die with me
  or perhaps
  it may not be
  so dramatic
  but simple,
  and you will sicken gradually,
  clothes,
  with me, with my body
  and together
  we will enter
  the earth.
  At the thought of this
  every day
  I greet you
  with reverence, and then
  you embrace me and I forget you
  because we are one
  and will go on facing
  the wind together, at night,

the streets or the struggle,
one body,
maybe, maybe, one day motionless.'

(*A moment. Mini looks at Teddy.*)

MINI: What was that?
TEDDY: His 'Ode to Clothes.'
MINI: I like that.
TEDDY: Me, too.
MINI: There's always so much.
TEDDY: What.
MINI: That you can't reach. That you never get to. Even with time.
TEDDY: Yes.
MINI: You could . . . keep going . . . if you wanted.
TEDDY: Until what?
MINI: I don't know. Something farther along.
TEDDY: I know that.
MINI: You don't want to?
TEDDY: All I'd be is farther along. I want to be with you.
MINI: Then you want to be nothing.
TEDDY: I've come far enough.

(*They look at each other. A moment. Then Teddy points to the material, etc. on the table.*)

TEDDY: You know what you're going to do then?
MINI: (*Looking down.*) What—with this?
TEDDY: Yes.
MINI: No. But that's the way I like it.
TEDDY: Take a break then?
MINI: Sure. What for?
TEDDY: How about a ride?
MINI: Now?
TEDDY: Yes.
MINI: It's dark.
TEDDY: Not for a good hour or two.
MINI: Where?
TEDDY: I don't know. Anywhere you want.
MINI: (*Putting her things down, moving to Teddy.*) Really?
TEDDY: Sure.
MINI: Up Lincoln Blvd. to the park?
TEDDY: Sure.
MINI: Or up the coast along the beach?

TEDDY: We could do that.

MINI: All the way to Zuma?

TEDDY: We might make it.

MINI: Or maybe just to Malibu Canyon. We could wind across to that tunnel where all the names are scratched in the rock. Maybe we could scratch ours.

TEDDY: Sure.

MINI: No, it's wrong to do that. We don't need to add to it. We'll pass through the tunnel and I'll try to count the lights—you'll watch the road—and then we'll get on the Ventura at Las Virgines and come through the Valley to the San Diego.

TEDDY: All right.

MINI: Or we could just take the Santa Monica through Palms past the Rosedale Cemetery over to downtown. And then up the Harbor and Pasadena to Eagle Rock.

TEDDY: You have to take the Golden State and Glendale to get to Eagle Rock.

MINI: The Pasadena will get you there and you pass that beautiful park— Arroyo Seco. Then you just go up Figueroa and over on Colorado.

TEDDY: The Golden State's much better and you pass Elysian Park.

MINI: Still, the Pasadena will get you there.

TEDDY: But what's in Eagle Rock anyway?

MINI: Nothing. Actually I'd rather get off the Harbor and go over the Santa Ana and San Bernadino to where the Long Beach comes in near Durango. Remember that clover-leaf with all the girders and pillars?

TEDDY: Yes.

MINI: It's a marvelous sight.

TEDDY: Yes it is. But far away.

MINI: Well, maybe we should just stay around here.

TEDDY: We could.

MINI: Take Lincoln down past the Marina.

TEDDY: All right.

MINI: Or over to Seventh and ride by the store.

TEDDY: Yes, that would be nice.

MINI: Remember what that block used to look like, Teddy?

TEDDY: Of course I remember.

MINI: We could even stay for a while, then come back up Ocean to the Pier. Or keep going on the Pacific Coast, like I said.

TEDDY: All right.

MINI: There's that antique store with the fabric barrels just before the Palisades.

TEDDY: Yes.

MINI: We could stop and check it out.

TEDDY: Yes.

MINI: I remember we enjoyed ourselves there more than once.
TEDDY: Yes.
MINI: Or we could just stay in the car, pass by.
TEDDY: Yes.
MINI: Same difference in the end.
TEDDY: Yes.
MINI: What do you think?
TEDDY: Whatever you say.

(*Slow fade to black during the final exchanges.*)

SCENE 4

In the dark, sound of an auto-wind mechanism on an electronic camera. Then after a moment pops from flashbulbs briefly illuminate the room in the darkness. Two men, one with a camera taking pictures. Hahn and his Assistant. Lights up. They are alone in the room.

HAHN: Will you look at this place? Do you believe it?

(*The Assistant with the camera says nothing. Hahn walks around the room.*)

HAHN: I don't believe it. (*He looks at some of the cat bowls, turns to the Assistant.*) Did you get this?

(*The Assistant moves to Hahn, aims his camera down at the floor, shoots a picture.*)

HAHN: And make a note of the smell. What do you think—cats?

(*Both walk around the room picking up things, examining them, etc.*)

HAHN: How can people live like this? Nobody can live like this. (*Picking up a dish.*) How long do you think this has been here? Couldn't scrape it off with a chisel. Whatever it is.

(*Hahn looks at his Assistant. The Assistant moves to him, looks at the dish. Hahn nods. The Assistant takes a picture of it. Hahn puts the dish down, moves away.*)

HAHN: Why don't you open a window? It really stinks in here.

(*The Assistant moves upstage to the windows, goes to raise the roll blind, but knocks a plant in a small pot from the ledge to the floor. He turns, looks at Hahn. Hahn looks back, says nothing. The Assistant raises the blind, opens a window.*)

HAHN: The plants are watered at least. Although I don't see how they live in this air. Maybe we should have our masks. And gloves. (*Walks around some*

more.) And what are all these books? (*Picks one up off a pile, flips through it.*)
Poetry. (*Drops it to the floor, takes another one.*) More poetry. Who buys poetry
books and then dumps them on their floor with garbage and cat shit? (*Walks
to the desk upstage.*) Look at this. Piles of them. (*Pulls a book out from one of the
support piles under Teddy's desk. The wood tips and falls to the floor along with the
papers and the cactus on top of it.*) Jesus . . . Do you think that was supposed to
be . . .

(*The Assistant raises his camera to take a picture. Hahn stops him.*)

HAHN: No, no. Let me try and fix it.

(*The Assistant backs away. Hahn tries to do something with the fallen books. But he only
makes matters worse.*)

HAHN: Jesus . . . (*He drops the books and walks away. Pointing to the door stage left:*)
What's through there?

(*The Assistant goes to the door, opens it, leans through to look.*)

ASSISTANT: Garage.
HAHN: Same?
ASSISTANT: Just a car.(*He closes the door, comes back toward Hahn.*)
HAHN: So where are they? Out for a stroll? The report says shut-ins. And the
front door was wide open.
ASSISTANT: Didn't the report also say . .
HAHN: Yeah.
ASSISTANT: Well, maybe they're gone. Maybe they went and did it.
HAHN: (*Still walking around the room.*) I guess we'll find out. Christ, did you see
the bedroom? Those sheets? The whole place is . . . (*Sees Mini's wooden
chest.*) What's this? (*Opens it.*) Christ. Dolls. (*Reaching in.*) It's full of dolls.
(*Taking one out.*) Kind of cute. (*Looks around for a place to put it. Sets it on the
floor, takes another.*) Some of them . . . (*Sets the second doll down near the first.*)
All right, I've had enough. Just get some shots of the outside and let's get
out of here.

(*Hahn and the Assistant take one more look around and get ready to go. But Teddy, Mini,
and Ruda then appear in the doorway stage right. Hahn and the Assistant look at them.*)

TEDDY: Who are you?
HAHN: Who wants to know?
TEDDY: We live here.
HAHN: Oh . . . Well, please come in. I'd like to—

MINI: (*Seeing her chest open and the dolls on the floor.*) My dolls. (*She goes to the chest, kneels, and starts to put the dolls back inside.*)
TEDDY: (*Looking around.*) What's going on here? What have you done?

(*Hahn looks at his Assistant, points to Mini kneeling before her chest. The Assistant quickly moves to Mini, begins to snap pictures of her. Mini looks up, surprised, frightened, and blocks her eyes from the flashes of the camera with one hand. Teddy goes to her.*)

TEDDY: (*To the Assistant.*) What are you doing? What is this?

(*The Assistant turns on Teddy, snaps a picture. Teddy stops, momentarily blinded, raises a hand to his eyes. The Assistant takes one or two more shots of him, then moves back to Hahn.*)

HAHN: (*Moving to Ruda.*) Are you the daughter?
RUDA: Yes.
HAHN: My name is Hahn. I'm with the county.

(*Hahn reaches to shake hands with Ruda. Ruda looks at his hand, doesn't take it.*)

HAHN: May I talk to you? In private?
RUDA: (*Going to Teddy and Mini.*) You get out of here.
HAHN: Please. It would be much better for all of us if you would—
RUDA: (*Interrupting.*) I said out.
HAHN: Please, Miss, you'll leave us no choice. People can't live . . . like this. If you won't talk with us you'll only force us to use conservatorship.

(*Ruda looks at him, says nothing.*)

HAHN: Please. I'll only need a minute of your time.
RUDA: All right. But outside.
HAHN: As you wish. (*He turns to go, then looks back at Teddy and Mini.*) Shame . . .

(*Hahn exits stage right followed by the Assistant. Ruda looks at Teddy and Mini, then follows Hahn out. Teddy and Mini are silent, still recovering. After a moment:*)

MINI: (*With her hands still at her eyes.*) Teddy?
TEDDY: (*Looking around the room.*) Yeah.
MINI: What—
TEDDY: Now they've done it.
MINI: What . . .
TEDDY: Look what they've gone and done. My books. The desk. (*Seeing the*

overturned pot on the floor.) Look at this.

MINI: What.

TEDDY: Did they do anything to your dolls?

MINI: Who are they?

TEDDY: Did they hurt them?

MINI: Who are they?

TEDDY: They're taking the house.

MINI: Who?

TEDDY: They're taking us.

MINI: Who?

TEDDY: I knew this would happen.

MINI: What's happened?

TEDDY: Just what I said. But they won't get us without a fight. Do you hear me? We'll fight if we have to.

(*Ruda comes back in stage right. Alone now. Teddy sees her, stares.*)

TEDDY: That's why you came for us? To let them break into our home behind our backs?

RUDA: No, Daddy, I—

TEDDY: Look what they've done here.

RUDA: I didn't know about this, Daddy. Honestly. I just wanted to talk.

TEDDY: Talk. That seems to be our mistake where you're concerned. Look at what it's done for us. (*Looks around the room at the mess, then goes back to Mini on the floor.*)

RUDA: I'm sorry, Daddy. I just—

TEDDY: It won't stop us, Ruda. Do you hear me? Not you. Not this. Nothing will. Now.

(*Ruda looks at her parents who kneel on the floor by the open chest. She starts to say something, then stops. A moment. Then lights down.*)

Act II

SCENE 1

Lights up on the room. The desk and the piles of books which were disturbed are now restored. Mini's dolls are back in the chest. The clutter of before, but it is once again Teddy and Mini's clutter. Teddy, Mini, and S. Fishman, a bearded attorney. Teddy with some papers in hand. Mini at the table with her starter box and materials. She works on her doll.

TEDDY: Thanks for coming, Mr. . . .

FISHMAN: Fishman. S. Fishman.

TEDDY: Yes. Well, thank you, Mr. Fishman. It's nice of you.

FISHMAN: We try to be of help. And if people can't get out—

MINI: (*Without looking up from her work.*) We can get out.

FISHMAN: (*Smiling.*) Yes, of course, Mrs. Dwyer.

MINI: We can get out any time we want. We didn't want to. Not for this.

TEDDY: Mini.

MINI: Well, it's true.

TEDDY: Of course it's true. But the man's made a housecall. Out of kindness. We should be grateful. (*To Fishman.*) I'm sorry, Mr. Fishman. All my wife means is that we thought it might be better to discuss this in private, here, where we can . . . be alone.

FISHMAN: I understand, Mr. Dwyer. Strictly off the record.

TEDDY: They've sent us these papers. I can't even read them.

FISHMAN: May I see?

TEDDY: Not past the title anyway. That's why we called.

FISHMAN: May I see them?

TEDDY: (*Holding a sheath of papers in front of him.*) Conservatorship, it says. Same thing the gimp from the county said when he was here. To Ruda.

FISHMAN: May I see, Mr. Dwyer?

TEDDY: Oh . . . yes, of course.

(*Teddy hands Fishman the papers.*)

FISHMAN: Who is Ruda?

TEDDY: Our daughter.

MINI: Not if I have anything to say about it. This is all her doing. We tried to include her in our plans and what does she do—she turns on us. If it wasn't for her we wouldn't even be talking to you. No lawyer has ever set foot in a Dwyer household. If my mother—

TEDDY: (*Interrupting her.*) Mini.

MINI: Oh . . . I am sorry. No offense, Mr. Fishman.

FISHMAN: (*Looking up from the papers, smiling.*) No offense taken, Mrs. Dwyer. This *is* a conservatorship suit, Mr. Dwyer. The county alleges that you and your wife are unfit to take care of yourselves any longer. There are affidavits alleging incompetence. (*Flipping pages.*) From neighbors. From City Social Services. From . . . your daughter. There are records of . . . police complaints. Utilities for non-payment. The city. And, of course, the county. Which seeks to become conservator.

TEDDY: What does that mean?

FISHMAN: They would assume control of your money, property, etcetera, and then administer your estate for you.

TEDDY: Our estate? You mean once we're dead.

FISHMAN: No, Mr. Dwyer. A will would direct management after death. Conservatorship seeks fair and competent management for those incapable of it in life. Usually elderly or disabled persons without family.

TEDDY: Well, that's not us. They can't just take our things, can they?

FISHMAN: Not exactly take them. It's more a re-ordering procedure. To see that property is, in fact, maintained. But an award to the county would be highly unlikely in this case.

TEDDY: Why?

FISHMAN: Because you have family. Your daughter is even involved in the case.

MINI: Involved. I told you she started it. One day we're talking to her, the next we're in court.

FISHMAN: You must have been aware of these proceedings, Mrs. Dwyer. This suit is quite far along.

MINI: All we did was talk to them.

FISHMAN: Who exactly is 'them?'

MINI: Well, Ruda. Then that Finter woman.

FISHMAN: The social worker.

TEDDY: I guess.

MINI: And the police. And then the man with the camera.

FISHMAN: And why were the police here?

MINI: Bobby DeNiro.

TEDDY: And the weeds.

FISHMAN: I'm sorry?

TEDDY: Bobby's one of our cats. He doesn't care for some of the neighbors.

MINI: Or their children. They torment him with these popping things. They're pistols that pop. The cretins aim at him and shoot, so naturally he goes for them. Got one in the face once. Nasty scratch but the little punk deserved it.

FISHMAN: The parents, however, didn't see it that way.

TEDDY: That's right. And they added the part about the weeds just to get back at us.

MINI: The copper told us. The one they called.

TEDDY: An eyesore, he called us.

MINI: Not us—the yard.

TEDDY: It's us they're talking about.

FISHMAN: Yes, well, in any case, neglect of household is listed several times here. Cross-verification is strong basis for a suit of this type.

MINI: Cross what?

FISHMAN: The same story told by more than one witness.

MINI: Now they're witnesses. They started out as people just wanting to talk.

FISHMAN: Did anyone suggest to you that you didn't have to talk to them, Mrs. Dwyer?

MINI: Yes. The Finter woman. But then she threatened us. Said it was for our own good and that if we didn't talk she'd have to make out a bum report on us.

FISHMAN: She actually put it in those terms?

TEDDY: Yes.

FISHMAN: (*Writing on his pad.*) Well, that's a start. And what about this county person—Hahn?

TEDDY: Never said a word to him. Never even met him.

FISHMAN: But he's filed a detailed report here describing the inside of your house.

TEDDY: That's right. He broke in one time when we were out. Ruda set it up, took us for a ride. Then he and his man broke right in and destroyed the place for their pictures.

FISHMAN: What do you mean?

MINI: Just what he said. They came in and knocked everything around. Broke pots on the floor. Pushed over Teddy's desk. Even got into my doll chest. And they snapped those cameras right in our faces.

FISHMAN: You're saying they created a mess here and then photographed it as evidence?

TEDDY: That's right.

FISHMAN: You actually saw them do this?

TEDDY: Well, no. We were out with Ruda, like I said. But when we left everything was in ship-shape, like now, and when we came back there they were stepping on Mini's dolls and kicking my books around.

FISHMAN: Do you have any way of proving this?

TEDDY: Well, the pictures. And my system. Everything has a place here. Any disruption is obvious.

FISHMAN: (*Looking around at the cluttered room.*) Yes . . . What pictures, Mr. Dwyer?

TEDDY: Of the room.

FISHMAN: You mean . . .

TEDDY: Yes, the ones they took. Hahn and the lean-to he was with.

FISHMAN: I see. I was hoping you meant some you yourselves had taken. Before Mr. Hahn's little visit. Snapshots even.

MINI: Not a chance. Only pictures in this house are things made by hand or kept in the head. Dwyers don't believe in cameras. Never have.

FISHMAN: I'm sorry to hear that, Mrs. Dwyer.

MINI: Well, don't be. We've never suffered because of it.

(*Fishman looks from Mini to Teddy. A moment.*)

FISHMAN: Frankly, you do seem competent enough to me. Certainly as the law defines the word. And you have money, correct?

TEDDY: More than we'll ever spend.

FISHMAN: Then I'm afraid I don't understand. The main basis for the suit seems to be, as you say, cats and weeds.

MINI: Now you're talking.

FISHMAN: Nothing a little cleaning wouldn't take care of.

TEDDY: I'll clean the damn yard myself.

FISHMAN: And keep an eye on your cats?

TEDDY: I'd watch them, yes.

FISHMAN: You would promise this at a hearing?

TEDDY: Certainly.

FISHMAN: Then to be honest, I don't think they have a case.

TEDDY: Well, what do you know? Did you hear that, Mini?

MINI: I'm here.

TEDDY: Finally someone on our side.

MINI: If we'd never said anything in the first place there wouldn't be any sides. This is still Ruda's fault.

FISHMAN: Yes, you mentioned that before, Mrs. Dwyer. What exactly happened with your daughter?

TEDDY: She didn't understand.

MINI: She turned on us, is what happened. The ingrate. I didn't want to tell her in the first place. It was Teddy's idea.

TEDDY: I thought it only fair.

FISHMAN: Excuse me, but tell her what?

MINI: Why, about our plan, of course.

FISHMAN: I'm sorry, Mrs. Dwyer. What plan?

MINI: Our plan. To kill ourselves.

FISHMAN: I beg your pardon.

MINI: I said to kill ourselves. I'm sure it's in the papers there . . . isn't it? Teddy? Did I . . .

TEDDY: (*Looking at Fishman.*) We assumed . . . that you . . . You'd better look at the papers again, Mr. Fishman. I would guess . . . the Finter woman's part.

FISHMAN: (*Looking at Teddy and Mini.*) Yes. . . . Maybe I'd better. (*Fishman finds the report from Mrs. Finter in the papers, examines it for a long moment. Then he looks up slowly.*) I see. Is this true what she says?

MINI: What?

FISHMAN: That one of you is ill and that you both claim to be contemplating . . . suicide because of it.

MINI: No it isn't.

TEDDY: Mini, he's here to help.

MINI: We're not contemplating anything. We've made up our minds.

FISHMAN: All right. Then would you like to tell me about it, Mrs. Dwyer?

MINI: I don't know.

FISHMAN: I *am* here to help if I can.

MINI: Famous last words . . .

TEDDY: We need someone on our side, Mini.

MINI: What for?

TEDDY: To buy us time. Maybe we shouldn't have told Ruda, like you said. But we did. And now we're in this. So if Mr. Fishman is willing to help—

MINI: If . . .

TEDDY: (*To Fishman.*) We want what we're entitled to: to do as we please with ourselves. We've had what we wanted in this world. We've done all we care to do. We're happy. We're satisfied. Now we're ready to go.

FISHMAN: But only one of you is ill. Isn't that correct?

TEDDY: We've lived together; we want to die together.

FISHMAN: An admirable sentiment, Mr. Dwyer.

TEDDY: It isn't a sentiment. It's the truth. It's earned.

FISHMAN: But you can't just—

TEDDY: (*Interrupting.*) You can't, you can't—is that what we're going to get from you, too? We were told you'd be different.

FISHMAN: Please, I assure you I sympathize with your predicament. If it is, in fact, your predicament. But I must also weigh the facts and represent them to you within the context of the law. That is my obligation as an attorney. Now may I ask which of you is ill?

MINI: No.

FISHMAN: I'm sorry?

MINI: So am I but we're not going to tell you.

FISHMAN: (*Holding up the papers.*) I'm sure it's in here somewhere, Mrs. Dwyer.

MINI: Then you find it. The more we tell, the more trouble we get ourselves into.

FISHMAN: I can see how you might feel that way, Mrs. Dwyer, but—

MINI: You can see, you can see . . . You see nothing.

FISHMAN: On the contrary, Mrs. Dwyer. I see what is before me and what is, in all likelihood, to become of it. I see two people in trouble who I believe are asking for help. Which is why I came here. To offer that help.

MINI: Offer away.

FISHMAN: I need to understand first, Mrs. Dwyer. I need the facts.

TEDDY: Facts . . . What we need is time.

FISHMAN: Excuse me, Mr. Dwyer, but what for?

TEDDY: What?

FISHMAN: Well, if you really feel as you claim to then what do you want with time? Why not just go ahead with this so-called plan and do yourselves in? In fact, why haven't you done it already?

MINI: Because it would be giving in. They'd be cheating us out of what we have left. We'll say when. We'll know when. It'll be our decision on our terms.

TEDDY: Exactly. We just want you to buy us that time, Mr. Fishman. Stop this conservator thing long enough—

FISHMAN: For you to ready yourselves?

TEDDY: Yes.

FISHMAN: I'm sorry, Mr. Dwyer. I'm afraid I can't do that.

TEDDY: Why not?

FISHMAN: I have to be honest with you. If I were to get you off knowing what I now know of your plans and you were to then carry out those plans, I would not only be morally accountable—I would also be an accomplice to a criminal action. I could be held responsible on legal grounds for your deaths.

TEDDY: We would make it clear you weren't responsible. In writing if you like.

FISHMAN: The law doesn't work that way, Mr. Dwyer. Your written statement would be proof positive of my prior knowledge.

MINI: It's no use, Teddy. He's one of them, too.

FISHMAN: I'd be lying if I didn't tell you this, Mrs. Dwyer. Conservatorship can be fought. But not on these grounds. If anything, your reasons would probably serve to speed the process. So that the court might protect you from yourselves.

MINI: Protect us from ourselves. That's a good one.

FISHMAN: I'm sure you can understand the law's position, Mrs. Dwyer.

MINI: I'm afraid not, Mr. Fishman. We Dwyers are people of sense.

FISHMAN: Then I'm afraid I'll have to decline the case. If you really intend to persist with this . . . plan, that is.

MINI: We do.

FISHMAN: Then I could be considered an accomplice even now. The law says a witness to the mere planning of a crime must come forward. And while suicide itself is no longer considered a crime as such, aiding and abetting a suicide—which the two of you are doing for each other and which I would be doing for you both—definitely is.

MINI: Great. Another witness.

FISHMAN: (*Standing, laying the papers down.*) It's obvious, however, that we all have reason to think of this . . . talk . . . as confidential. Your request was to keep it strictly off the record as was my intention when I agreed to come to your home. I am not without feeling, Mr. and Mrs. Dwyer. And if your situation is truly as you represent it then I am . . . sorry for you. As I said, I cannot on the basis of what you have told me accept your case, but the law protects confidential inquiry between attorney and prospective client and, as such, I am prepared to say nothing. Or that this meeting did not, in fact, even occur.

MINI: Listen to that, Teddy. He's prepared to say nothing. And with all those words.

TEDDY: We just want to be together.

FISHMAN: I understand, Mr. Dwyer.

MINI: But you're not prepared to say so.

TEDDY: We know what we're doing. Doesn't that count for anything?

FISHMAN: Yes, it does, Mr. Dwyer. It makes your crime a willful one. I *am* sorry.

(*Fishman walks away from them and picks up his briefcase. Then he turns back.*)

FISHMAN: Do you really think you can . . . do this? I mean, you have it worked out?

TEDDY: Yes.

FISHMAN: You know . . . how?

TEDDY: Yes.

FISHMAN: An actual plan?

TEDDY: Yes.

FISHMAN: You're very brave people.

TEDDY: Not really. We're just trying to act sensibly.

(*Fishman looks at them again.*)

FISHMAN: Well, I wish you . . . I don't know. What do I wish you?
TEDDY: Luck.
MINI: Or a hospital room.
FISHMAN: Yes . . . well . . . luck then. Either way. Goodnight.
MINI: Good-bye, Mr. Fishman.
FISHMAN: Yes. Good-bye . . . Mrs. Dwyer. Mr. Dwyer.

(*Fishman looks at them, hesitates, then exits quickly stage right. From offstage, sound of the front door opening, then closing.*)

TEDDY: Well, so much for that.
MINI: Lawyers . . . To think we even let one in the house.
TEDDY: ¿Qué pasán a los hombres olvidados?
MINI: (*Going back to her doll.*) You can say that again.
TEDDY: I've been saying it all day. I woke up with it in my ears this morning. How long has it been, would you say?
MINI: Since the last time?
TEDDY: Yes.
MINI: Beats me. Remember where you picked it up yet?
TEDDY: No idea.
MINI: Well, you know what? I think it would be a fitting thing to leave behind. It would give them something to think about. All the Fishmans.
TEDDY: What do you mean?
MINI: Just that on a single piece of paper: '¿Qué pasán a los hombres olvidados? Signed, T. and M. Dwyer.'
TEDDY: Maybe . . . maybe . . .
MINI: Could you imagine the looks on their faces when they saw it? Someone like him? Or that Finter woman?
TEDDY: They wouldn't even know what it meant.
MINI: Or that Hahn character? He'd crumple it and tell everyone we were nuts. 'Qué pasán a what? They were nuts. Both of them.' Teddy?
TEDDY: Hm.
MINI: What *does* it mean?
TEDDY: Hm? Oh . . . I . . . (*Going to his desk, looking in his notebook.*) I asked the Nelkins' gardener. Hold on. Right, here it is. Of course. ¿Qué pasán a los hombres olvidados? What happens to the lost ones?
MINI: What happens to the lost ones? I like it . . . I'm about ready, Teddy.
TEDDY: (*Looking at her, startled.*) For what?
MINI: To stuff this. The face is inked on. I need to see it filled.
TEDDY: Oh. You scared me.
MINI: (*Smiling.*) Oh. . . . Sorry.

TEDDY: All right. Is it to the drawers then? We're through with the Fishmans and the Finters and the Hahns once and for all?

MINI: (*Putting down the doll.*) Yes, to the drawers. I'll pick only our finest.

TEDDY: (*Moving to the doorway stage right.*) Save my light blue.

MINI: (*Following.*) We'll take care of ourselves. Just like always.

TEDDY: (*Almost singing.*) Save my light blue.

MINI: No lawyers in this house.

TEDDY: Save my light blue.

MINI: No one but us in this house.

TEDDY: Save my—

(*Just as they reach the doorway, sound of their telephone ringing—a broken, muffled ring. They stop, turn back.*)

TEDDY: Well, what do you suppose that is? I'll get it.

MINI: You'll have to find it first.

(*Teddy has to search for the phone behind piles of his books. Finally he finds it, picks it up.*)

TEDDY: Hello? . . . Yes . . . Oh hello, Mrs. Nelkin . . . What? . . . Oh, I see . . . Well, I'm sorry . . . Yes, I am. Terribly . . . I will, yes . . . Oh, that isn't necessary. I'll take care of it myself . . . No, there's no need to do that, Mrs. Nelkin. Please. Don't . . . Yes, I'll be right over . . . No, it won't happen again. I promise . . . Yes, thank you for calling me and not them. I'll be right over . . . Yes. Good-bye.

(*Teddy hangs up the phone, can't help but smile.*)

MINI: Bob?

TEDDY: Yes.

MINI: What did he do now?

TEDDY: Good one this time.

MINI: (*Coming to him.*) What? Tell me.

TEDDY: Jumped up on the new one's high chair and puked all over the tray.

MINI: Did he!? Well, he's even more sensitive than we knew.

TEDDY: There's more.

MINI: What do you mean?

TEDDY: There was a bird's head in it.

MINI: In what?

TEDDY: The puke. They're all sick over there. And the baby's screaming. She says she'll call the police.

MINI: Mrs. Nelkin?

TEDDY: Yes. I've got to go over.

MINI: All right. What about Bobby?

TEDDY: He's fine. Puked and ran. Right out the window.

MINI: Good for him!

TEDDY: (*Rushing out stage right.*) You stay here. I'll be back.

MINI: (*Calling after him.*) All right. Tell her if she'd put screens on her damn windows like normal people none of this would happen. And as for you, Bobby DeNiro—good for you! (*Smiling.*) Good for you!

(*Mini stabs at the air in front of her and laughs to herself alone in the room. Lights down.*)

SCENE 2

Lights up. Mini in the house. Teddy in the garage. Over the course of several minutes Mini moves about the room and carefully attends to all her plants. With her she has a case which holds her tools: scissors, rags, aerator, misting bottle, plant food, etc. She trims each one, cleans the soil, washes any leaves or stalks with milk, shines them, then waters and mists them. 'Care for the living,' she mumbles to herself, 'care for the living.' During this time Teddy puts the finishing touches on the polishing of their car in the garage. He uses a chamois polishing cloth and occasionally whistles. When he finishes this he walks a circle around the Bonneville and smiles at it. Then he moves to a corner of the garage and slowly pulls a large cardboard box out in front of the car. He removes what looks like a painter's drop cloth and unfurls it on the hood of the car. He carefully folds it into a long rectangle and then picks it up, takes it to the door at the rear of the garage and stuffs it tightly against the bottom. Then he returns to the box, repeats this with a second cloth. Then what looks like a beach towel comes out of the box and Teddy takes it to the window and hangs it over the glass on hooks he has placed there. He stands still for a moment and looks around the garage. Then he returns to the box, bends over, and removes some type of corrugated hosing. He holds it up, looks at it. But then the phone rings inside the house. Mini begins to look for it in the room. Teddy calls out:

TEDDY: Mini? Gonna get that? Mini?

(*She doesn't answer him but picks up the phone after several rings.*)

MINI: Hello . . . Yes, speaking . . . Yes . . . Yes . . . I don't understand. What story? . . . In what paper? . . . No, I haven't. The boy doesn't come this early. Who is this anyway? . . . Look, I think you've got a wrong number . . . No, I won't . . . You tell me who you are first . . . Well, I don't talk to strangers. Least of all over the phone. And I don't know what you're talking about . . . No. Goodbye.

(*She hangs up the phone but stands there looking at it afterward. Teddy opens the door from the garage, leans in.*)

TEDDY: What was that?
MINI: Nothing. Wrong number. What are you up to?
TEDDY: Nothing much. Just checking out the car. How about you?
MINI: Fixing my plants.
TEDDY: They all right?
MINI: Most of them.
TEDDY: The cactus?
MINI: It'll come back.

(*Mini goes back to the plant she was working on. Teddy watches a moment, then goes back into the garage. He looks around again, walks to the drop cloths, shoves them to see that they're tight against the door. He nods, then picks one up, piles it on top of the other and lifts them both, returns them to the box near the car. He also goes to the window, starts to take down the towel. But then the phone inside rings again. Teddy turns, listens. Mini picks it up. Teddy takes the towel, drops it in the box, pushes the box back in the corner, and goes to the door. He opens it, goes back in the house, listens as Mini talks.*)

MINI: Hello? . . . Yes, speaking . . . What? Who is this? . . . What story? Look, if this is some . . . No, no I haven't . . . Well, I might just do that . . . You tell me . . . Yes, that's right . . . Yes, I did . . . Miniature Dwyer's . . . Santa Monica . . . No, a long time ago . . . Well, yes, I still do . . . Here at home . . . Well, you let me see this story first and then I'll tell you . . . Fine, you do that . . . Fine, good-bye. (*She hangs up, again looks at the phone, this time slightly stunned.*)
TEDDY: (*At the door.*) Now what was that?
MINI: They say there's a story in the paper.
TEDDY: Who says?
MINI: I don't know.
TEDDY: What kind of story?
MINI: About us.
TEDDY: The afternoon paper?
MINI: I guess. They wanted our address. One of them remembered the store.
TEDDY: But who were they?
MINI: I don't know.
TEDDY: A story about us?
MINI: That's what they said. They knew all about it.
TEDDY: About what?
MINI: Us.

(*Teddy looks at her, then walks her to the couch.*)

TEDDY: You sit down. I'll be right back.

MINI: Where are you going?

TEDDY: Out front. To see if the paper's here yet.

MINI: He remembered the store . . .

(*Teddy looks at Mini again, then exits stage right. Sound of the front door opening off-stage. Then Teddy coming back in, the door closing. Teddy re-enters stage right with a newspaper.*)

TEDDY: I don't see any story. (*He starts flipping through the pages.*) Nothing here. . . . (*Still flipping.*) Nope . . . Nope . . . (*Starting on the second section of the paper.*) Something about the store? I don't see—(*He stops, is silent. Mini looks up slowly. Teddy has stopped on something, is reading it to himself.*) God damn it . . .

MINI: What.

TEDDY: (*Still reading.*) God damn it . . .

MINI: What.

TEDDY: God damn it . . . (*Now looking up from the paper.*) God damn it.

MINI: What is it? Let me see.

TEDDY: (*Handing Mini the paper.*) Fishman.

MINI: (*Mini takes the paper, finds the story. Reading out loud.*) 'Attorney To Represent Couple In . . . Right-To-Die Case. Attorney S. Fishman of The Santa Monica Legal Clinic announced today that he intended to accept a case he and the clinic had previously turned down. The case involves an elderly Santa Monica couple, Mr. and Mrs. Ted Dwyer, who are being sued by the county for conservatorship over their expressed desire that they be allowed . . .' (*She looks up from the paper.*) You mean he went to them and told? Everything?

TEDDY: Looks that way.

MINI: What for?

TEDDY: It says he had a change of heart after he thought about it.

MINI: So he went to the paper? Why didn't he come to us?

TEDDY: Lawyers like to see their hearts exposed. In print.

MINI: But now it's all over the city. What happens if—

(*The telephone rings again. Teddy and Mini stop, look at each other.*)

TEDDY: Let me get it this time. (*Goes to the phone, picks it up.*) Hello? . . . No, it isn't . . . No, we aren't . . . No, I'm not . . . You must have the wrong number . . . Yes, right name but wrong number. Good-bye. (*Hangs up.*) Takes care of that. You have to just—(*The telephone rings again. Teddy looks at it, picks it up.*) Hello? . . . No. You've got the wrong number. Sorry. (*He slams the phone down, looks at Mini. A moment. Then it rings again.*)

MINI: Jesus Christ in the sky . . .

(*Teddy just picks it up this time and presses the button to disconnect the line. Then he sets the receiver down leaving it off the hook.*)

MINI: What do we do now?

TEDDY: Disconnect the phone.

MINI: And if they find out the address? It's not tough once you know the number.

TEDDY: That's why they're calling. To see if we're the ones. We just keep saying no.

MINI: It won't work. They'll come. Who are they anyway?

TEDDY: Last one said a reporter.

MINI: Oh, great.

TEDDY: We could use them I suppose.

MINI: Sure. Just what we need—blood-suckers crawling all over us. Is that what you want? Teddy?

(*Teddy doesn't answer because Ruda has just entered through the doorway stage right and he has seen her. Mini doesn't notice but she sees Teddy staring.*)

MINI: What are you looking at?

(*Teddy still doesn't answer. Mini then turns on the couch.*)

MINI: Ruda . . . Where did you come from?

RUDA: The door, Mother. I still have my key.

MINI: Well, give it back. You're no longer welcome in this house.

RUDA: Please, Mother, we need to talk.

TEDDY: Talk . . . A man opens his mouth and the world stomps its way in.

RUDA: Daddy—

MINI: You use your father's tongue as a welcome mat.

RUDA: And you prefer the fools you've gone to? The newspapers?

MINI: We didn't go to any damn newspaper.

RUDA: Well, someone did.

TEDDY: It was Fishman.

RUDA: Your lawyer.

TEDDY: That's what he's calling himself apparently. But it's news to us.

RUDA: It's all out of hand. I never for one minute intended—

MINI: Intended—how many wasted lives in that word?

RUDA: All I wanted was for you to talk to someone. Someone who might be able to help.

MINI: There is no such someone in this world, girl. When are you ever going

to learn? We're on our own in this life. All of us. If there was anything I
thought I made clear to you—

RUDA: 'You make your own bed. And then you lie in it.' 'You stake out
a corner. And then you stay in it.'

MINI: Well, some of it got through, I see.

RUDA: All of it, Mother. And it's why you're making no sense to me.

MINI: What are you talking about?

RUDA: You, Mother. You and Daddy. Neither of you would be the ones to
give up. No matter what the circumstances. I can remember sitting in Daddy's chair here, years ago, watching you work. 'Look at this,' you would
say, 'look at this tiny thread. It's as much a part of this world as you or I.'
Do you remember, Mother?

MINI: But everything would be wrong. I wouldn't have my work. I wouldn't
even have my hands.

RUDA: But you'd be alive.

MINI: Not by my definition of the word.

RUDA: You're afraid, aren't you? You're afraid of the pain.

MINI: Pain . . . How old are you, Ruda? You must be forty if you're a day.

RUDA: Not quite, Mother. Still have a few months to go.

MINI: Excuse me. It's just that when I was your age—in fact, your age exactly
—I knew real pain. I had you.

RUDA: Why, thank you, Mother.

MINI: You can't do it, you can't do it, they were all screaming. They said I
was too old. Can you imagine!? Too old at thirty-nine. I told them to go
jump. Grin and bear it, my mother said. So that's what I did. In spite of the
pain. I just lay there on their green table grinning.

RUDA: Maybe you should have listened to them, Mother. Think what you
could have spared yourself.

MINI: Oh, child, you haven't a brain in that head. Where do you suppose it
went? Into a pot? Or the pretty salt air . . .

RUDA: I have a brain, Mother. The one you gave me. In spite of what you
wanted. Or should I put it another way—didn't want.

MINI: Now what are you trying to say?

RUDA: Only what you know to be true. That your daughter is unlike you and
your mother before you and her mother before her.

MINI: Don't be ridiculous. Dwyers beget more Dwyers. It is our—

RUDA: (Interrupting.) What, Mother—duty?

MINI: Well, yes, if you want to put it that way.

RUDA: It's you who wants to put it that way. More of the old grin and bear it.
Mini for her mother.

MINI: No. You're putting words into my mouth.

RUDA: Yes, I am. And maybe they're the words you wanted to say to your
own mother. Way back then. 'I don't want children. I don't need children.

I won't have children.'
MINI: No! Stop!
RUDA: Sew my lips, Mother. Wasn't that how it went when I talked too much?
You'd sew them together, you said, like one of your dolls.
MINI: Only when I was working. And even then—
RUDA: I should have *been* one of your dolls. You've never cared for the fact that
I couldn't be finished. That I would never join the others in the trunk so
you could move on.
MINI: It was you who left this house.
RUDA: I did what I was raised to do: get out of your sight.
MINI: I wanted to be left to myself, not left. There's a difference.
RUDA: Yes, Mother, there is. And I just want you to know that I'm going to
leave to this world exactly what you want—what you've always wanted—to
leave to me: an absence. An absence of Dwyers.
MINI: Don't say that.
RUDA: Why not, Mother? All I have to give you at the age you gave me my life
. . . is your death.

(*Pause. Mini stares at Ruda.*)

MINI: You don't give that to me. No one does. (*She walks out of the room.*)
TEDDY: Ruda.

(*Ruda turns to Teddy.*)

TEDDY: We're not doing this to you. We're doing it to ourselves.
RUDA: But you made me a part of it. You brought me down here.
TEDDY: I know. That was my fault. Your mother was against it and I should
have listened to her. I insisted you had to know. I—
RUDA: You wanted to see me, Daddy.
TEDDY: Yes.
RUDA: You wanted to see me. For you.
TEDDY: No, I—
RUDA: Yes, Daddy. And I love you for it. But this was for you, not me.
Mother was right about the way I would react and you know it. If you real-
ly wanted to do this you should have just left me out of it.
TEDDY: I thought you'd be able to understand. I thought if we explained—
RUDA: You'll never explain this to me.
TEDDY: This isn't like you. This should make sense to you. As it does to us.
RUDA: This is one of those things that makes sense in the mind . . . but not in
the flesh . . . I'd take care of you, Daddy. After she was gone.
TEDDY: Ruda, don't.
RUDA: I mean it. You're still the only man I've ever cared about.

TEDDY: That's wrong. I don't want to hear this again.

RUDA: Why? Because you know it's true?

TEDDY: No. Because it's in the past. You have a life of your own now. Up there. You're always saying how much you like it. Your work, your place, even your business is good.

RUDA: Yes, it is. That's true.

TEDDY: Then what?

RUDA: I'm still . . . alone.

TEDDY: You're a young girl. You have your whole life ahead of you.

RUDA: I'll be forty years old next January, Daddy. And I still call you Daddy. This is funny . . . I didn't even want to come down here when you called. I love being with you but it also . . . hurts so much.

TEDDY: Maybe I tried too hard to make up for your mother. I don't know. I certainly never intended . . .

RUDA: Right. Like Mother says—intended . . . (*She turns away from him.*) Listen to me, Daddy. All I came here today to say was that the County has made everything clear now. It's no longer just talk—it's real. From here on in, it's either depend on me or depend on strangers.

TEDDY: We'll depend on no one, Ruda.

RUDA: You'll have to, Daddy. Eventually.

TEDDY: Who says so?

RUDA: It's the way it is.

TEDDY: Not in this house.

RUDA: In every house. The court will rule against you. You'll have no choice.

(*Mini appears in the doorway up right, has apparently been listening.*)

MINI: We'll have our choice, Ruda. Go back to Carmelcorn.

RUDA: I can't, Mother.

MINI: Yes you can. Just point your car to the sea. The road will take care of the rest.

RUDA: No, Mother, it won't. Before I leave I have to know I've found a way to say one thing I've been trying to say since I first walked in: that I love you, both of you. So just tell me—how am I supposed to say that? By forcing you to live? Or by letting you . . . die?

TEDDY: Ruda.

RUDA: Daddy?

TEDDY: We love you, too. Now . . . good-bye.

(*Ruda looks at Teddy, fights back tears. Then she runs to him, throws her arms around him. Teddy embraces her as well. After a moment she steps back, looks at Mini who looks away. Ruda hesitates, then runs from the room. Sound of the front door opening, slamming offstage.*)

MINI: (*After a moment.*) She understands. But she doesn't understand.

TEDDY: I guess it was too much to expect.

MINI: There is a brain in that head.

TEDDY: I just thought somehow . . .

MINI: I don't know why we should be so surprised. Independence is what we've always asked of her. Still, when it comes back at you . . .

TEDDY: Yes. It hurts. Because you've loved.

MINI: (*Looks at him.*) Teddy?

TEDDY: (*Turning, looking at her.*) I know.

MINI: We have no choice now, do we?

(*Teddy walks to the phone, puts the receiver back on the hook. The phone rings almost immediately. He takes the receiver off, again disconnects the line.*)

TEDDY: Not that I can see.

MINI: They'll be cheating us out of some of our time.

TEDDY: But think of the alternative.

MINI: They'll stop us, won't they.

TEDDY: Guaranteed.

MINI: Well, I don't mind then.

TEDDY: Me either.

MINI: You're sure?

TEDDY: 'It happens that I am tired . . .
   I am tired of my feet and my nails
   and my hair and my shadow.
   It happens that I am tired of being a man . . .'

MINI: What's that called?

TEDDY: 'Walking Around.'

MINI: Good title.

TEDDY: Yes.

MINI: You're serious then?

TEDDY: I'm serious, yes.

MINI: In that case I have something to show you. If you think there's time.

TEDDY: Is it important?

MINI: I would say so.

TEDDY: Then there's time. What is it?

MINI: (*Getting up.*) Something. Close your eyes.

TEDDY: Why? Is it a surprise?

MINI: No. I just like the way you look with your eyes closed.

TEDDY: (*Smiling, then closing his eyes.*) All right, all right.

MINI: (*Moving to her chest in the corner.*) Now keep them shut.

TEDDY: (*A little wobbly on his feet.*) Don't worry.

MINI: (*Opening the chest.*) No cheating.

TEDDY: (*Opening one eye to stop from swaying.*) I'm an honest man.
MINI: (*Taking a doll from the chest.*) Here we are.
TEDDY: Open them?
MINI: (*Moving to him with the doll.*) No, no, I'm coming.
TEDDY: (*Closing his eyes again.*) All right. Tell me when.

(*Mini looks at him, then changes her mind, goes to the table where she sets the doll so that it sits upright on the edge. The doll's face looks very much like Mini's.*)

MINI: Just one more minute.
TEDDY: Say the word.
MINI: (*Now turning around.*) All right. Now.
TEDDY: Open them?
MINI: Yes.
TEDDY: (*Opening his eyes, momentarily losing his balance, then re-gaining it.*) What is it? I don't see.
MINI: Over here.

(*Teddy turns, sees the doll. He walks slowly to the table, examines it for a long moment.*)

TEDDY: Well, well . . . will you look at that? Will you . . . look . . . at . . . that?
MINI: Do you like it?
TEDDY: Like it—I could learn to love a face like that.
MINI: Oh, Teddy.
TEDDY: It's true.
MINI: What about the work?
TEDDY: Elegant, as always.
MINI: I tried a new stitch around the edges.
TEDDY: Still experimenting, eh? Right up to—(*Stops himself.*)
MINI: That's right. Let it be known that Miniature Dwyer was never afraid of taking a risk. Even in her final moments.
TEDDY: That they will know.
MINI: And you really like the face?
TEDDY: It's lovely. Almost a self-portrait, isn't it?
MINI: The face behind my head. I've seen it. And I'm satisfied.
TEDDY: Then it was you all along.
MINI: A little of me. A little of my mother. See the cheeks?
TEDDY: Yes, but the eyes . . .
MINI: Right. A little of Ruda. Do you think she'll notice?
TEDDY: Maybe some day.
MINI: Good. It's the way I'd like to be remembered. As understanding what it was I was made of. And that she was part of that. In spite of . . .
TEDDY: Yes . . . And me? What about me?

MINI: You know where you are, Teddy. The insides.

TEDDY: Who's ever going to see that? They'd have to tear it open.

MINI: And that's as it should be. As it was. You do like it then?

TEDDY: Yes, I like it. It may even be your best.

MINI: (*Going back to the chest.*) As long as it's among my best—that's all I care about. (*Taking out more dolls, bringing them to the table.*) So they say 'she quit at her peak; it was not giving up.'

TEDDY: (*Watching as Mini sets them up next to the new one.*) That they'll say. I can guarantee it.

MINI: That she knew what she was doing. A mind conscious of itself.

TEDDY: Readily apparent.

MINI: (*Going back for more dolls.*) A mind undulled by pain.

TEDDY: It's certain.

MINI: (*Setting them up on the table.*) A mind at work. Even in her final moments.

TEDDY: Just like her mother.

MINI: (*Smiling.*) Yes.

TEDDY: Who was quite a woman.

MINI: Yes.

TEDDY: And who had quite a daughter.

MINI: Yes.

TEDDY: Who had a daughter of her own and then went the same way.

MINI: Yes.

(*The dolls are now set up in a line extending the entire outer edge of the table, the new one at the center.*)

MINI: There. How about that?

TEDDY: Quite a collection.

MINI: It is, isn't it?

TEDDY: Yes.

MINI: And think of all the others. Scattered all over. Who knows where?

TEDDY: Yes.

MINI: I'm pleased. I'm satisfied. I'm . . . ready.

TEDDY: Good.

(*Teddy looks at her. A moment. Then he smiles, steps forward, and undoes his belt buckle and the top button on his pants.*)

MINI: Teddy? What are you doing?

TEDDY: I've got something to show you, too. (*He continues to open his pants which have a button fly.*)

MINI: Oh, Teddy.

TEDDY: (*Continuing.*) I'm serious.

MINI: What. I see the buttons. They're good as new.
TEDDY: (*Continuing.*) No.
MINI: What then? (*She sees.*) Oh . . . Your light blue.
TEDDY: (*At the same time.*) My light blue.

(*They both laugh. Mini then goes to Teddy and they embrace. After a moment they separate.*)

MINI: Well . . . anything else then?
TEDDY: (*Looks at her.*) One more thing.
MINI: The will. Did you do what we said, Teddy?
TEDDY: You be the judge.

(*Teddy takes a paper from inside his Neruda book on the desk. He unfolds it, holds it up. He reads.*)

TEDDY: To whom it may concern:
'. . . In the margin of these lines
you will have found your name,
I care but precious little,
we talked of nothing else
than a hell of a lot more,
why you are and why you aren't
and this happens to everyone,
no one can work out everything:
when all accounts are done
we all turn out rich have-beens
now ranked with the new poor.

So I leave to those who barked
my hiker's eyelashes,
my preference for salt,
the address of my smile,
so that they steal it all
discreetly if they can:
since they could hardly kill me
I cannot stop them now.
Let them not wear my clothes
and not appear on Sundays
with slices of my corpse
unerringly disguised.
I left no one alone,
they're hardly going to spare me,

it'll be seen no matter:
they will publish my socks.'

¿Qué pasán a los hombres olvidados?
T. and M. Dwyer.

MINI: Hear, hear.

TEDDY: You like it?

MINI: Very much. Let's leave it with the dolls. Over here.

TEDDY: It's from his 'Autumn Testament.' The last line of course being mine.

MINI: Of course. (*She takes the will and places it in the lap of the new doll at the center of the table. Then she looks back to Teddy.*) Anything else then?

TEDDY: Not that I can think of.

MINI: What about Bobby and the others?

TEDDY: They're on their own. The sooner they learn, the better.

MINI: I suppose so. (*Smiling.*) Maybe the Nelkins will take some of them in.

(*Teddy looks at her, smiles.*)

MINI: Teddy?

TEDDY: Hm.

MINI: How does it work again? Not by choking? We won't smell anything?

TEDDY: We'll smell plenty. But we'll be unconscious before any choking. The carbon monoxide gets into your blood, eats up your oxygen from the inside out. Not unlike—

MINI: The way Finnerman said I'd—

TEDDY: Yes. But faster. And without the pain.

MINI: Well, that's . . . nice.

TEDDY: Yes . . . All set then?

MINI: (*Looks around the room for a moment.*) I guess.

TEDDY: (*Going to the door to the garage and opening it.*) Then let's go.

MINI: (*She goes to the cactus on Teddy's desk, places a hand on it—at first affectionately but then squeezing hard. She grimaces at the pain from the needles.*) Yes . . . let's. (*She moves to Teddy at the door. She starts to step into the garage, then stops.*) You don't want anything with you? A book?

(*Teddy looks at Mini. Then they both suddenly break into laughter.*)

MINI: Good one, huh? A book.

TEDDY: Yes.

(*They both look at each other, then away and very slowly around the room. Teddy reaches to a wall switch, shuts off the lights. Then they step into the garage, Teddy pulling the door shut behind them.*)

TEDDY: It'll just be a minute here. (*He goes to the corner of the garage, pulls the cardboard box out again. He opens it, takes one of the drop cloths out, again unfurls it on the hood of the car and folds it neatly into a rectangle.*)

MINI: What's that for?

TEDDY: (*Taking it to the back of the garage.*) The door.

MINI: Hm?

TEDDY: (*Putting it down against the door.*) The door. Have to plug the cracks.

MINI: I thought you had a hose.

TEDDY: I do. But you still have to plug the cracks.

MINI: Oh. I thought it would be just the hose.

TEDDY: (*Coming back for the second cloth.*) No. The cracks, too. (*Folding it.*) It'll just be a minute.

MINI: All right. (*Watching Teddy.*) This is exciting, isn't it?

TEDDY: (*Taking the second cloth to the door.*) Hm?

MINI: This is exciting. My heart is beating.

TEDDY: Yes.

MINI: Good way to go. With your heart beating.

(*Teddy finishes with the cloths, then goes to the box for the corrugated hosing.*)

MINI: Oh, there's the hose.

(*Teddy takes it to the rear of the car.*)

MINI: Is it strong?

TEDDY: Yes, it's corrugated.

MINI: Where did you get it?

TEDDY: (*Kneeling to place the hose over the tail pipe of the car.*) Where America shops. Sears.

MINI: (*Laughing.*) Oh, that's a good one. You should write that in your book, Teddy.

TEDDY: (*Standing, opening the trunk of the car.*) I did. (*He reaches into the trunk, fixes the hose, then eases the door back down just short of the latch.*)

MINI: Where is it anyway?

TEDDY: What.

MINI: Your book.

TEDDY: The desk. Front left leg.

MINI: Didn't you want it out somewhere?

TEDDY: It's needed where it is. (*Now coming around to Mini.*) There we are.

MINI: All set?

TEDDY: Yes. All set.

MINI: With everything?

TEDDY: With everything.

MINI: The hose is ready?
TEDDY: The hose is ready.
MINI: And the cracks are plugged?
TEDDY: The cracks are plugged.
MINI: Then I guess we're all set.
TEDDY: We're definitely all set.
MINI: (*Looks at him.*) Well . . . what do we do then?
TEDDY: (*Going to the car, opening the door.*) Just get in.
MINI: (*Moving to the car.*) Like we were going for a drive.
TEDDY: Exactly.
MINI: Where to?

(*Teddy looks at her. They laugh. Then Mini suddenly puts her arms around Teddy.*)

MINI: I love you, Teddy.
TEDDY: I love you, too, Miniature Dwyer.
MINI: (*Breaking off.*) Well then . . . let's go.

(*Mini gets in the car. Teddy follows pulling the door shut behind him. Sound inside the car is miked, giving the impression of a sealed glass booth.*)

TEDDY: Let's throw a little light on the subject. (*Turns the dome light on above them.*) There. Now . . . window up.(*Rolls up the window.*) Door locked. (*Pushes the button down.*) Now . . . all I have to do is take the key, put it in the ignition, leave it in park, brake on, and then I just—
MINI: (*Interrupting.*) Teddy.
TEDDY: Hm.
MINI: We're doing the right thing, aren't we?
TEDDY: You're not having second thoughts now.
MINI: Not for me.
TEDDY: For who then?

(*Mini doesn't answer.*)

TEDDY: Me?

(*She still doesn't answer.*)

TEDDY: What is it?
MINI: You can go back in the house, get in bed, say you were taking a nap, that you didn't hear, that you didn't know, that you—
TEDDY: (*Interrupting her.*) Now why would I want to do that?
MINI: You wouldn't want to?

TEDDY: Not on your life.

MINI: I wouldn't hold it against you.

TEDDY: I know that.

MINI: It's speak up now or—

TEDDY: Forever hold my peace.

(*Teddy turns the key in the ignition. Sound of the engine coming on, then idling smoothly.*)

TEDDY: It's sensible, nothing more.

MINI: That wasn't hard, was it?

TEDDY: Just a turn of the key.

MINI: Same one we've used all along?

TEDDY: Never once replaced it.

MINI: (*Sliding over to his side.*) Talk to me, Teddy.

TEDDY: All right.

MINI: I remember when you bought this car. Cinco de Mayo, wasn't it? 1961? You drove up in front of the store and you beeped.

TEDDY: Right onto the sidewalk.

MINI: You had a straw hat from downtown.

TEDDY: They were giving them out free in the showroom. Sombreros. You mean all you have to do is buy a car, I asked. That's right, the gimp answered, and the hat is yours. In that case, I said, I'll take it. You should have seen the look on his face. A hat for the price of a car. Those were the days. (*Laughs.*)

MINI: I closed the shop and we drove to my mother's. I remember walking in, down that long hallway that smelled like a wet cracker. She was taking a bath in that tiny room in the back, a bottle of beer on the tile beside her. 'We bought a car,' I said. 'Who—you and Roosevelt?' she asked. 'Teddy,' I said, 'Teddy Dwyer. Same name as ours.' 'Just like the Roosevelts,' she answered, 'a Dwyer marries a Dwyer.' Then she asked me to hop in. 'Hot one today,' she said. She was naked and the tile above her head was chipped. And pink. Like her body. Like her. It was shortly after that that she . . .

TEDDY: Yes.

MINI: And it was like I always said, wasn't it? She was at work?

TEDDY: Yes.

MINI: And she didn't suffer?

TEDDY: Not for long anyway.

MINI: Teddy?

TEDDY: Hm.

MINI: It smells.

TEDDY: Make your way . . .

MINI: Bad as Bobby's litter box.

TEDDY: Make your way . . .

MINI: Or that time Ruda left a taco in the glove compartment and it sat for two days.

TEDDY: Another day and you make your way.

MINI: Hot sauce and all. Teddy?

TEDDY: Hm.

MINI: Remember?

(*Nothing now but the sound of the engine idling for a moment or two. Then in the house two figures appear in the doorway stage right. A Television Newsman and a Cameraman he has brought with him. The Cameraman is outfitted with lights and a porta-pak video camera.*)

CAMERAMAN: We can't do this. We can't just barge in here without asking.

NEWSMAN: Why not?

CAMERAMAN: For one thing, it's against the law.

NEWSMAN: Hey, we're on their side. What are they going to care? A little face on the six o'clock and they'll be kissing our butts like everyone else. (*Seeing the dolls on the table.*) Well, well . . . this is the place, all right. Get a shot of this.

CAMERAMAN: You sure?

NEWSMAN: Come on. What's the matter with you?

CAMERAMAN: I just don't want any trouble.

NEWSMAN: Come on. Just get a shot of this and then we'll wait outside. OK?

CAMERAMAN: If you say so.

NEWSMAN: I say so.

(*The Cameraman switches on his light, aims his camera at the dolls, the room, etc.*)

NEWSMAN: You know, I smell something.

CAMERAMAN: (*Turning off the camera.*) What?

NEWSMAN: (*Walking toward the door to the garage.*) I smell something. A car running.

CAMERAMAN: What?

NEWSMAN: There's a car running. (*Now at the door.*) In here.

CAMERAMAN: Jesus, it's them.

NEWSMAN: Exactly. Get that camera ready.

CAMERAMAN: For what? Let's get out of here.

NEWSMAN: Don't be ridiculous. Get the camera ready.

CAMERAMAN: You're crazy.

NEWSMAN: Just follow me.

(*The Newsman takes hold of the door to the garage, opens it, goes inside. The Cameraman follows. They see Teddy and Mini in the car.*)

CAMERAMAN: My God. Get a window open.
NEWSMAN: Get a shot of that.
CAMERAMAN: Are you crazy? Get that door. Get them out of there.
NEWSMAN: I'll get the door. You get the picture.
CAMERAMAN: I can't breathe.
NEWSMAN: (*Screams.*) Get the picture!
CAMERAMAN: You're crazy.
NEWSMAN: Get the picture!

(*The Cameraman finally raises his light and camera. A flood of light across the hood and windshield of the car, Teddy and Mini inside. Then blackout.*)

SCENE 3

Lights up. Mini on the couch, a Doctor over her administering oxygen through a plastic mask. Ruda and Policeman stage right. Mini's dolls are lumped together in a single pile at one end of the table. Teddy seems to be staring at them.

DOCTOR: She'll need some caring for but she'll be all right.
RUDA: And my father?
DOCTOR: Observation certainly.
RUDA: Where? County?
DOCTOR: Unless you prefer someplace else.
RUDA: Can they be together there?
DOCTOR: I doubt it. Not under the circumstances.
RUDA: What about somewhere else?
DOCTOR: Technically, Ma'am, they're under arrest.
RUDA: They just wanted to be together.
DOCTOR: Hm?
RUDA: They just wanted to be together.
DOCTOR: Funny way of showing it.
RUDA: They meant no harm to anyone . . . else.
DOCTOR: The law is the law.
RUDA: My mother was sick.
DOCTOR: Don't worry. We'll take good care of her. Officer?
POLICEMAN: (*Turning to the Doctor.*) One at a time or both together?
DOCTOR: Hm?
POLICEMAN: To the van. One at a time or both of them together?
DOCTOR: Does it matter?
POLICEMAN: Cameras outside, sir. I'd say one at a time.

DOCTOR: All right. Whatever.

POLICEMAN: (*Looks at Teddy.*) I'll take this one first. And then come back for her. Will you be wanting a stretcher, sir?

DOCTOR: Well, she can't very well walk, can she?

POLICEMAN: I don't know, sir. That's your decision. I just thought with the crowd out there . . . Stretcher then?

DOCTOR: Yes, a stretcher.

POLICEMAN: If you say so. (*Moving to Teddy.*) All right, friend, up 'n' at 'em. (*Taking Teddy by the arm, then turning to Ruda.*) You're welcome to come along, Ma'am. Might look better out front, you know.

RUDA: Thank you. I think . . . I'll wait with my mother.

POLICEMAN: If you say so. Be back with the stretcher then.

(*The Policeman takes Teddy but then sees he has one of Mini's dolls in his hand.*)

POLICEMAN: Let's leave that here now. (*He takes the doll, tosses it back on the pile with the others.*) That a boy. Come on now. That's it.

(*He leads Teddy off stage right. Sound of the front door opening and closing offstage.*)

DOCTOR: Don't worry. He'll be all right. They all get these ideas at one point or other.

RUDA: Think so?

DOCTOR: You spend your life trying to avoid it and then all of the sudden you find yourself wishing for it. The difference is these two seemed to know what they were doing.

RUDA: Yes.

DOCTOR: Well, we'll take care of them. And you'll see, some day you'll be sitting with them and they'll thank you. Look what we would have missed, they'll say. You wait and see.

RUDA: I will.

(*Ruda looks at Mini, then goes to the couch, kneels. The Doctor moves off to one side, begins to write on a clipboard.*)

RUDA: Mother? Can you hear me? Mother?

(*Mini opens her eyes wide, looks up at Ruda.*)

RUDA: You need me. Maybe for the first time. I understand now. What you were doing. And what I've been doing. And you . . . and Daddy . . . belong together. Dwyers do beget Dwyers. Do you hear me, Mother? I'll see that things are done your way. I'll get you out.

(*Mini looks at Ruda, then over at the Doctor who is busy writing. She then reaches up, takes the oxygen mask off of her own face.*)

MINI: (*Almost whispering, but with resolve.*) We'll do it again, Ruda.
RUDA: (*Nodding assent.*) I know, Mother.

(*Mini stares into Ruda's eyes for a long moment, looks puzzled. Then she slowly reaches for Ruda's face, touches it. A moment. Then with suddenness, Ruda and Mini embrace.*)

RUDA: I know . . .

(*Lights down.*)

END

Hajj
The Performance

Lee Breuer

Hajj was first performed in its entirety at the New York Shakespeare Festival in May 1983, with the following cast:

Performed by Ruth Maleczech

Director: Lee Breuer
Sets and Lights: Julie Archer
Video: Craig Jones
Music: Chris Abajian
Taped Performers: Phil Schenk (father); Lute Ramblin (child)
Technical Director: David Hardy

Hajj-Part One was first presented as a work-in-progress as part of the Wooster Group Visiting Artists Series in May 1982. It was later presented as part of the National Video Festival by the American Film Institute in Los Angeles and Washington, D.C. at the Kennedy Center in June 1982. *Hajj*-Parts One and Two were presented for the first time at the California Institute of the Arts in March 1983.

Lights discover the Performer seated, back to audience before a low makeup table with a large triptych mirror that shows her triple reflection to the audience—tile surface, Arabic motifs, a clutter of toiletries and makeup paraphernalia. She has previously put up her hair, blocked out her eyebrows and put on alcohol. Now she attaches an elastic headband and applies the six tapes requisite for an on-stage face lift. Then she applies liquid base. Her voice is amplified.

Three closeups of the performer appear in the three planes of the triptych mirror. The effect is achieved by the placement of color video monitors behind one-way mirrors connected to three cameras in a reverse studio configuration—three closed circuit systems functioning simultaneously. Performer speaks to herself and simultaneously her reflections.

I HAVE NOTHING TO HIDE .

She appears to blow out the images as if they were candles and repeats—

I HAVE NOTHING TO HIDE .

while reaching for eyeliner. The eyeliner is in a set of nine colors mounted in a plastic display case. It resembles an enlarged electronic calculator or adding machine. The eyeliners are in actuality buttons that activate phrases of computer programmed music that allude to electronic calculating machines. The music plays.

A camera closeups a price tag on a hairdryer reading "$99.98." The performer reads—

NINETY-NINE NINETY-EIGHT .

Performer, utilizing hairdryer to dry makeup base, shown in close shot says—

I CAN TAKE ANYTHING .

She activates "eyeliner" computer—music pours forth. She continues—

TWO HUNDRED A WEEK LESS SOME SOCIAL SECURITY .

More "cash register" music. She sings—

THE MAN THAT I MARRY
WILL COME CASH AND CARRY—

"Cash register" bells with a conga beat—

I HEAR MY MUSIC PLAYING .

A camera begins a very slow, sensuous pan in extreme closeup of all the bells and bottles on the table that continues throughout the following.

—sonorous, silvery bells play—

THIRTY PIECES OF SILVER .

The Performer applies, between each line, various colors of liner and rouge. Each time she touches a color of her "palette," the color acts as a computer button and music pours forth.

I'LL PAY YOU TOMORROW .

A closeup of a kleenex—on it is written "$5.09."

FIVE O NINE .

She takes the kleenex from the box, uses it, crumples, tosses.

I'LL PAY YOU THE DAY AFTER TOMORROW .

Another closeup of kleenex—on it written "$7.42."

SEVEN FORTY-TWO .

She takes from box, uses, crumples, tosses.

I'LL PAY YOU HALF ON SATURDAY .
THEN IF I CAN GET A—

Closeup of kleenex with words "check cashed" written—

CHECK CASHED—
I'LL DROP THE REST OFF MONDAY
BEFORE SEVEN O'CLOCK .

Music—eight bells. She corrects herself.

EIGHT .

Music—ten bells. The extreme closeup camera pan is now showing the tiny bells scattered around the table that produce the bell sounds.

TEN .

—twelve bells—

I KNOW YOU NEED IT .
I'M NOT TRYING TO RIP YOU OFF .
TWELVE .

—thirty quick bells—

TWELVE-THIRTY .
THIRTY BY FRIDAY
AND THE REST PAID
BY THE FIRST OF THE MONTH .

Bells play—first half of Big Ben motif—

EVEN

—second half of Big Ben motif—

STEVEN .

Bells play first half of Mendelssohn's "Wedding March" motif. She says to her reflection—

I LOVE YOU .

—second half of "Wedding March" motif.

I NOW PRONOUNCE YOU
A POUND OF FLESH.
TWO-NINETEEN A POUND.

The extreme closeup pan of the objects on the table comes to rest on a blond wig as for a child. The Performer's hand caresses it on camera in the manner of a filmic insert. She says—

I LOVE MY DADDY.

A close shot of the body of a sleeping child about eight years old, the camera panning the full length of the body. The image floats across all three mirror/monitors like a dream or memory—sound of wind and distant sheep bleating. The Performer's memories are shown, as here, by pre-recorded imagery on tape that is patched into the closed-circuit systems at the appropriate times. The live, closed-circuit camera work then stands for her mentation and associations in the present as distinct from the pre-recorded taped sequences which elucidate her memories and daydreams from the past.

Over the image of the child, she says—

THE DAY BEFORE YESTERDAY,
THE TRUTH PUT ME TO SLEEP.
A HAIL STORM ON MY FINGERS
DID NOT WAKE ME.
NOR A LIGHT SHINING IN MY EYE.

—a distant phrase of Al Adan Al Charhi, *the Arabic call to prayer, is heard—*

THE PROPHET OF LOSS
SANG TOO FAINTLY.
I HEARD NOT SCRIPTURE.

Closeups of the Performer—profile, then from reverse profile—pan across the mirrors. She is putting on mascara.

THE PROBLEM IS CASH.
THAT'S A LIE.
THE PROBLEM IS CASH FLOW.
THAT'S A LIE.
THE PROBLEM IS FLOW
DON'T YOU KNOW.

Closeup pans in opposite direction. She puts on lipstick.

LIES! (A STUDY IN COST ACCOUNTING)
LIES! (A CHRONICLE OF EXPENDITURES)
LIES! ALL LIES! ALL—

Video image of Performer's face, tightly cropped, in a hand mirror.

MY LIFE SUCKS.

She lights a cigarette.

BIG BUCKS.

Blows out image—activates computer music, which alludes to a telephone ringing.

I'LL GET BACK TO YOU.
PENNIES FROM HEAVEN.

Ringing continues.

I'LL GET BACK TO YOU.
SEVEN COME ELEVEN.

—continues.

I'LL GET BACK TO YOU.

She blows smoke. Amplified, it resembles a jet plane. Cameras zoom over the table. The image resembles an aerial view.

SEVEN FORTY SEVEN.

Performer reclines with her head propped against the table—smoking the cigarette. Reverse angle closeups of her on mirror monitors.

I HAVE A SPIRITUAL LIFE.
PACKAGE INCLUDES—

A single bell tone introduces each.

FOOD.
SHELTER.

PEDIATRICIAN .
TUITION .
GRADUATED ALLOWANCE .
SUMMER CAMP .

Side cameras' closeups slowly recede.

TRAVEL .
LOAN .
LAWYER .
BAIL .
SHRINK .
PENSION .
ASCENSION .
FUNERAL STONE
INSCRIBED, "HERE LIES A SPIRITUAL LIFE" .

ONE HUNDRED TWENTY-TWO THOUSAND EIGHT HUNDRED
FORTY-ONE DOLLARS AND TWENTY-EIGHT CENTS . NONE OF
THIS IS TAX DEDUCTIBLE AT PRESENT, BUT THERE'S A BILL
PENDING .

*As she smokes, her face is replaced by closeups of the cigarette smoke on the mirror/video
screens.*

THERE IS A WOMB OF AIR
BETWEEN MY FEET AND THE FLOOR .
THERE IS A WOMB OF SILENCE
BETWEEN YOUR VOICE AND MY EAR .
THERE IS A WOMB OF LIES
BETWEEN MY MIND AND LIFE .
I'M A PEA IN A SHELL GAME .
DON'T BET ON ME .
FIVE'LL GET YOU—
—THREE .

*Here begins a long memory sequence on videotape, utilizing various combinations of the
mirror/video screens. We see mysterious and lyric views of an old World War II Army
truck, still and in motion—on roads and in an open field—snow on the ground. Once we
see a close shot of a hunting rifle on the truck seat, and the Performer lying by it superimposed. She reaches for the gun. Suddenly the sound of thunder. The truck and its occupants—the Performer as a Child, and an adult, perhaps her Father—are traveling. The
journey has spiritual overtones, a pilgrimage of sorts.*

The Child, riding, speaks to the camera in closeup. The Child says

I SING OF YOU ALEX WHO I KILLED . OF COURSE I DID . AND
THANK YOU . DEAR . . .

The Performer joins the Child, lips synching.

. . . FOR EVERY FANTASY I REAPED . AND CURSE YOU . PRICK .
I OWE YOU MONEY . YOU'VE BEEN DEAD FOR HALF MY LIFE .
YOU ARE MY HALF LIFE . LOVE . YOU DATE MY ART . . .

. . . *The Child's voice drops out, leaving the Performer's voice post-synchronizing the image of the Child. She is now dressed identically to and made up to resemble the Child in the truck. An old patchwork quilt around her shoulders, blond wig, face lift with youthful-seeming base and coloration, the same orange bandana the Child wears in the image. Her voice seeks to recreate the Child's phrasing.*

. . . I SEE MY ART IN THE GREEN GLOW OF RADIUM . ALWAYS
LESS BY HALF . I SEE THIS GAME . AS CUTE AS ARCHAEOLOGY .
I'M GOING TO PAY YOU . BABY . WATCH ME DIG YOU UP AND
STUFF IT UP YOUR ANUS MAGNUS . WATCH ME WRITE THIS . I
SING OF YOU .

Over an image of the truck receding into the twilight—country desolate, winter road—the Performer's face (live, closed-circuit) is superimposed on the pre-recorded sky. She speaks, less now in the Child's phrasing.

ONCE . ONCE A LIFE WALL PAPER SMOKES . YELLOW LEAF
CLUSTERS FLARE . FALL . FLAKE AWAY UNDER MY BATHED
BARE FOOTPRINTS . ONCE . ONCE . ONCE A LIFE THE CLOCK .
THE DEMON READS ALOUD . THE WRITING ON THE OTHER
WALL . A CALL TO PILGRIMAGE .

Other images of the truck appear simultaneously traveling other roads.

LO AND BEHOLD . WE'RE ON OUR WAY . FOLLOW THE BOUN-
CING BALL . THE SUN LOOKS LIKE A MELTED DEUTCHMARK .
IT ACETYLENE'S THE SCENERY . ROADS . RIVERS . ROCKS LIKE
CRAP ON THE TEN BELOW SNOW . I THINK OF YOUR RIBS AND
YOUR LIFE IN MY MIND . . .

The mirrors go black. Then light headlamps shine through the two side mirrors, making them allude to headlamps of the truck, and the mirrors to windshields.

. . . THE SUN GOES OUT . SSSSST . LIKE A MATCH INTO A WAVE . WE'RE ON OUR WAY TO CHEATS BAY . SSSST .

Headlamps go out.

. . . LIGHTS OUT . LET'S DRIVE IN DARKNESS .

The mirror/screens show views from inside the speeding truck—left and right closeups of the rear view mirrors showing winter trees, streams and mountains speeding by; center the winding road over the hood. The sound track—a Dervish chant, The Mawlid-Invocation Of The Divine Name, *over the truck motor. The head of the Performer making a sign of the devil with her fingers is superimposed over the windshield—the image is of the Child riding in the truck. She growls in a devil's voice.*

READY OR NOT . AL . HERE I COME . WITH CASH . MY CHECK'S NO GOOD . DEAD MAN . I COME TO SODOMIZE YOU WITH A ROLL OF JACKSONS .

The Performer dances against the images of the speeding truck—speeding forward and backward, by rearview mirror reflection—at the same time. She spins as Dervish and simultaneously mimetically drives the truck like a child playing with a steering wheel. Vocally she roars as the motor which, electronically altered, appears to become a blood curdling scream. The onrushing truck swerves off the road and careens into the mouth of a mountain cave like the opening of an Egyptian tomb. And the screens go black.

The sound of a deluge of rain, an echoing gun shot—echoing like the thunder. The image of rain splattering over a rock. In the rock, the Performer's face superimposed—weeping. She mourns.

IF I SELL THIS . ALEXANDER . I WILL MOVE YOUR BONES TO PERSIA . WANT TO BET ME . CONQUEROR OF ASIA . PUT YOUR MONEY WHERE YOUR MOUTH WAS .

In the center of the triptych a memory image. The truck in a blizzard of snow. The Child, under the quilt, struggling home to an old weathered farm house. Inside, the Child held in the Father's arms, being rocked to sleep, speaks as if in a dream . . .

IF ONLY I CAN TALK TO YOU . ALI . LOVINGLY . . .

The Performer, on closed circuit in the side mirror/screens, looking like the Child, appears to hold herself in her own arms in the same position. They continue speaking together.

. . . HERE IN THE MOON BLANCHED KITCHEN OF MY DREAM-

ING . POWDER SNOW BLOWING IN A GENIE GUST . OR IN THE
BATHTUB OF MY MEMORY . LIT BY NOSTALGIA'S CANDLE .
SHADOWS OF CATS ON THE SHADOWY WALL CHASING
SHADOWS OF MICE ON THE CEILING . . . MOUSE . . . BLIND
MOUSE . . . IF I . . . IF I CAN TALK TO YOU WITH A TONGUE
FRESH LICKED . BY A TONGUE FRESH LICKED . I WILL BE BET-
TER . EVERY TIME A LITTLE BETTER BLED OF PRIDE.

A black out—all video goes dead.

ALEX . ALEX YOU GO DEAD ON ME .

*The Performer now speaks without amplification and unenhanced by video. She changes
her makeup, wig, costume and character to that of a woman, half martyr, half
whore—strangely like the Child decayed. She completes her makeup with the insertion of
three bejewelled teeth fitting over her own.*

. . . YOU ARE THE ONE I CAN'T PAY OFF . I CAN'T PUT OFF
YOUR BILL . UNTIL . THE DAY AFTER TOMORROW . WHEN I
SCORE . I'LL SCORE FOR MORE THE DAY I EULOGIZE MY
OWING . UNHAPPILY YOU'RE THROUGH . THERE'S JUST NO
COMING THROUGH FOR YOU . YOU DONE ME . SEE . I AIN'T A
GOOD GUY . I CAN'T SUCK MY ABSOLUTION FROM YOUR COL-
LARBONE . AND YOU CAN'T CRY .

LOVE IS MONEY . ALEX . MONEY . LOVE . THAT'S ALL YE NEED
TO KNOW . THE TERMS . I OWE YOU FORTY DOLLARS ALEX-
ANDER OF THE EARTH . NOW LET'S DO BUSINESS .

I CAN'T TALK TO YOU . I TALK TO MONEY . MONEY KNOWS
ME . WE MAKE DEALS --- HEY ALEX . THROW ME A LINE . I'LL
WRITE IT ON YOU WITH MY FINGERNAIL BELOW YOUR SPINE .

ONCE YOU DIE YOU LIVE FOREVER . ONCE YOU'VE LIVED
YOU'RE GOOD AS GONE . ONE'S THE BILLING . ONE'S THE FEE .
UP YOUR BLACK BONE BABY . CASH ME . IN SECRECY .

*She takes a flashlight in hand and speaks to men in the audience, one by one, searching out
the darkened faces, holding and releasing them with the flashlight beam.*

HOW STRANGE THE NIGHT . ALEXIS . SLEEPING WITH YOU IN
THE SEVENTEENTH ARRONDISEMENT RIGHT ON THE STONES
. THE COBBLESTONES . AU COIN DE LIEBE STRASSE UND

GEMUTLICH PLATZ . FUCK . ON THE FUTON . FUCK . IN THE
MUMMY BAG . OH OH NON DIMENTICARE ALEX . I SLEPT
WITH YOU ON VIA DOLCE UNDER THE LAMBRETTAS . FUCK .
IN SLEEPING CARS EN ROUTE TO BEAUTIFUL CHAMPAGNE UR-
BANA . GATEWAY TO THE CANYON . COLDWATER CANYON IN
THE HOT TUB UNDER THE FAN IN FRONT OF THE FIRE ON TOP
OF THE TURK . ISH . CAR . PET .

WEST SIX SEVEN PUSH B THREE . FUCK . EAST SEVEN COME
ELEVEN PUSH C FOUR . BY THE CLIFFS . "CLIFF!" . OVER
WATERS . "WATERS!" . IN THE DARK SIDE OF THE WINDOW
ON THE SNOWY SKY INTO WHICH SO MANY BLACKBIRDS FLY .
ALEX !

Bells play a little lullaby. She sings

I HEAR MY MUSIC PLAYING .
I HEAR ALL MY LOVES . THEY'RE SINGING .
LISTEN . ALEX . I HEAR WHAT I'M SAYING .
ALEX . LISTEN . ALL THE PRAYER BELLS STOPPED RINGING .

*She dances. The bottles and bells syncopate like a belly dance. She holds the flashlight in her
crotch and seduces the audience with its beam.*

STRANGE THE NIGHT . ALEXIS . SLEEPING WITH YOU ON THE
SET OF HOTEL UNIVERSE . THE KEYS TO HOTEL UNIVERSE
ARE IN MY POCKET . UNDER THE MAT . AT THE DESK IN AN
ENVELOPE . BY THE FLOWER POT SECOND FROM LEFT . FUCK .
RIGHT . FUCK . LEFT. THE KEYS TO HOTEL UNIVERSE ON KEY
RINGS WITH INITIALS . A B C D E F G H I J K L M N O OH OH .

*The face of an old man appears in the center video. The image pans from one old man's
face to another echoing the manner in which she lit faces in the audience.*

THE KEYS TO HOTEL UNIVERSE ON KEY RINGS . 1 2 3 . 4 5 6 7 . 8 9
0 . 1 2 3 4 . HELLO . I HEAR YOU . YOU'RE THE ONE THAT RINGS
A LITTLE DEAD .

*The Performer's face in color, superimposed over the black and white portraits of the old
men, appears to search them out while speaking. Her hand in closeup on the side mir-
ror/screens clicks keys like* zil *to the continuing rhythm.*

THE GRAY EYE LOOKING INWARD . BLACK EYE DARTING

FROM SIDE TO SIDE . AN EAR . TICK TICK TICK . TO THE
GEIGER COUNTER OF OBSESSION . EAR TO DECAY . HALF LIFE
THAT FITS THE HALF LIFE . ME HALF YOU. YOUR FACE AP-
PEARS IN OTHER FACES . EYES SWIM UP IN OTHER EYES .
YOUR TOUCH TOUCHES ME . IT'S OTHER FINGERS . YOUR
DEATH RINGS . TING A LING . IN EVERYTHING .

*The Performer's face in color comes to rest precisely superimposed over the face of Alex in
the black and white photograph. He appears to come alive as her lips move over his. She
says*

RIGHT HERE . I WRITE . HERE I COME . BACK . IN LOVE WITH
YOU AGAIN . AGAIN . ALEXANDER READ MY WRITING . OPEN
YOUR EYES . JANUS HEADED GHOST OF MAN NAMED FEAR OF
LIFE . NAMED FEAR OF LIFE TO COME .

*Closed-circuit closeup pans of the Performer left and right mirror/screen and super closeup
of her mouth—jewelled teeth flashing—center.*

LOVE IS MONEY . ALEX . MONEY . LOVE .
AND THAT'S NOT ALL .
YE NEED TO KNOW THAT
HATE IS OWING .

*Music of the bells and bottles distorted, strange, echo. Makeup table glows—infernal light.
Smoke. She walks on the table searching with the flashlight beam. We see her bare feet on
video labor through the darkness.*

SPECULATION . THAT I FIND YOUR GRAVE BY TORCHLIGHT .
IN THE DUTY WINTER . FOG LIGHTS ON THE RIVER ICE . I
CAN'T BELIEVE MY EYES . GLOW OF AMBER . GLOW OF FIRE
FLOWING   UNDERNEATH . HOW DEEP WE ARE DEAR
GENTLEMAN .

MY SOUL IS SMOKING . AS I LIVE AND BREATHE . MY TONGUE
IS ORANGE . MY WEAPON IS GREEN . MY NAME IS DEBTOR .
THE UNFORGIVEN . MY VISION IS A DEBTOR'S PRISON .

*On video, the flashlight picks out her black dressing gown thrown on the corner of the
makeup table. She lifts it. Under it, appearing on all three monitors, is a life-like latex
mask of Alex Lujak, lying on the dark background of tiled surface like a death mask. She
sits down on the table and prepares the mask to put it on. As she speaks, her amplified voice
changes register electronically till her range and texture is that of an old man. As she speaks,*

she sheds the vestiges of the woman—earrings, wig, jewelled teeth.

ALEXANDER LUJAK WAS SEVENTY-ONE WHEN HE KILLED
HIMSELF WITH A DEER RIFLE IN THE BEDROOM OF HIS HOME
. IT WAS RAINING . HIS DAUGHTERS HAD LEFT HIM, ONE FOR
A BLACK MAN, THE OTHER FOR A JEW . A FIRST SON AND
NAMESAKE, AGED TWO, HAD DROWNED IN AN IRRIGATION
DITCH . HE LEFT THE CHURCH . TWENTY-EIGHT YEARS
LATER, A SECOND SON, CHILDLESS, HAD HAD HIMSELF
VASECTOMIZED, WHICH TERMINATED DESCENT THROUGH
THE MALE LINE . HIS WIFE, NETTIE, HAVING UNDERGONE
SHOCK TREATMENTS, WAS NOW INSTITUTIONALIZED . THE
PREVIOUS YEAR HE HAD SUFFERED A PULMONARY EDEMA
AND HAD ACTUALLY DIED FOR SIXTY SECONDS . IN THE LAST
MONTHS, TRY AS HE MAY, HE COULD NOT STOP SMOKING .

The Performer puts on the mask and assumes the character of Alex Lujak.

The memory, in pre-recorded video images of Alex and his daughter preparing to journey by truck, accompanies the narration. Twice a closeup of the Performer in the mask of Alex appears superimposed over a stylized image of rain—the leit motif of the memory.

DESPITE HIS POLISH NAME, HE WAS A CROAT . BORN IN
RUMA, YUGOSLAVIA JULY 6, 1912, THE SECOND OF FOUR . HE
EMIGRATED WITH HIS PARENTS TO A SMALL FARM NEAR
CLEVELAND, OHIO . MARRIED IN 1937, WITH A GRAMMAR
SCHOOL EDUCATION, HE WORKED IN A STEEL MILL DURING
THE SECOND WORLD WAR—CONTRACTING, AS A RESULT,
SEVERE BRONCHIECTASIS . HIS LUNGS INFLAMED AND
WEAKENED FROM INHALING SMALL BITS OF STEEL, HE SET
OUT IN 1947 IN AN OLD ARMY TRUCK WITH THE FAMILY FUR-
NITURE PILED IN THE BACK FOR THE CLEAN AIR OF THE
DESERT AROUND PHOENIX, ARIZONA, TAKING WITH HIM HIS
DAUGHTER, AGED EIGHT, FOR COMPANY .

HE ARRANGED THE FAMILY FURNITURE IN THE BACK OF HIS
TRUCK JUST AS IT HAD BEEN IN HER ROOM AT HOME—SO SHE
WOULD NOT BE AFRAID TO GO TO SLEEP WHEN THEY STOP-
PED BY THE SIDE OF THE ROAD .

The memory imagery shows the truck pulling off the road and entering the crypt-like cave that we saw earlier through the windshield of the careening truck before the sound of the gun shot.

Live closed-circuit images of Alex watch in profile from the side monitors, the memory im-age in the center of the truck in the enormous cave—like the entrance to a mine—travels with its lights on. Then stops by a rock wall. The Father, his face never once seen, lifts the sleeping Child from the cab and puts her to bed in her own bed in the back of the truck. We see the arrangement of the furniture as has been described. We see the figure of the Father take up the deer rifle and prepare to sit up all night guarding the Child—tapping the gun strangely with his fingernail. Slowly we pull back to show Father, Child, gun and room inside the truck inside the grave.

The Performer in the mask continues to speak with an old man's voice, but subtly it starts to change and evolve back into her own.

LATE IN LIFE, AND WITH DOUBTS AND FEARS AS TO THE WISDOM OF HIS ACTIONS, AFTER A SON WAS BORN AND THE FATHER AND THE DAUGHTER WERE ESTRANGED, HE GAVE TO HER A SUM OF MONEY—AS A LOAN . FOR HIM SO GREAT A SUM THAT THE AMOUNT WAS NEVER MENTIONED IN THE HOME . IT WAS SPOKEN OF AS "FORTY DOLLARS" AS ONE SPEAKS OF FORTY DAYS AND NIGHTS OF FLOODING, OR OF WANDERING FOR FORTY YEARS . UNFORTUNATELY, FATE CONSPIRED TO PREVENT REPAYMENT BEFORE DEATH IN-TERVENED . UNFORTUNATELY, ALEXANDER LUJAK DIED AFRAID OF BEING CHEATED .

The Performer's voice is now completely her own.

O PRIMITIVE MAN . HUNTER . FISHER . GATHERER OF SPARE PARTS . WHO DIES NOT OF LOVE . DIES OF SHAME .

I LOVE THIS ROOM . I WANT TO DIE IN THIS ROOM . AND I WOULD . HAD NOT I HAD THE NEED TO DO YOU . POETIC JUSTICE . HAD NOT I OWED YOU . BEYOND JUDGING . BEYOND LOVING . THIS GUARDING OF YOUR DYING . NOW . THE WAY YOU GUARDED . THEN . MY SLEEPING .

JEALOUSLY .

JEALOUSLY I SING OF YOU . ALEX . WHO I KILLED . OF COURSE I DID . THE LOSING OF YOU . IS THE FINDING OUT—THE PASS-ING . IS THE PASSING OVER INTO—MINE BEYOND JUDGING . BEYOND LOVING . YOU ARE MYSTERY .

The electronically created old man's voice suddenly takes over again.

I LOVE THIS ROOM . I WANT TO DIE IN THIS ROOM . AND I WOULD . HAD NOT I HEARD THIS CALL TO PILGRIMAGE . THIS KNOT OF GOD IN MY THROAT . DROP OF GOD ON MY EYELASH . THIS DEEP DREAMING HOME . WHERE YOU ARE WAITING . FLOATING . DANCING .

The Performer in the mask dances the dance of pilgrimage against the "rain of memory" in the mirrors to the ecstatic music of the end of The Mawlid-Invocation Of The Divine Name.

At the conclusion of the dance, she faces the audience and rips the latex mask in half. Half remains clinging to her face. Half she throws down.

I WANT TO KILL AND LOVE IN THE IDENTICAL MOTION . IN THE IDENTICAL WORD . IN THE IDENTICAL DEVOTION . I WANT NOT ONE IMPOSSIBLE THING . BUT TWO . OUT OF NOT ONE IMPOSSIBLE NEED . BUT TWO . CALLED NOT ONE IM-POSSIBLE NAME . BUT TWO . I AM NOT ONE IMPOSSIBLE ONE . BUT TWO .

ACCORDINGLY .

HERE IN THE DARK BOX OF MY THROAT . I BRING YOU BACK TO LIFE . I RIP YOU OFF—

She rips off the remaining portion of the mask.

—FOR ALL TO SEE JUST HOW ALIVE A CORPSE CAN BE . IN MY BODY . ALEXANDER . YOUR CHARMED BONES TAKE ON A CER-TAIN GLOW .

The Performer returns to the dressing table, puts on her robe and puts cold cream on her cheeks.

YOU CAN'T LEAVE ME . THAT PLAN HAS A FLAW .
WE'LL NEVER SORT EACH OTHER'S ATOMS OUT .
WE ARE UNDER SENTENCE OF A BOYLE'S LAW .
FOR HOPE'S DISPERSAL IN CHAMBERS OF DOUBT .

The lights go out.

END

Clear Glass Marbles

and

Rodeo

Jane Martin

Clear Glass Marbles was first performed at the Actors Theatre of Louisville during the '81 Shorts Festival, opening November 7, 1981 with the following cast:

Performed by Sally Faye Reit

Rodeo had its American premiere at the same time with the following cast:

Performed by Margo Martindale

Director: Jon Jory
Sets: Paul Owen
Lights: Jeff Hill
Costumes: Jess Goldstein

Clear Glass Marbles

A young woman is standing next to an end table with a lamp on it, holding a crystal bowl filled with ninety clear glass marbles.

LAURIE

The day my mother found out she was dying she asked me to go out and buy her these clear glass marbles. Dad and I hadn't even known she was ill which was nothing new. Whenever you asked my mother if she was ill she would throw things at you, sesame buns, the editorial page, a handful of hair ribbons. "Do not," she would say, "suggest things to suggestible people." Anyway, I brought her the marbles and she counted ninety of them out and put them in this old cut-glass bowl which had been the sum total of great Aunt Helena's estate. Apparently, the doctor had given her three months and she set great store by doctors. She said she always believed them because they were the nearest thing to the Old Testament we had. "I wouldn't give you two bits for these young smiley guys," she'd say, "I go for a good, stern-furrowed physician." She wouldn't even have her teeth cleaned by a dentist under fifty. So she counted out ninety clear glass marbles and set them in the bowl on her bedside table. Then she went out and spent twelve hundred dollars on nightgowns. She said, "In my family you are only dying when you take to your bed, and that, my darlings, is where I am going." And she did. Oh we hashed it around. Dad said she couldn't possibly be dying but the doctors convinced him. I told her it seemed a little medieval to lie in state up there but she said she didn't want to be distracted from what she loved, us, and what she wanted to mull . . . And she said there was nothing outside except drugstores and supermarkets and drycleaners and that given her situation they were beneath her dignity. I asked her what she intended to do up there and she said study French, visit with us, generally mull and maybe call a few pals. Study French. She said she had made a pledge to herself years ago that she would die bilingual. Dad and I cried a lot, but she didn't. He was fun to cry with. From then on the doctors had to come see *her* because, as she put it, she *came in* with a house call and she was *going out* with a house call. And all day, every day, she would hold one of these marbles in her hand. Why? She said it made the day longer. Mother had her own bedroom. That was the way it always was, for as long as I can remember. She called my father "The Thrasher." Dad could really get into a nightmare. Apparently early on in the marriage he had flipped over and broken her nose and that was it. Separate beds. Her room was very spare really. Wooden floors, an old steel-and-brass bed, oak dresser, bedside table, and don't ask me why, a hat rack. No pictures on the walls. She never understood how people could look at the same darn thing day after day. She said it was bound to "deflate the imagination." We'd sit with her after dinner and talk about "issues." She told us she was too far gone for gossip or what we ate for lunch. Then we'd all turn in and in a little while, just before I'd drift off I'd hear this . . .* (*She rolls one of the marbles across the stage floor.*) Happened every night. After the third or fourth day I saw one on the floor and started to pick it up but she said "leave it." She said it very sharply. I asked, "How come?" She said she was "learning to let go of them." (*From now on the actress frequently rolls marbles across the stage, indicated hereafter by an asterisk, ending up at last with only one.*) Oh, she passed the time. There were things she wanted. She made out a list of children's books from her own childhood and we got as many of them as we could find from the library. She said they were still the only good books she'd ever read.*

She wrote notes to, I don't know, maybe sixty or seventy people, and they told us later on that they were sort of little formal goodbyes, each of them recalling some incident or shared something, not very significant, but the odd thing was that in each one she included a recipe. A recipe in every one of them.

We got out the big cookie tin full of snapshots that somehow never became a scrapbook. She liked that. She showed my father how to do the medical insurance and how she handled the accounts. We went through her jewelry.* She wrote down the names of the roofers and plumbers and air-conditioning people. She called it "wrapping it up." "Well, this is good," she'd say, "I'm wrapping it up."*

She had the television moved up in her room and she called me aside to say that it was entirely possible that she might reach a stage where she really wouldn't know what she was watching but that I must promise her that I'd keep it on P.B.S.

Later on, when it started getting hard,* she told Dad and me that she would like to spend more time alone. "I'm afraid," she said, "that I'm going to have to do this more or less by myself." She said that she was glad, and she hoped we would be, that this was arranged so that you got less attached to the poeple you loved at the end. The next period isn't worth going into, it was just . . . hard. (*She picks up the bowl of marbles.*) Do you know that from the very beginning down to the very last she never admitted to any pain. Never. She called it "the chills." The last thing she asked for was a picture we had in the front entrance hall of a labrador retriever she and Dad had owned when they were first married. He was, she said, a perfectly dreadful dog. "When you are young," she said, "you believe in the perfectibility of dogs."

I was in bed two weeks ago Wednesday toward dawn, then this . . . (*She pours the rest of the marbles on the floor. When they have stopped rolling, she speaks.*) Dad and I ran in there. The bedside table was turned over and she was gone. Dead. When the emergency medical people got there they found this . . . (*She opens her hand to disclose one more marble.*) The rest spilled when the table fell, but this one was still in her hand.

I keep it.

I keep it in my hand all day.

It makes the day longer.

BLACKOUT

Rodeo

A young woman in her late twenties sits working on a piece of tack. Beside her is a Lone Star beer in the can. As the lights come up we hear the last verse of a Tanya Tucker song or some other female country-western vocalist. She is wearing old worn jeans and boots plus a long-sleeved workshirt with the sleeves rolled up. She works until the song is over and then speaks.

BIG EIGHT

Shoot—Rodeo's just goin' to hell in a hand basket. Rodeo used to be somethin'. I loved it. I did. Once Daddy an' a bunch of 'em was foolin' around with some old bronc over to our place and this ol' red nose named Cinch got bucked off and my Daddy hooted and said he had him a nine-year-old girl, namely me, wouldn't have no damn trouble cowboyin' that horse. Well, he put me on up there, stuck that ridin' rein in my hand, gimme a kiss and said, "Now there's only one thing t' remember Honey Love, if ya fall off you jest don't come home." Well I stayed up. You gotta stay on a bronc eight seconds. Otherwise the ride don't count. So from that day on my daddy called me Big Eight. Heck! That's all the name I got anymore . . . Big Eight.

Used to be fer cowboys, the rodeo did. Do it in some open field, folks would pull their cars and pick-ups round it, sit on the hoods, some ranch hand'd bulldog him some rank steer and everybody'd wave their hats and call him by name. Ride us some buckin' stock, rope a few calves, git throwed off a bull and then we'd jest git us to a bar and tell each other lies about how good we were.

Used to be a family thing. Wooly Billy Tilson and Tammy Lee had them five kids on the circuit. Three boys, two girls and Wooly and Tammy. Wasn't no two-beer rodeo in Oklahoma didn't have a Tilson entered. Used to call the oldest girl Tits. Tits Tilson. Never seen a girl that top-heavy could ride so well. Said she only fell off when the gravity got her. Cowboys used to say if she landed face down you could plant two young trees in the holes she'd leave. Ha! Tits Tilson.

Used to be people came to a rodeo had a horse of their own back home. Farm people, ranch people—lord, they *knew* what they were lookin' at. Knew a good ride from a bad ride, knew hard from easy. You broke some bones er spent the day eatin' dirt, at least ya got appreciated.

Now they bought the rodeo. Them. Coca-Cola, Pepsi Cola, Marlboro damn cigarettes. You know the ones I mean. Them. Hire some New York faggot t' sit on some ol' stuffed horse in front of a sagebrush photo n' smoke that junk. Hell, tobacco wasn't made to smoke, honey, it was made to chew. Lord wanted ya filled up with smoke he would've set ya on fire. Damn it gets me!

There's some guy in a banker's suit runs the rodeo now. Got him a pinky ring and a digital watch, honey. Told us we oughta have a watchamacallit, choriographus or somethin', some ol' ballbuster used to be with the Ice damn Capades. Wants us to ride around dressed up like Mickey Mouse, Pluto, crap like that. Told me I had to haul my butt through the barrel race done up like Minnie damn Mouse in a tu-tu. Huh uh, honey! Them people is so screwed-up they probably eat what they run over in the road.

Listen, they got the clowns wearin' Astronaut suits! I ain't lyin'. You know what a rodeo clown does! You go down, fall off whatever—the clown runs in front of the bulls so's ya don't git stomped. Pin-stripes, he got 'em in space suits tellin' jokes on a microphone. First horse see 'em, done up like the Star Wars went crazy. Best buckin' horse on the circuit, name of Piss 'N'Vinegar, took one look at them clowns, had him a heart attack and died. Cowboy was ridin' him got hisself squashed. Twelve hundred pounds of coronary arrest jes fell right through 'em. Blam! Vio con dios. Crowd thought that was funnier than the astronauts. I swear it won't be long before they're strappin' ice-skates on the ponies. Big crowds now. Ain't hardly no ranch people, no farm people, nobody I know. Buncha disco babies and dee-vorce lawyers—designer jeans and day-glo Stetsons. Hell, the whole bunch of 'em wears French perfume. Oh it smells like money now! Got it on the cabie T and V—hey, you know what, when ya rodeo yer just bound to kick yerself up some dust—well now, seems like that fogs up the ol' TV camera, so they told us a while back that from now on we was gonna ride on some new stuff called Astro-dirt. Dust free. Artificial damn dirt, honey. Lord have mercy.

Banker Suit called me in the other day said "Lurlene . . ." "Hold it," I said, "Who's this Lurlene? Round here they call me Big Eight." "Well, Big Eight," he said, "My name's Wallace." "Well that's a real surprise t' me," I said, "'Cause aroun' here everybody jes calls you Dumbass." My, he laughed real big, slapped his big ol' desk an' then he said I wasn't suitable for the rodeo no more. Said they was lookin' fer another type, somethin' a little more in the showgirl line, like the Dallas Cowgirls maybe. Said the ridin' and ropin' wasn't the thing no more. Talked on about floats, costumes, dancin' choreogaphy. If I was a man I woulda pissed on his shoe. Said he'd give me a lifetime pass though. Said I could come to the rodeo any time I wanted.

Rodeo used to be people ridin' horses for the pleasure of people who rode horses—made you feel good about what you could do. Rodeo wasn't worth no money to nobody. Money didn't have nothing to do with it! Used to be seven Tilsons riding in the rodeo. Wouldn't none of 'em dress up like Donald damn Duck so they quit. That there's the law of gravity!

There's a bunch of assholes in this country sneak around until they see ya havin' fun and then they buy the fun and start in sellin' it. See, they figure if ya love it, they can sell it. Well you look out, honey! They want to make them a dollar out of what you love. Dress *you* up like Minnie Mouse. Sell your rodeo. Turn *yer* pleasure into Ice damn Capades. You hear what I'm sayin'? You're jus' merchandise to them, sweetie. You're jus' merchandise to them.

BLACKOUT

Native Speech

Eric Overmyer

for Melissa Cooper

Native Speech was produced by the Los Angeles Actors' Theatre on June 18, 1983, with the following cast:

Hungry Mother	*John Horn*
Loudspeaker/Freddy Navajo	*Christine Avila*
Free Lance	*Candy Ann Brown*
Belly Up	*Al Stevenson*
Charlie Samoa	*Miguel Fernandes*
Johnnie Sucrose	*Billy Edgar*
Jimmy Shillelagh/Crazy Joe Navajo	*Enrique Kandre*
Janis	*Robin Ginsburg*
The Mook	*John LaFayette*
Hoover	*Henry Bal*

Director: John Olon
Sets: A. Clark Duncan
Lights: Barbara Ling
Costumes: Fred Chuang
Music: Sharon Smith

Characters:

Hungry Mother
Loud Speaker (a woman's voice)
Free Lance*
Belly Up
Charlie Samoa
Johnnie Sucrose (a transvestite)
Jimmy Shillelagh
Janis*
The Mook
Hoover
Freddy Navajo*
Crazy Joe Navajo

*women

Notes: Hungry Mother and Janis are white. The Mook and Free Lance are black. They are an impressive, attractive couple: a Renaissance Prince and Princess. Belly Up is black, middle-aged, somewhat older than Hungry Mother; a large man, an ex-sarge, the outline of his chevrons still visible on his fatigue jacket. Hoover, Freddy Navajo, Crazy Joe Navajo, Charlie Samoa, Johnnie and Jimmy should be played by Asian-American, Hispanic, or Native American actors. They should *not* be played by white actors.

Freddy Navajo is a woman. Loud Speaker is an unseen, amplified, *live* voice: one of those ubiquitous, bland, cheery woman's voices heard in airports, shopping malls, or on the Time of Day recording.

Johnnie Sucrose is a transvestite, a convincing one. The drag should be accomplished.

The following parts can be doubled:
  Freddy and Loud Speaker
  Jimmy and Crazy Joe

This reduces the cast from twelve to ten. Doubling is not preferable, so care should be taken to make clear that doubling is an economic, not aesthetic, choice.

Except where indicated, Hungry Mother's voice is *not* amplified during his broadcast monologues. We hear his voice as he hears it, not as it is heard over the radio by his listeners.

Hungry Mother should never make contact with, play to, or acknowledge the theatre audience. He is isolated in his studio, alone in the world.

Setting:

Hungry Mother's underground radio station, and the devastated neighborhood which surrounds it. The studio is constructed from the detritus and debris of Western Civ: appliances, neon tubing, automobile parts. 45's. Cultural artifacts. *Junk.*

Outside, a darkening world. Dangerous. The light is blue and chill. It is always twilight, always winter.

"If he was not as dead as the cold lasagna on which the tomato sauce has begun to darken, I was a Dutchman. The gaudy and, in the absence of blood, inappropriate metaphor actually came to mind at the moment, as a willed ruse to lure me away from panic—the fundamental purpose of most caprices of language, hence the American wisecrack."
—Thomas Berger, *Who is Teddy Villanova?*

AUTHOR'S NOTE: *Native Speech* was originally to have been produced at the Chelsea Theatre Center, New York, in January, 1981, by Robert Kalfin, directed by Paul Berman, with Dwight Schultz as Hungry Mother. While we were in rehearsal, the Chelsea was forced to close its doors, for financial reasons, after many years of operation. *Native Speech* was subsequently presented as a stage reading at Playwrights Horizons, New York, January 1982, and at Center Stage, Baltimore, May 1983. Both readings were directed by Paul Berman, with Dwight Schultz and Stephen Markle as Hungry Mother. *Native Speech* opened June 18, 1983, at the Los Angeles Actors' Theatre, directed by John Olon.

I would like to thank the following friends who have sustained me through this long, difficult process of bringing the play to light: Jeff Brooks, Arnold Cooper, Elinor Fuchs, Jim Harris, Robin Hirsch, Michael Howard, Michael Landrum, John Olon, and Dwight Schultz. I owe a special debt to Paul Berman and Steven Dansky, who have worked for years on the play's behalf, and to Robert Kalfin, whose support and unflagging encouragement have kept me in the theatre.

Act I

The Studio. Hungry Mother. Red lights blinking in the black. A needle scrapes across a record. A low hum. Hum builds: the Konelrad Civil Defense Signal. He bops with the tone, scats with it. The tone builds, breaks off. Silence. Hungry Mother leans over the mike, says in a so-good-it-hurts voice:

HUNGRY MOTHER: O, that's a hit. Hungry Mother plays the hits, only the hits. I want some seafood, mama. (*Beat.*) This is your Hungry Mother here—and you know it.

(*Lights. Hungry Mother is a shambly, disheveled man in his late thirties. The Broadcast Indicator—a blue light bulb on the mike—is 'on.' And so is Hungry Mother.*)

HUNGRY MOTHER: (*Cooool.*) Static. Dead air. Can't beat it. With a stick. Audio entropy. In-creases ever-y-where. Home to roost. Crack a six-pack of that ambient sound. (*Beat.*) You've been groovin' and duckin' to the ever-popular sound of "Air Raid"—by Victor Chinaman. Moan with the tone. A blast from the past. With vocal variations by yours truly. The Hungry Mother. (*Beat.*) Hard enough for you? (*A little more up tempo.*) Hungry Mother here, your argot astronaut. Stick with us. Solid gold and nothing but. Hungry Mother be playing the hits, playing them hits, for you, jes' for youuuu . . . (*Full of manic now.*) Uh-huh! Into the smokey blue! Comin' at you! Get out de way! Hungry Mother gonna hammer, gonna glide, gonna slide, gonna bop, gonna drop, gonna dance dem ariel waves, til he get to you, yes you! Razzle you, dazzle you, blow you a-way! This one gonna hammer . . . gonna hammer you blue! (*Drily.*) Flatten you like a side of beef, sucker. (*Mellifluous.*) This is WTWI, it's 7:34, the weather is *dark*, dormant species are stirring, cold and warm bloods both, muck is up, and I'm the Hungry Mother. The weather outlook is for continued existential dread under cloudy skies with scattered low-grade distress. Look out for the Greenhouse Effect . . . We'll be back, but first—a word about succulents— (*Beat. Flicks switches. Then, subdued, reasonable.*) We're coming to you live, from our syncopated phonebooth high above the floating bridge in violation of *several* natural laws, searching, strolling, and trolling, for the sweetest music this side of Heaven. (*Beat. Then:*) Back at you! This is the Hungry Mother, just barely holding on, at WTWI, the cold-water station with the bird's-eye view, on this beautifully indeterminate morning, bringin' you monster after musical monster. Chuckin' 'em down the pike, humpin' 'em up and over the DMZ, in a never-ending effort to make a dent in that purple purple texture. And right now I've got what you've all been waiting for—Hungry Mother's HAMMER OF THE WEEK! And Mother's Hammer for this week, forty-seven with a silver bullet —"Fiberglass Felony Shoes"—something slick—by Hoover *and* the Nava-jos. (*Now modest, compassionate, friendly, slightly patronizing.*) And, as always, behind every Mother's Hammer of the Week—there's a human being. And a human interest story. You're probably hip to this already, but I'm gonna lay it on you anyway. Hoover—is a full-blooded, red-blooded *Native American.* (*Slight pause.*) Hoover had a monster a few years back: "Fiberglass Rock"—just a giant on the Res. And elsewhere. That, *mais oui,* was before the tragic accident in which Hoover—ah, I don't know if this is public knowledge—but, o why not grovel in gore? (*Bopping.*) With the fallout from his titanium monster, "Fiberglass Rock," Hoover put something down on a pre-owned dream, a Pontiac Superchief, drive it *away.* A steal. A *machine.* Four on the floor and three on the tree, a herd of horses under the hood! (*Mock melodrama.*) Four flats. Cracked axle. Hoover—his heart as big and red as the great outdoors—goes down . . . with a wrench. The Superchief slips the jack—and pins Hoover by his . . . pickin' hand. (*Beat.*) WIPE OUT! (*Beat.*) Crushed dem bones to milk. (*Rising frenzy.*) But now he's back. Back where he belongs! With the aid of a prosthetic device! Back on the charts again! PIONEER OF PATHO-ROCK! (*Slight pause. Then: warm, hip.*) Many happy returns of the day, Hoover, for you and yours. (*Flicks switches. Mellow.*) The sun is up, *officially,* and all good things, accord-ing to the laws of thermo-dynamics, must come to an end. Join us—tomorrow—for something approaching solitude. WTWI now relents and gives up the ghost of its broadcasting day. (*He flicks switches. The blue light, the Broadcast Indicator, goes 'off.'*)

(*Over the loudspeakers, a woman's voice,* live.)

LOUD SPEAKER: Aspects of the Hungry Mother.

HUNGRY MOTHER: (*Reading from a book of matches.*) Succes without college. Train at home. Do not mail matches.

LOUD SPEAKER: Hungry Mother hits the streets.

HUNGRY MOTHER: (*To Loud Speaker.*) I be gone . . . but I lef' my name to carry on.

(*Hungry Mother shuffles into the street. Free Lance approaches. They recognize one another, tense, draw closer. They do a street dance, slow, sexy, dangerous. Freeze. They release. Free Lance slides back and out.*)

LOUD SPEAKER: Hungry Mother after hours.

(*Hungry Mother slides into the bar where there is a solitary figure drinking.*)

HUNGRY MOTHER: Belly Up.

BELLY UP: Say what?

HUNGRY MOTHER: Belly Up, it's been a coon's age.

BELLY UP: I know you?

HUNGRY MOTHER: Think it over.

BELLY UP: Buy me a drink.

HUNGRY MOTHER: City jail.

BELLY UP: (*Checks him out.*) Hungry Mother. What it is, Mom, what it is. How's it goin', Home? How goes the suppurating sore?

HUNGRY MOTHER: It's coming along. Thank you.

BELLY UP: (*Grinning.*) Hungry Mother. Whose tones are legion. Hungry Mother, voice of darkness. Impresario of derangement. Tireless promoter of patho-rock. The man who'll air that wax despair.

HUNGRY MOTHER: When no one else will dare.

BELLY UP: The quintessential Cassandra. The damn Jonah who hacked his way out of the whale. Hungry Mother, the bleating gurgle of those who've had their throats cut.

HUNGRY MOTHER: You give me too much, Belly Up, my boy. It's all air time. Air-waves access, that's what it's all about. I just prop 'em up over the mike and let 'em bleed—gurgle gurgle pop short.

BELLY UP: Credit where credit is due.

HUNGRY MOTHER: (*Black, Southern preacher.*) Why, thank you, Brother Belly. It's a comfort to know that, a genuine solid comfort. My cup is filled with joy to know that someone's *really* listening. Why, late at night and on into the dawn, I have my doubts, I surely do. Casting my pearls—over the brink—

BELLY UP: (*Picking it up.*) Into the trough. On a wing and a prayer. Before the swine of despond. (*Pause.*) Not so, Hungry Mother, not so; not a bit. Your words hang on the barbed wire of evening, glistering in the urban nether vapors like a diamond choke chain on black satin.

HUNGRY MOTHER: Belly Up, you have the gift, you surely do. It's a wonder you don't pursue some purely *metaphorical* calling.

BELLY UP: My sentiments precisely. Please indulge me as I continue to flesh out my figure . . . Hungry Mother turns tricks quicker than a dock-side hooker hustling her habit. He fences insights, pawns epiphanies. And we redeem those tickets in nasty corners. You the laser wizard. The magnetic pulse. The cardiac arrest. The barbarians have smashed the plate glass window of Western Civ and are running amok in the bargain basement. (*Slight pause. Hungry Mother applauds.*) Thank you. Transistor insights. Diode data. Crystal-tube revelations. That why we dial you in, Mothah.

HUNGRY MOTHER: You and who else?

BELLY UP: You'd be surprised. (*Pause.*) I got a chopper on the roof.

HUNGRY MOTHER: What? (*Belly Up winks and laughs. Hungry Mother, puzzled, pauses for a moment, then pushes on.*) Look, I got a question for you. Say the hoodlums, punks, pervos, perps, feral children, coupon clippers, and all the other bargain basement thrift shoppers, say they skip Housewares. Sporting goods. Electronic lingerie. Junior misses. All the lower floor diversions. And go straight for the suites at the top.

BELLY UP: (*Laughs.*) I got a chopper on the roof! Got my own sweet chopper to take me outa this! See? I anticipate your question. Like I anticipate the situation. And the answer. An-ti-cipate. Got to have that getaway hatch, Mother. Got to have it. Even a fool can see what's comin'. (*Slight pause.*) You're *sensitive*, Mother. We can read you like a rectal therm. Any little fluctuation. Fuck Dow Jones. We got the good stuff. (*Slight pause.*) We tune you in, we know when to split. Any little fluc. You our miner's canary, Mother. We hang you out there on the hook, and hope you smell the gas in time. You croak—we go.

HUNGRY MOTHER: I'll try to give you five.

BELLY UP: Man, five is all I ask. My ears are glued.

HUNGRY MOTHER: Keep those cards and letters coming. So I know you're still glued.

BELLY UP: Don't sweat. As long as you still singing, we still listening. When you on the air, we say "Hosannah!"

HUNGRY MOTHER: Say "Hungry!," sweetheart.

(*They toast. Darkness. As Hungry Mother walks back into the studio his amplified voice booms over the PA:*)

HUNGRY MOTHER: (*On tape.*) Hoover is crawling back from near annihilation, a mighty mean accident for the little red man—(*Lights. Hungry Mother freezes at the mike.*)

LOUD SPEAKER: Further aspects of the Hungry Mother—*revealed*! For the very first time—the Hungry Mother in jail!

(*The jail appears in a flash of light: Charlie Samoa and Johnnie and Jimmy. Disappears. Lights up on Hungry Mother. He breaks freeze. Flicks switiches, blue light* 'on.')

HUNGRY MOTHER: (*High-speed.*) Career-wise, a mighty mean accident, a tough break for the little red man. We'll be back with the Prick Hit of the Week—ha, ha, oh—Freudian faux pas—Pick Hit of the Week, "Nuking the Chinks," by Dragon Lady and the Flying Paper Tigers, but first—a word about peccaries . . . Friends—like so many vanishing species, these ugly little critters need your help. A tusk or two, a hoof, a stewpot of glue. It's all over for them, but what about their by-products? (*Dramatic.*) Next week—blue whales and dog food. (*Mellifluous.*) This is WTWI, the station with no visible means of support, this is a weekday, this is the Hungry Mother, blistering the dusk to dawn shift, grinding 'em down and pulling 'em out, monster after effervescent monster. Holocaust warnings are up. They continue to machine-gun survivors outside our studio. And the ozone keeps oozing away! And now—Mother's got what you've all been waiting for—nearly an hour of unrelieved agony! Twilight Desperation News! Brought to you by Universal Antipathy—Universal Antipathy, engendering tensions all over the globe—and by Sorgum—a fast food whose time is ripe ripe ripe! Invest in sorghum futures today! And now the hour's top headlines. (*Newscaster tones, a teletype effect:*) "Killer Bees from Brazil Drop Texas Rangers in Their Tracks" . . . "Starfish Finish Off Great Barrier Reef" . . . quote, "The sky's the limit," endquote . . . One last note for you nature lovers: fossil fuels now coat 87 percent of the known universe. Those slicks are tough. No wonder dry-cleaning costs an arm and two legs . . . On the international beat, expatriate citizens of the island of Malta are demanding restitution from the community of nations. Malta was mugged early yesterday by two large black countries with hydrogen knuckles . . . it sank without a trace. Shades of Krakatoa. The usual measures to contain the radio-active dusk are being implemented with, as one official so succinctly put it, little, or no, chance of success. We'll have more this hour on the latest in genetic mutation, both here and abroad, but first—late, and leg, breaking sports . . . (*Hungry Mother picks up a pair of mechanical birds, and winds them into motion: they waddle and squawk. To the birds.*) You're brilliant and you're blue . . . conjugal bijou babies. Doves of love. Beaks of lazuli, warbles of tin. (*The birds wind down and halt. Intones.*) Wound down. (*He eats beans from a can.*) Interlude In Which Beans Are Eaten.

LOUD SPEAKER: The authorized autobiography of the Hungry Mother. The truth—with a twist!

HUNGRY MOTHER: First . . . lemme say . . . unequivocally—and between bites—that the Hungry Mother was made, not born. Not of woman born. Heh heh heh. Puts me up there with the all-time greats, right? I want to be most emphatic about this. The Hungry Mother is—my own creation. Nom de wireless! Home-made man! So fine!

LOUD SPEAKER: Hungry scat! Mother doo wop!

HUNGRY MOTHER: (*To the mike, sings.*)

Put on your felony shoes
Put on your felony shoes
Everybody gonna want you to
Put on your felony shoes
Come on wit' me
We gonna cut somethin' loose
We gonna boost
Something fine
And shiny and new
If you'll jes'
Put on your felony shoes!

LOUD SPEAKER: And now—number one with a dum-dum—Mother's Hammer Too Hot To Handle!

HUNGRY MOTHER: And now, getting tons of extended hot air play in S and M loading zones and up and down the leather docks from coast to disco coast—the newest from Hoover and the Navajos—parvenu of patho-rock —"Fiberglass Creep and the Rotating Tumors!" (*He begins teletype noise, and speaks gravely.*) Police today busted a waterfront distillery, arresting twenty-seven adults. The distillery produces a wine brewed from the sores of children, which is quite popular locally and in the contiguous states, and easily available without a prescription. The cops said the kids were kept in cages underneath the piers because quote, the salt water facilitates the festeration process, endquote. The perpetrators will be arraigned tomorrow on tax evasion charges, and the children, several hundred of them, have been released into the custody of leading lending institutions . . . (*Upbeat.*) The blockbuster scoop this solid-gold weekend—thousands of citizens roaming the streets in states of bliss-out and fat poisoning. Watch out for those psycho-paralytic hallucinations! They can be tricky! Speaking of weather, the outlook through the weekend remains bleak. Our five-day forecast calls for continued historical uneasiness mingled with intermittent bouts of apocalyptic epiphany, and occasional oxygen debt—under cloudy skies. So wear your rubbers . . . (*Jaunty.*) This has been the Agony News Hour, an exclusive twilight feature of WTWI, with your host, the Hungry Mother. Stay tuned for "Name My Race," the game guaranteed to offend nearly everyone, brought to you by Ethnic Considerations, dedicated to exacerbating racial tensions through violence—Ethnic Considerations, a hallmark of the Twentieth Century, don't leave home without them. (*He holds a stack of letters impaled on bowie knife. He plucks off the top letter and reads it in a cheery DJ voice.*) "Dear Mother: My boyfriend has a fishhook in the end of his penis. This makes congress difficult. Even painful. What can I do about it? Signed, Afraid to Swallow." (*He crumples it up and tosses it away.*)

Eighty-six *that*. Prick Hit of the Week. Cranks. Who do they think they're kidding. I'm not just fooling around here. (*Next letter.*) "Dear Mother: My husband is an unreconstructed Stalinist. He refuses to de-Stalinize, knowing that recantation would expose him as an accomplice to the most heinous crimes of this vile century. This ideological rift has been the recrudescent cause of numerous domestic conflicts and, I believe, threatens the dialectic of our marriage. Just yesterday I suggested opening bi-lateral summit talks on the question of rehabilitating Trotsky for the family shrine of revolutionary heroes, and he broke my jaw. Dear Mother, for the sake of the children, what do you suggest? Signed, Just a Bourgeois Social Fascist At Heart." (*Slight pause.*) Dear Just A Bourgeois: I suggest a fight to the death with needle-nosed pliers. (*He tears it up.*) What's happening to the language? It's scary, Jim. The Great Nuance Crisis is upon us. One last letter for this fiscal year. (*A Cheery DJ voice.*) "Dear Mother: I listen to you every night. You are a great comfort to me. I don't know what I'd do without you. Please help me, Mother. It hurts so bad I can barely talk. Signed, Desperate." (*Slight pause.*) Dear Desperate . . . For once I'm at a loss for words. (*Slight pause.*) Perhaps you've mistaken me for your natural mother. I'm nobody's mama, sweetheart. (*Slight pause.*) Dear Desperate, I can't help you—if you don't give me something more to go on. Who are you, where, and what's troubling you, Bunky. Please try and nail it down a little closer, dear . . . Friends, got an *esoteric* problem? Send it to Mother and he'll devour it for you. And now it's time once again for— *The Big Dose, A Taste of Things To Come*, when the Mother lets you in on what it's really gonna be like once the rude boys start playing for keeps. So here it is, tonight, at no extra charge, Hungry Mother brings you more than two hours of—dead air. Enjoy.

(*Flicks switches. Blue light "off." Shrugs into an overcoat and goes into the street. Encounters Free Lance. They do their dance, as before. Freeze. Slight pause.*)

LOUD SPEAKER: Hungry Mother—Street Solo!

(*He runs downstage scatting some "theme" music. At the appropriate moment:*)

LOUD SPEAKER: And now! Heeeeeeere's . . . HUNGRY!!

HUNGRY MOTHER: (*Bopping.*) Could be Japanese! . . . Genetic . . . engineering! Charnel—numbah—five! *Smoke!* (*Changing gears.*) Friends . . . let's have a chat. Heart to heart. Would Mother hand you a bum steer? . . . As you know, the suggested agenda topic for today's luncheon is . . . Why Do De Gu'mint Be De Boz Ob De Scag Trade, or . . . Methadone—Magic or Madness? . . . But I, uh, I have something of more immediate import to . . . impart. (*Slight pause.*) Friends . . . let's talk about . . . crude drugs.

(*Clears throat.*) Brothers and sisters, I was down at the Hotel Abyss the other day, down at that old Hotel Abyss, when I chance to run into an old old friend of mine. A legend in his own time. A man who knows the score. Who never lets the sun get in his eyes. A man with no holes in his cosmic glove . . . I am speakin' of course about . . . Cocaine Ricky. (*Slight pause.*) Your friend and mine. (*Slight pause.*) Brothers and sisters, Cocaine Ricky tell me there be some mighty cold stuff goin' 'round out there, and I just want you to watch it. Very very cold. Ice cold. Dude be pushin', be pushin' it as snow. You know? Snow fall. Snow job. Snow blind. Snow go. (*Slight pause.*) Ain't snow. It's *Lance.* Lance. (*Slight pause.*) Instant death. (*Slight pause.*) Powdered nerve gas. (*Slight pause.*) Government issue. Sooo cooold. Huh!

(*Hungry Mother and Free Lance enter the studio. She is dressed to street-kill.*)

FREE LANCE: This place looks like a Cargo Cult beach head. You always had a knack for dives, Mother.

HUNGRY MOTHER: Thank you very much.

FREE LANCE: I don't truck with the radio much. It doesn't occur to me. It's not one of my . . . habits. I don't have time for media. What I'm saying is—I haven't caught your show.

HUNGRY MOTHER: Fuck you very much.

FREE LANCE: Don't be bitter.

(*Slight pause.*)

HUNGRY MOTHER: Where you live dese days, honey chile?

FREE LANCE: On the docks.

HUNGRY MOTHER: Couldn't cotch me down dere, anyways.

FREE LANCE: Armegeddon Arms. Condos de rigueur. Sing Sing singles. Know them?

HUNGRY MOTHER: No, but I know the neighborhood. Intimately. (*Black again.*) Watchew dew down dere, woman? You ain't involved with dem child distillers, is you?

FREE LANCE: I don't believe so. Not to my knowledge. It hasn't come to my attention. You ought to come visit me, Mother.

HUNGRY MOTHER: I should, it's true.

FREE LANCE: It's much nicer than this, really. Chrome furniture. It'd be a change.

HUNGRY MOTHER: I don't get out much. Don't leave the 'hood. I'm cooped.

FREE LANCE: Cooped.

HUNGRY MOTHER: Up.

FREE LANCE: It's very outre, you know. Swank and chic in the nastier neighborhoods. I just crave the danger. It's narcotic. And there's really nothing to worry about. The building itself is just the best. Impregnable. White boys from Missoura.

HUNGRY MOTHER: I can appreciate that.

FREE LANCE: Eliminates the Fifth Column spectre. My parents *never* hired black servants. No mammies for me. Don't tell me about race loyalty. When push comes to shove, I mean. Save on silver, too. And being near the water gives me a warm feeling.

HUNGRY MOTHER: For a quick and hasty exit.

FREE LANCE: When the time comes. We've made the arrangements. There won't be any trouble. When the time comes.

HUNGRY MOTHER: You'll take some casualties, of course.

FREE LANCE: When the time comes. Probably. Of course. One learns to live with one's losses.

HUNGRY MOTHER: Don't one? That reminds me. (*He flicks switches: blue light "on." Red-hot.*) Back at you, sports, this is *the* Hungry Momma, the one and only, the original Hungry Momma, accept no substitutes, coming at you out of the blue-black on this elusive weekday ay-em in a possibly transitional stage in the floodtide of human affairs. Let the historians decide. You've been listening—to more than two hours of—*dead air.* C'est frommage. The time just got away from me there, mon cher. We'll be phasing out our broadcasting day with vanishing species animal noises, what a hoot. And we'll finish off with a new one, got it in the mail today, from the purveyors of patho-rock, Hoover and the Navajos, their latest— "Fibreglass Repairman!" (*Sings a slow blues, keeping the beat with handslams. Sings:*)

I'll insulate yo' home
I'll fibreglass yo' phone
An' I'll Navajogate
The little woman
Befo' yo'
Back is turned.

(*Low-key.*) Just breaks my goddamn heart. Sayonara, kids. I'll be back later in the week at my regularly unscheduled time. So—keep dialing and keep *hoping.* This is the Hungry Mother, the man who put the *hun* back in hungry, reminding you to stay cool, take it light, and say—*Hungry!* (*Slight pause, then cool and bureaucratic.*)

WTWI has now pissed away
Its broadcasting day. (*Hungry Mother switches the blue light "off."*)

FREE LANCE: I'm surprised you don't lose your license.

HUNGRY MOTHER: Tell you the secret of my success. Nobody hears me. This tube gear eats it. Raw. I got a radius range of under a mile. Barely covers one police precinct. I'm very proud of my precinct. It ain't much, but it's home. I pledge allegiance to my precinct . . . Nobody *lives* up here. 'S all bomb-outs. Gutted projects. Arsonated rubble.

FREE LANCE: Listener response?

HUNGRY MOTHER: Rubble don't write a lot of post cards. The junkies call me sometimes. *Hit* Line requests. Sugar Bear and Oz. They call on their anniversary. Four years, a mutual monkey. Many happy returns of the day. Born to junk.

FREE LANCE: One hears stories.

HUNGRY MOTHER: It's been known to happen.

FREE LANCE: About you, dear. One hears them. In the air. Snatches. All over. Faceless celeb. You ought to take precautions. You have more listeners than you think. Than you might imagine.

HUNGRY MOTHER: Funny you should say that. I have been getting more letters. Got one today, it was a mistake. She mistook me. It's a serious letter.

FREE LANCE: Aren't they all?

HUNGRY MOTHER: Just crazy. This one was crazy, too. But serious.

FREE LANCE: What are you going to do about it?

HUNGRY MOTHER: What can you do about it?

FREE LANCE: Respond.

(*Pause.*)

HUNGRY MOTHER: She wants help.

FREE LANCE: Then help her.

HUNGRY MOTHER: How?

(*Pause.*)

FREE LANCE: I've changed my name.

HUNGRY MOTHER: Ah.

FREE LANCE: I've *altered* it.

HUNGRY MOTHER: I remember. You were into brand names. Rumor had it. "Canned Soup."

FREE LANCE: Generic. Not brand, generic. That one didn't stick.

HUNGRY MOTHER: I'm not surprised. "Polish Vodka."

FREE LANCE: Very tasty. I was all over the society pages. But I gave it up when I left the Agency. It's Free Lance now.

HUNGRY MOTHER: Oooo. Evocative. (*Slight pause.*) I prefer Polish Vodka.

(*Slight pause.*)

FREE LANCE: If wishes were horses.

(*Slight pause.*)

HUNGRY MOTHER: If the river was whiskey.

(*Slight pause.*)

FREE LANCE: You've always been the Hungry Mother. Ever since I've known you. (*Pause.*) I work for the Mook now.
HUNGRY MOTHER: The Mook. Oh my.
FREE LANCE: Again. That's how I heard about you. That's how I tracked you down.
HUNGRY MOTHER: The Mook? Listens to me?
FREE LANCE: Faithfully.
HUNGRY MOTHER: It's almost an honor. In a patho-spastic sort of way.
FREE LANCE: He told me you were back on the air.
HUNGRY MOTHER: I'll have to upgrade my shit. Can't have no cut-rate shit if the Mook's tuned in.
FREE LANCE: You ought to be more careful. The Mook's worried about your license.

(*Slight pause.*)

HUNGRY MOTHER: I don't have no license. And I'd bet my momma he knows that. His momma, too. How's his reception? Where's he based?
FREE LANCE: He *floats*.

(*Pause.*)

HUNGRY MOTHER: Why'd you go back?
FREE LANCE: Oh, honey. (*Laughs.*) Oh, honey. I'd drink his bathwater. (*Beat.*) I did super at the Agency. It was dull, darling. Dull as crushed rock. For them. On my own, it's a breeze. *Free Lance.* Don't you just dig the shit out of it? (*Pause. Cool smile; sardonic.*) I *love* the way he beats me, Mother. Swell hands. Something of a setback for personal liberation, right Mother? (*Slight pause.*) I tried to cut him loose.
HUNGRY MOTHER: You sure you're not involved with those kids? Ask Mook.
FREE LANCE: Mook doesn't do kids. You're very tender, Mother, but I could never count on you. Maybe after the revolution.
HUNGRY MOTHER: Right. The coup d'etat will make us straight . . . Thanks for stopping by, uh, Free Lance. Always nice to see you.
FREE LANCE: You, too, Mother. Like old times. Good, yes?
HUNGRY MOTHER: Absolutely golden. Better than a poke in the eye with a sharp stick. The best of them.

FREE LANCE: Don't become a stranger, Mother.

(*She drifts into the street. Hungry Mother slides into the bar. Belly Up is drinking, alone. He's wearing his old sergeant's fatigue jacket, the shadow of the chevrons still visible on the sleeve.*)

BELLY UP: You're taking off like a target-seeking, heat-sensitive, laser-directed, anti-personnel device. Stuffed with shrapnel. *Plastic* shrapnel. (*Laughs.*) Cluster bomb, Mom. Cluster bomb! (*Slight pause.*) Plastic shrap don't x-ray. That's the holy beauty of it. X-rays can't cope. Can't lo-cate it. Can't dig it out. (*Slight pause.*) Cluster fuck. (*Slight pause.*) Hungry Mother, the voice of the voiceless, the articulator of the ineffable, the thing that goes bump in the night. I never miss a show.

HUNGRY MOTHER: I wish I could say the same.

BELLY UP: You're getting better. More conscientious. Know what I saw? In a window. A record. By Hoover and the Navajos.

(*Long pause.*)

HUNGRY MOTHER: Outstanding. (*Pause.*) Was there a picture? What'd they look like?

BELLY UP: No picture. Crazy thing. It came in a fibreglass dust jacket. I got that shit up my ass. It burns like hell. Gets into every damn nook and cranny. Fibres. They're far out. They're a far out group. Insulation. Navajogation. Kills me. This—?

HUNGRY MOTHER: Patho-rock.

BELLY UP: Knocks my socks off. Patho-rock. I love it. Better than mime for the blind. Heaps better. "Thermal Underwear Cathedral!" "Fibreglass Felony Shoes!" "Carcinogenic Kisses Told A Tale On You!" Can you dig it? Blows me away. You ought to have them on the show.

HUNGRY MOTHER: Don't bug me, Belly Up. I just get this stuff in the mail.

BELLY UP: From the record company.

HUNGRY MOTHER: From *nobody*. It just floats in on the tide.

BELLY UP: You're gonna break 'em, Mother. You're gonna break 'em big. When I saw them in a store I was fibreglassted. Heh heh. I had no idea they were for real. I thought you . . . *created* them, you know? The holy power of PR.

HUNGRY MOTHER: So did I. In a way, I mean. As far as I know, I don't know if there really is a "Hoover and."

BELLY UP: I purchased it.

HUNGRY MOTHER: LP or single?

BELLY UP: LP. A botanica. Voodoo boutique. Haitian herb shop. I was on the prowl for a pack of mojo and a slice of John the Conqueroo. Saw it in amongs the loas and the gris-gris.

HUNGRY MOTHER: That's a good sign. That's encouraging. Those places are more underground than I am. Maybe we can nip this in the bud. I'd hate for it to get out of hand. I never intended to inflict Hoover and the Navajos on the general public. Something like this. A trend.

BELLY UP: Maybe they're ready for it. Look at it this way—Hungry Mother, hit maker!

HUNGRY MOTHER: Right. Just another top-forty jock. Sounds good. I want it. I need it. I want to have impact . . . I'm a fucking artist, man. I want to be taken seriously.

BELLY UP: To which end?

HUNGRY MOTHER: The bitter end, natch. Tell me, Belly, to what do you attribute my sudden surge of popularity?

BELLY UP: To the fact you're coming in loud and clear. Everywhere I go, Hungry Mother, that's who folks be talkin' bout.

HUNGRY MOTHER: Where do you go?

BELLY UP: Dark places. Places that slide. Places that aren't quite solid underfoot. You're becoming very big on the fringes. Amongst the rubble. Don't be downcast. You're articulating a definite need.

HUNGRY MOTHER: Don't think I'm not grateful. I like it. I love it. Here I thought I was only reaching my local rubble, and now you tell me I'm a smash in the rubble all over town.

BELLY UP: An idea whose time has come.

HUNGRY MOTHER: It's a heavy responsibility. Walk me home, Belly Up.

BELLY UP: Sorry. Not at this hour. I don't leave the bar.

HUNGRY MOTHER: What are you afraid of?

(*Pause.*)

BELLY UP: Get your hungry ass over here on time, I'll give you a lift. Back to the World.

HUNGRY MOTHER: I hear you. (*Slight pause.*) I hear you. (*Beat.*) Belly Up, I keep getting these letters.

(*The bar fades. Hungry Mother on the streets.*)

LOUD SPEAKER: Aspects of the Hungry Mother. The Hungry Mother in Jail.

(*The jail scene appears: Charlie Samoa, and Johnnie and Jimmy in silhouette.*)

HUNGRY MOTHER: This is a flashback. A reprise. I don't think I care for this right now.

LOUD SPEAKER: Manana, manana. You're just postponing the inevitable. It's on the playlist, baby. This is a very *tight* playlist.

HUNGRY MOTHER: Maybe later. How about? I want a reprieve from this reprise.

LOUD SPEAKER: (*Miffed.*) You're just postponing the sooner or later, babe.

HUNGRY MOTHER: Fuck off.

(*Jail fades. Hungry Mother runs into the studio and flicks the blue light ''on.''*)

HUNGRY MOTHER: Hey! This be your happy, hopping, high-speed Hungry Mother—doin' it to you before you can do it to yourself. Our special this hour, Hungry Mother's Horoscope—a penetrating peek at the Big Zee. So stick around and watch the Mother scope it and dope it—just for you. Also on the bill this o-bliterated amorphous morn—*broken glass* . . . and—Hungry Mother's Consumer Guide to Junk, where to score and what to pay, where to shoot and what to say, all the places and all the pushers, why not have the best possible habit in this, the Best, of all possible worlds? But first—this hour's top headlines. (*Teletype sound and newscaster voice.*) That illegal cordial made from kid pus is still circulating. Several deaths have been reported . . . More mastodon sightings in the North Cascades . . . Wolves in the outlying districts—if you're walking in the suburbs this morning, *remember*—Wolf Warnings are up. Pedestrians are advised to travel in packs and exercise the usual precautions . . . We'll be back after something brief. This is WTWI, and this is the Hungry Mother, live—if you call this living, from our Twilight Studios. Remember to say, ''Hungry!'' And now, another interminable episode of ''Sexual Shadow Land,'' the show that's sweeping the station. (*Rod Serling:*) His was an ordinary fetish—with a difference— (*Phone rings.*) I'll get it. (*Flicks switches.*) You're on the air! Hey there!

JANIS: (*Live, over P.A.*) Hello? (hello? hello?

HUNGRY MOTHER: Turn down your radio! Please! Turn it down!

JANIS: What? (what? what?

HUNGRY MOTHER: Turn that radio down! Turn it down! You're on the air! Trust me!

JANIS: Okay! (okay! okay! (*When Janis next speaks, the echo and feedback are gone.*) Better?

HUNGRY MOTHER: Much! I'd starve on feedback. What can Mother do for you? What can you do for Mother?

JANIS: Oh, Mother, I know. I listen to you all the time. I sit by the radio. I wait. I don't want to miss you. I hardly go out anymore. I don't.

HUNGRY MOTHER: You sound like a fan.

JANIS: Believe me, I am . . . I am. I don't go out anyway. But—I am. A fan. It's a comfort.

(*Pause.*)

HUNGRY MOTHER: Yes? Was there something else? You're killing my air.

JANIS: My name is Janis, Mother. I'd like to see you. You don't know me. I'm a stranger. We've never met.

HUNGRY MOTHER: Sure. C'mon up.

(*Slight pause.*)

JANIS: This is serious. I want to meet you. (*Slight pause.*) Mother. I really need to see you. Please . . . Can you tell me how to get there?

HUNGRY MOTHER: Sure. Ah, it's One Marauder Avenue, just past Faghag Park. Always hungry to have visitors in the studio, little lady. (*He hangs up. Looks pointedly at the "on" blue light.*) Whatever happens. Hang loose. Go with the flow. Everything is everything.

(*The jail scene appears. Hungry Mother walks into it. The Trio regards him ravenously.*)

CHARLIE SAMOA: My name is Charlie Samoa.

HUNGRY MOTHER: Right away.

CHARLIE SAMOA: And these are . . . the Samoans. (*Indicating the transvestite.*) Johnnie Sucrose—take a bow, sweetie—and Jimmy Shillelagh.

HUNGRY MOTHER: Charmed, I'm sure. My name is . . . uh, professionally I'm known as, uh, aka—

CHARLIE SAMOA: We know who you are—

JOHNNY SUCROSE: There's no need to shit us—

JIMMY SHILLELAGH: We never miss a show—

JOHNNIE SUCROSE: We'd know the golden tones anywhere. We're big big fans of yours.

CHARLIE SAMOA: But we got a question. The question is—what are you doing here?

JOHNNIE SUCROSE: Not that we mind, you understand—

JIMMY SHILLELAGH: Not that we're thrilled—

CHARLIE SAMOA: Even honored—

JOHNNIE SUCROSE: But it comes as something of a shock—

JIMMY SHILLELAGH: To say the least.

CHARLIE SAMOA: We hope it does not have to do with your superb radio show—

JOHNNIE SUCROSE: Of which we never miss a single segment—

JIMMY SHILLELAGH: At considerable risk to ourselves in view of the multiple restrictions pertaining to the use of, access to, and ownership of tube gear and ghetto blasters in this, ah, ah—

JOHNNIE SUCROSE: *Penal* institution.

CHARLIE and JIMMY: Yeah.

HUNGRY MOTHER: You guys are desatively bonnaroo. A matched set.

Siamese triplets, joined at the mouth. I predict a great future for you, should you consider it. Give me a call when you get out.

(*Pause.*)

CHARLIE SAMOA: Answer the question.
JOHNNIE SUCROSE: It behooves me.
JIMMY SHILLELAGH: Believe me.
CHARLIE SAMOA: Believe him.

(*Slight pause.*)

HUNGRY MOTHER: Criminal mischief . . . I . . . mmm . . . I shattered a sub-way window. (*Slight pause.*) With a golf club.

(*Pause.*)

CHARLIE SAMOA: *Why?*
HUNGRY MOTHER: I was . . . *sore.*

(*Pause.*)

JOHNNIE SUCROSE: How many strokes?
HUNGRY MOTHER: Just one. (*Slight pause.*) Nine iron.
JIMMY SHILLELAGH: Good choice.

(*Pause.*)

CHARLIE SAMOA: Penny ante, Mother, strictly penny ante.
JOHNNIE SUCROSE: We are very disappoint.
JIMMY SHILLELAGH: Although at the same time greatly relieved that this does not have to do with your illegal yet highly entertaining radio program.
HUNGRY MOTHER: Oh, no. Not on your sweet. It's not illegal, anyway. *Para-legal.* I've never had any trouble. Nobody listens.
CHARLIE SAMOA: We do.
JOHNNIE SUCROSE: We're interested—
JIMMY SHILLELAGH: We're concerned—
CHARLIE SAMOA: We're anxiety-ridden.
JOHNNIE SUCROSE: You don't have a license.
HUNGRY MOTHER: What a bitch. They license every goddamn thing in this goddamn city. You need a license to change a light bulb and a permit to take a piss.
CHARLIE SAMOA: Good thing, too. Where would we be without social order?

You got to maintain it.

JOHNNY SUCROSE: Very impor-*tant*.

JIMMY SHILLELAGH: Somebody's got to do it. Gotta have that social scheme.

CHARLIE SAMOA: A modicum of status quo.

JIMMY SHILLELAGH: To go along with a lot of expensive tube gear and no visible means of support. And no license.

HUNGRY MOTHER: Very acute. Ah . . . where do you get your dope on me?

CHARLIE SAMOA: We asked around.

JIMMY SHILLELAGH: We checked the score.

CHARLIE SAMOA: We heard it through the grapevine.

(*The Samoans laugh raucously, then subside.*)

HUNGRY MOTHER: And that's how you come to be such . . . fans.

CHARLIE SAMOA: Thereby hangs a tale. It begins with a grudge. As most tales do. I was free-lancin'. That's my thing. A little liason. A middle-man shuffle 'tween U.S. Guv Intelligence cats and a certain Kuomingtang warlord. Local scag baron . . . Am I boring you? Got a minute?

HUNGRY MOTHER: Not at all. I mean certainly, yes, most certainly, I do.

CHARLIE SAMOA: Where am I?

JOHNNIE SUCROSE: (*Suggestively.*) The Golden Triangle.

JIMMY SHILLELAGH: Enmeshed in webs. High intrigue.

JOHNNIE SUCROSE: Boo-coo bucks.

JIMMY SHILLELAGH: So fine.

JOHNNIE SUCROSE: *Sweet.*

CHARLIE SAMOA: Put a lid on it. Oh by the way, Mother, your junk reports are . . . very helpful—somewhat fanciful—but very informatical in a metaphorical sort of way. We're grateful, Mother. Say thank you, boys and girls.

JOHNNIE and JIMMY: Thank you, Mother.

(*Long pause.*)

HUNGRY MOTHER: You're not supposed to take that . . . sure. Sure.

CHARLIE SAMOA: We think you got your finger on something. Some sort of . . . pulse. But I digress. (*Sniffs.*) In the course of negotiating these delicate, er, negotiations, I happened to run into certain disagreements with, that is to say, run afoul of an associate more of colleague actually, concerning in connection with distribution rights . . . very complex. This *gentleman* . . . in order to press me, in order to, I suppose, exert a primitive kind of leverage—kidnapped my daughter. (*Pause.*) When this rather crude ploy failed to have the desired effect, he did something very unpleasant to her. (*Pause.*) Nobody pushes me around. I want you to understand, Mother, that she'll be alright. I'm convinced of that. My daughter means everything to me. You know that, don't you Mother? Her mother was a *slut*, but she means everything to me. (*Pause.*) I went to his apartment house. I walked past the doorman. He didn't even see me. I'm a ghost. I walked up the back stair. Two at a time. No hurry, I was in no hurry. I rang the bell. Bang bang. I put the muzzle up, the muzzle of my magnum up—against the eyehole, the glass peephole. I rang the bell. He came to the door. I could hear his footsteps. He slid the cover back. Ffffffffffttt. The cover of the peephole back. Click. Who could this be? His stomach's falling out. He couldn't see nothing, you understand. To him it just looked dark. But it was *steel*. (*Slight pause.*) He put his eye up to the glass. I make a clicking sound in the back of my throat. Click. Click. I shot him through the eye. Through the glass. That's how it was. I blew his fucking head apart. (*Pause.*)

HUNGRY MOTHER: Why are they in here?
CHARLIE SAMOA: Ask 'em.
HUNGRY MOTHER: Her. How can she be here?
JOHNNIE SUCROSE: I'm his conjugular visitor.

(*Slight pause. They laugh.*)

CHARLIE SAMOA: Pull the strings, Mom, you got to pull the strings.

(*They are laughing, shouting, pushing and shoving Hungry Mother—a mock mugging. At last Hungry Mother breaks away. A moment, then:*)

HUNGRY MOTHER: I have to be going now.
CHARLIE SAMOA: Take it light—
JOHNNIE SUCROSE: Everything'll be alright—
JIMMY SHILLELAGH: Uptight and out of sight!

(*They are laughing again.*)

JOHNNIE SUCROSE: Out of state! Out of state!
CHARIE SAMOA: That's good! Out of state! Johnnie, you kill me, babe!
JOHNNIE SUCROSE: Don't become a stranger!
JIMMY SHILLELAGH: Right! Right! Right!

(*Raucous laughter. They fade. Hungry Mother walks out and into the studio, up to the mike; blue light is still "on."*)

HUNGRY MOTHER: And while we're waiting for our mystery girl guest, here's Hungry Mother's Horo-scope. (*Mellifluous, honeyed.*) Virgo: your stars are black dwarves, be advised. But don't take it too hard, my dear. Thermodynamic entropy comes to us all. Libra: proceed with caution. A romantic entanglement may lead to a social disease. Sagittarius: your moon is in eclipse and your spouse in the house of your best friend. Taurus: your moon is in Uranus. Success is light-years away. Capricorn: copasetic! Aries: if you open your mouth, I wanna see some teeth. Leo: you were so ugly when you were born, the doctor slapped your mother. Gemini: once black, they never come back. Cancer: you've got it, what can I say? Tough nuggies. Moloch: take the first-born boy-child of every house—(*Phone rings.*) Hang on! The lines are burning up! (*Switch flicking.*) Hello? Maybe I'll turn this mother into a *talk* show! Hello! You're *radio*-active!

THE MOOK: (*Live, over P.A.*) The planets are propitious. Hello, Mother.

HUNGRY MOTHER: Hey.

THE MOOK: How's by you?

HUNGRY MOTHER: Passable.

THE MOOK: Long time you know.

HUNGRY MOTHER: Not long enough. You know?

THE MOOK: I'm looking for Free Lance.

(*Slight pause.*)

HUNGRY MOTHER: So'm I.

THE MOOK: I'll be right up.

(*Click. Hungry Mother stares at the blue light, still "on." He spears beans with a fork.*)

HUNGRY MOTHER: How long can he keep this up? Three beans, three prongs. One bean per prong, it's only fair. How long, ladies and gentlemen? Stick with me, friends, the suspense is killing.

(*Janis enters.*)

HUNGRY MOTHER: Like beans? (*Flings one.*) What's your opinion? (*Flings another.*) On the spot woman in the street interview how do you like your beans?

JANIS: Boiled.

HUNGRY MOTHER: Very good. You're right in step with the rest of America. Just another pedestrian. (*Flings a forkful of beans, striking Janis.*) Hey! Bull's eye! Well, maybe not a direct hit, maybe not *ground zero*, but certainly *close enough for jazz*, wouldn't you say? Yes, once again, that's—*close enough for jazz*! . . . You ought to do something about that bean stain, little lady. Isn't she pathetic, ladies and gentlemen?

(*Janis, wary, backs off. Pause.*)

HUNGRY MOTHER: Oh . . . yeah. Don't be alarmed. Just part of my standard Improvisation avec beans. Nothing to be ashamed of.

JANIS: Are you Hungry Mother? That's a stupid question. Of course you are.

HUNGRY MOTHER: The first.

JANIS: I'm Janis.

HUNGRY MOTHER: I figured.

JANIS: I called ahead.

HUNGRY MOTHER: Right.

JANIS: You said I could come up.

HUNGRY MOTHER: I thought you were another Janis. Different Janis. Janis I used to know.

JANIS: Oh. It's a common name. Not like Hungry Mother.

HUNGRY MOTHER: Aw shucks, that's just my nom de ozone . . . Give it time. The wave of the future. (*Pause.*) Something I can do for you?

JANIS: I wanted to see you.

HUNGRY MOTHER: You're the first, the very first! Hey! Reaching that wider audience! Hungry Mother has impact! It pays to listen! Kudos. Kudos are in order. My first fan. How's it feel, little lady? How do you like the studio?

JANIS: It's nice.

HUNGRY MOTHER: But small. Nice but small. But who knows, if this keeps up, this wild adulation, in twenty or thirty years I'll be able to (*Used Car salesman:*) trade it in on something nicer, yes, friends, why wait, empty those ashtrays and come on down . . . Beans?

JANIS: No. Thanks.

HUNGRY MOTHER: Something Japanese, perhaps. They do very well with that little shit. Transistors, crap like that. Minutia. A definitive talent for the diminutive, don't you think? Tell me, as my numero uno fano, do you find I have a sexy voice?

JANIS: No.

HUNGRY MOTHER: Robust. Virile. Vaguely Mediterranean. Like a swollen sack of coffee beans.

JANIS: No. (*Slight pause.*) Soothing. Possible.

HUNGRY MOTHER: I see.

JANIS: There's pain. In your voice . . . I came to talk to you. I need to talk to you. Don't be cruel.

(*Slight pause.*)

HUNGRY MOTHER: Rings a bell. I have a famous sinking feeling. You ain't my first guppy.

JANIS: No. No.

HUNGRY MOTHER: Damn. (*Peering.*) Auto-graph hound? Woof. Woof.

JANIS: I recognize the pain.

HUNGRY MOTHER: Do you?

JANIS: It's like my own. Familiar. Similar. Like what I feel at night. In my chest. Your voice sounds like that. That pain.

(*Pause.*)

HUNGRY MOTHER: You're Desperate, aren't you?

JANIS: (*Flushing.*) No, no, I would never that would be over—

HUNGRY MOTHER: No no no no no. That's how you sign your letters. Desperate.''

JANIS: Yes.

HUNGRY MOTHER: Janis Desperate. Jesus.

(*Pause.*)

JANIS: I want you to help me.

HUNGRY MOTHER: People in hell want ice water.

JANIS: What? What does that mean? What is that supposed to mean? I want you to help me. Please.

HUNGRY MOTHER: It's a joke, Janis Desperate. A joke.

JANIS: I don't get it. I don't see anything funny.

HUNGRY MOTHER: You're not concentrating. Is all. Now pay attention. This is Pop Analogy Number One. Rock 'n roll Metaphor. You might just cop on to what I'm laying down—dig? You can't always get what you want. But if you try sometime. You get what you need. (*Slight pause.*) I hate to be the one to break it to you sister, but people in hell don't *want* ice water, they *need* it. And—guess what? They *don't* get it . . . Do you get it?

(*Pause.*)

JANIS: I don't feel good, Mother. I know you know what I'm—I know you feel the same.

HUNGRY MOTHER: I'm asking do you get it. You're asking me to help is the joke. I'm laughing. I'm larfing. You'd better larf too.

JANIS: I know you know how I feel.

HUNGRY MOTHER: Not a glimmer.

(*Pause.*)

JANIS: I don't have any furniture in my place. Nothing. A radio. I play the radio. Full blast. To keep the junkies away. They run through the building at night. Up and down the stairs. Fire escape. Rip the copper out of the walls. The wiring. There's no water. No light. They steal the stoves. The gas crawls up the wall. (*Slight pause.*) I turn it up. Way up. Radio. Play it all night. Afraid to sleep. They run through the building all night. Scratch the walls. (*Slight pause.*) I said that. (*Slight pause.*) That's how I found you, Mother. One night. Down at the end of the dial. Before dawn. Strange voice. Cracked. Had a crack in it. Down at the end of the dial. Pain in it. (*Slight pause.*) Thanks for turning up. You were so faint at first. When I first found you. Just a crackle. Clearer in winter than summer or spring . . . No, that's silly, but—my place is right across the park. I think the leaves must interfere? Anyway, lately—you're coming in as clear as a bell.

HUNGRY MOTHER: A lucky bounce offa the clouds. It's all in the angle, sweetheart. I'm 26,000 light years off-center.

JANIS: Incredibly clear. What I am telling you. What I am trying to say. For more than a year now your voice has really made the difference to me, Mother.

(*Pause.*)

HUNGRY MOTHER: Why don't you buy some furniture? Beanbag chairs. Shag rug. Plexiglass coffee tables. Big glossy books. Galopagos this and that. Austerity is salubrious but poverty can be painful. Cheer yourself up. Hanging plants, that's the ticket. Junkies don't truck with hanging plants.

JANIS: (*Trying again, in a rush.*) I felt you were lonely, you said you wanted letters, I could tell, I could tell you were, by your jokes, you were worried no one was listening, no one cared, no one was hearing you, so I wrote, I wrote you. I never dreamed, you know, of writing to a, a public person, a stranger, I wouldn't you know, infringe on someone's privacy . . . so I was really distressed when you read my letters over the air . . . but in a way that was alright, it was okay, it was like you were listening, like you were answering. I never expected you to—that's why I signed my letters Desperate, I thought—

HUNGRY MOTHER: That's the way God planned it.

JANIS: Mother, I didn't mean to write you just about me, my problems. I was going to cheer you up, believe me—

HUNGRY MOTHER: (*Trying to duplicate her voice precisely.*) Believe me.

JANIS: Oh, I do.

(*Pause.*)

HUNGRY MOTHER: Look, uh . . . what's on your mind?

JANIS: I just—want you to be my friend. A friend. Is that so much to ask?

HUNGRY MOTHER: Depends. Come here.

(*Janis moves to him.*)

JANIS: Okay.
HUNGRY MOTHER: Tight squeeze.
JANIS: That's okay. Cozier.

(*She sits. Hungry Mother puts an arm around her. She smiles, slightly. She relaxes, just a bit.*)

HUNGRY MOTHER: 'S nice, huh?
JANIS: Yeah. Yeah.
HUNGRY MOTHER: I . . . can't do it.
JANIS: What?
HUNGRY MOTHER: Janis, there's something I should tell you.
JANIS: (*Touching his face.*) Sssshhh, don't talk. You don't have to talk.
HUNGRY MOTHER: Yeah, there's something I should have mentioned earlier.
    (*Slight pause.*) You're lonely, right?
JANIS: Yes.
HUNGRY MOTHER: Well, I'm lonely too.
JANIS: Oh, Mother, I know you are. I know you are.
HUNGRY MOTHER: Well, darling—as one lonely person to another—(*Slight pause.*)—we're on the air!

(*Janis jumps to her feet, looks at the blue light.*)

JANIS: Oh. Oh.
HUNGRY MOTHER: (*Goes to mike.*) Wasn't that touching friends? You heard it
    here, first. Hang in there, there's more to come from Janis Desperate,
    much more.
JANIS: Bastard.
HUNGRY MOTHER: Sorry.
JANIS: Yes.
HUNGRY MOTHER: That's my style, sweets. Free-form free-fall. Wing it over
    the edge and see how long it takes to hit bottom.
JANIS: Jesus.

(*The Mook enters. A large man, elegant. Terrifying. A black Renaissance Prince.*)

HUNGRY MOTHER: Ah, Mook! Mook! I'm honored. Long time no you know.
    I believe you two, you know, too.
THE MOOK: You're off the beam. I haven't had the pleasure. Seen Free
    Lance?
HUNGRY MOTHER: How about her?

THE MOOK: I doubt it. You lookin' to get out of show business, Mother, and into an honest line of work? Whyfor you cute, Mom? She's nice, but the Free Lance I have in mind is nicer by far.

HUNGRY MOTHER: Right. Sorry. Mook. Janis. Janis. Mook.

THE MOOK: Enchante.

JANIS: Fine!

(*She stalks out.*)

THE MOOK: Whatsa matta for her? The rabbit died?

HUNGRY MOTHER: Naw . . . We just met.

THE MOOK: Mark my words, Mother. The price of fame is a paternity suit.

HUNGRY MOTHER: I'll watch my step.

THE MOOK: You'll know you're in the big time when you find you have five or six half-nigger brats who bear not the slightest resemblance to anyone you ever knew. (*Pause.*) Where's Free Lance?

HUNGRY MOTHER: Changed her name.

THE MOOK: You said she'd be here.

HUNGRY MOTHER: I said I was expecting her. I am. I still am.

THE MOOK: You ought to get out more, Mother. Away from the mike. Clear your head.

(*Pause.*)

HUNGRY MOTHER: Free Lance.

(*Pause.*)

THE MOOK: She didn't tell me. She was going to change her name. She just changed it.

(*Pause.*)

HUNGRY MOTHER: I could use more air.

THE MOOK: I liked Polish Vodka better.

HUNGRY MOTHER: To drink or on her?

THE MOOK: Both . . . *Simultaneous.*

HUNGRY MOTHER: I thought she was working for you.

THE MOOK: In this assumption our thoughts concur. (*They dap.*) Coincide. (*Dap.*) Collide. (*Dap.*) She's not treating me well, Mother. Or herself. She's going out on the limb of principles. I want her to come down. If you snag the drift of my metaphor.

HUNGRY MOTHER: I think I follow it.

(They begin a complicated dap, a hand jive.)

THE MOOK: Free Lance. That's rich.

HUNGRY MOTHER: Snap!

THE MOOK: It's a question of precedents. She needs her insurance, Mother, like a child needs her vitamins. And this is a world, Mother, as you well know, in which a child cannot hope to survive without a little luck and some kind of insurance.

HUNGRY MOTHER: Crack!

THE MOOK: She knows I cannot allow this. Not just my livelihood is threatened by her rash and precipitous action. What if my other ladies take it into their heads. I wouldn't want to see them get hurt.

HUNGRY MOTHER: Pow!

(They finish dap.)

THE MOOK: Exactly. Thank you, Mother, for extending my metaphor.

HUNGRY MOTHER: Not at all. Any time. *(Slight pause.)* Maybe she's lucky.

THE MOOK: I'm her luck. *(Slight pause.)* The thing that really gets my goat, Mother, that really galls the living shit out of me—is that she's setting this whole thing up like some kind of walking three-D cliche. Right offa the silver screen. Ruthless pimp with the cold as stone heart. Prosty with the tits of gold. They get down—to brass tacks. Small-time indy versus rapacious multi-national. Victory for free enterprise. yea. Sheep farmer whips cattle baron. Score one for the free fucking market and laissez-faire capital-ism. Creeping socialism crawl under de rock. Music up and out. *(Slight pause.)* The record's scratchy, Mother. A bad print. I seen it before. I heard it before.

HUNGRY MOTHER: Why'd she do it? She said she missed you.

THE MOOK: She saw it in the movies.

HUNGRY MOTHER: Oh.

THE MOOK: For Christ sake, I'll give you ten to one. She took it into her head . . . Mother, Mother. I'm chiding you, Mother. Tsk, tsk. In America—life—*(Strikes pose.)*—imitates—media!! *(Slight pause. Drops pose.)* Who should know better than you?

HUNGRY MOTHER: I hang my head. *(He does.)*

THE MOOK: I resent being put in this position. I resent being made to play some kind of classic American morality schtik. I resent being made archetypal. You know? It gives me a *black* burning sensation behind my eyes.

HUNGRY MOTHER: What are you going to do to her?

(Long pause.)

THE MOOK: Ask her to come in. Nicely. (*Slight pause.*) You were close.

HUNGRY MOTHER: (*Brusquely.*) Old days. Stone Age. Before I became the Hungry Mother.

THE MOOK: Don't kid me. You always been the Hungry Mother. From time immemorial . . . You comin' in loud and clear dese days.

HUNGRY MOTHER: Yeah?

THE MOOK: Right. Somebody's monkeyed with your volume.

HUNGRY MOTHER: Atmospheric turbulence. Sunspots. Geo-thermal radiation.

THE MOOK: You ought to watch your ass.

HUNGRY MOTHER: So everybody tells me. Christ, it's enough to make a corpse paranoid.

THE MOOK: Especially those Junk Reports.

HUNGRY MOTHER: Mook, they aren't for real.

THE MOOK: Oh, yes they are. Now they are. Every junkie in town, Mom. Every junkie, every narc, every pusher, every pimp. You the *source*, man, the Wall Street fuckin' Journal of Junk . . . Everybody knows you're illegal, Mother. It's not secret. Folks concerned. Highly concerned. There are rumors. Grand jury activity. They might get together. They might *convene.* This whole gig just might go titties up.

HUNGRY MOTHER: I can't explain it, Mook. This tube gear is shot. It's cream of shit. It's a miracle it gets off the block.

THE MOOK: (*Leans forward, very black, very deep.*) Tell it to the judge. (*Laughs, booming cackle.*) They taping you 'round the clock, little man.

HUNGRY MOTHER: (*Yelling.*) I don't broadcast around the clock!

THE MOOK: If only you'd keep a schedule, Mother. They don't want to miss a single spasm. A single spurt. Right now, they trying to ascertain just who listening. Besides themselves, I mean. A demo-graphic sample. To determine your threat extent. It's proving elusive.

HUNGRY MOTHER: I'll bet it is.

THE MOOK: Just a friendly gesture. If you see Free Lance, tell her to come on in. Just like the movies. It'll go easier. Plea bargain. One week only. Tell her that. (*The Mook heads for the door.*)

HUNGRY MOTHER: Hey, Mook.

THE MOOK: Yes dear?

HUNGRY MOTHER: You're on the air!

(*The Mook looks at the blue light a long moment. The he shakes his head and grins.*)

THE MOOK: Motha fucka! (*He exits.*)

(*Hungry Mother races to the mike.*)

HUNGRY MOTHER: Well, there you have it, gas fans, the heat is on! You heard it all, *live*, from the life of Hungry Mother, a true story. Cross my heart. If you'd like to participate in the life of Hungry Mother, just drop me a card—indicate your primary field of interest—philosophical, sexual, athletic, dinner, dress, or aperitif—and mail it to . . . Hungry Mother, Got To Get You Into My Life, Hubba Hubba Hubba Hubba, WTWI, Franz Fanon Memorial Tenement, Number One Marauder Avenue, just past Faghag Park. All entries will remain on file for use at my personal discretion. (*Weatherman.*) The long-range outcast for this weekend—*diptheria*! Followed by bubonic plague and intermittent spotted fever. Enjoy. Right now outside our studio—continued existential dread dappled with parapsychological phenomena, and streaked with low-grade anxiety. Speaking of weather, we'll have the latest prices for bone-marrow and rendering in a moment, but first . . . (*He slumps on stool. Silence. He returns to mike: teletype and newscaster.*) Flash news update. That acute distress has gone—*terminal*. Closed with a rush. Check it out. Other tidbits about our town . . . That dog rapist remains at large. Pet owners—do you know where your pets are tonight? Coming up in the near future—if there is one—heh heh, always the optimist, Mother, check it out! Always the optimist. *Lycanthropy In The Home*! Always a hairy subject, we'll have some tips on just how to deal with it. And we'll be talking to a bonafide cat burglar, and you'll find out *exactly* what they do with our furry friends . . . the fiends. We'll also have our Prick Hit of the Week, when you ladies can line up the sexual swine of your choice and sock it to him—right here in our soundproof booth. (*Mellifluous.*) That just about puts a merciful end to our broadcasting day here at WTWI, the twilight station with the demeanor that only a Mother could love. We'll top it off with our ever-popular Slumlord of the Day Award, we'll be back after somebody's briefs, but first—a word about *mange*. . . This is the Hungry Mother, wrapping it up here, boss, with a mouthful of joy buzzers and a handful of static, telling you to have a hopeful day, spelled with two ells.

(*Three individuals enter the studio: two men and a woman. We know them for:*)

HUNGRY MOTHER: Has to be— (*Long pause; then a whisper.*) *Hoover and the Navajos.*

(*Freeze. Tableau. Lights fade. Blue light still ''on'' in the black. Long moment. Snaps off. Blackout.*)

End of Act One

Act II

Black.

LOUD SPEAKER: The Rising *Pop*ularity of Hungry Mother . . . Beginning with— (*Blue light pops "on," silhouetting four-figure freeze:*) Tableaux Vivants! Avecs peaux rouges!

(*Lights up slowly on Hoover and the Navajos, and Hungry Mother. They remain still, as Hoover speaks simply, in the classic mode:*)

HOOVER: In the moon of grass withering . . . or perhaps in the moon of vanishing animals . . . I surrendered my people to General Howard. My heart was . . . *broke.* I said to him—the chiefs are dead. Looking Glass is dead. All the young men are dead. Or scattered like dry leaves. Or drowning in whiskey. My children chew bark. Their feet are frozen. The old women gobble dead grass and devil's brush. We are starving. My lungs are full of clotted blood. As I said before—from where the sun now sets, I will fight no more, forever. This is what I said to General Howard. (*Pause.*) So he gave me a job. (*Pause. Hoover holds up a brightly colored plastic package in one hand, and points to it with his other hand, on which he is wearing a black leather glove.*) Selling these . . . The snack that never grows old . . . Fiddle Faddle . . . That's how I became Chief Fiddle Faddle. (*Hoover flips down his shades. Pause. Grins.*) Just kidding.

(*The Navajos begin poking around in the studio. Hungry Mother takes over from Hoover at the mike.*)

HUNGRY MOTHER: Hey, hey! Hoover, fella, you really had me going there. I was brewing up some really fierce Apache crocodile tears. Isn't he something, ladies and gentlemen? We're here today with our special guests, Hoover and the Navajos—

HOOVER: Just kidding.

HUNGRY MOTHER: Yes, yes, just fooling around. Tell us, Hoov—a lot of us—

the listening and yearning audience—would like to know something more *about* Hoover and the Navajos. All they know is what I tell 'em, what I, you know, make up off the top. On the spur.

(*Very long pause, during which Crazy Joe lies on Hungry Mother's refrigerator and drinks from a bottle in a paper bag; Freddy polishes her shades and ceremoniously unwraps and chews a piece of gum; she rolls the foil into a ball and flicks it at Hungry Mother. Only then does Hoover speak.*)

HOOVER: You got it right. You got it right, Mother. You got it so right. Except in smallest details. No way you could miss. The light comes down on you . . . Smallest things. Our names. My friends. Mother, my companions . . . Crazy Joe Navajo. (*Crazy Joe burps delicately by way of greeting.*) Freddy Navajo. (*Freddy nods coldly. Hoover smiles.*) The light comes down on you, Mother. Indians are always silent. Having nothing to say. Ask your stupid questions.

HUNGRY MOTHER: (*After a slight hesitation.*) In the fawning fanmag manner, then—when did you write your first song? When did you first start playing the guitar? When did you decide to devote your lifestyle to music?

HOOVER: In the moon of rising expectations.

HUNGRY MOTHER: In the little magazine manner then—when did you first conceive, and begin to develop as a distinct genre of popular music, *patho-rock*? What sets *patho-rock* apart from other strands, such as goat-bucket blues or coon cajun cakewalks? Compare and contrast. Trace its evolution in a socio-historical context. How do you account for your obsession with fibreglass? Is it worthwhile speculating along psycho-sexual dysfunction lines?

HOOVER: In the moon of historical necessity . . . Out of the blue . . . Unrelenting bitterness, as long as the waters shall flow and the grass shall grow—you know the phrase? . . . And environmentally generated malignancy contracted as an immediate consequence of contact with the carcinogenic substance. In that order.

HUNGRY MOTHER: (*Brightly.*) I see. That's too bad!

HOOVER: In the moon of bowing to the inevitable. In the charnel moon of abject capitulation. In the blue moon of genocide. In the quarter moon of going completely off the wall . . . In the moon of *forced labor* . . .

HUNGRY MOTHER: Right. Got it. That's what gives your songs that grit, that nit, that *sliced life*. Tell me—and I'm sure your fans at home would be more than super interested too—where do you get those desatively bonnaroo titles like *Fibreglass God*?

HOOVER: I got drunk and fell on the floor.

(*Pause. Then Freddy stands.*)

FREDDY: Freddy Navajo here. Earth to Freddy. I hear voices. Indian voices. Mescalito. Coyote. Charlie Chan. Joan of Navajo speaks in my ear. It ain't easy to hear myself think—with all those voices going. All the old voices. Covered here today. Hoover did his Poetic Indian to his usual turn. (*Freddy and Crazy Joe applaud.*) Aplomb. Aplomb. And Crazy Joe's taciturn Drunken Injun is, as always, subtle and tragic. Impeccable. Correct.

(*Freddy and Hoover applaud. Slight pause.*)

CRAZY JOE: (*Ever so slightly slurred.*) Thanks.

FREDDY: A classic of its kind. You see my predicament? So many voices. A welter. A goulash. So hard to find a point of view. Which piece of history to vocalette.

HUNGRY MOTHER: (*Cheerily.*) How 'bout TB? You know, tuberculosis, Easter Seals for brown babes? Famine? Small-pox sleeping bags?

FREDDY: Hostility is always in good taste.

HUNGRY MOTHER: Uh . . . Freddy, what's the—why don't you do the new single?

FREDDY: Right . . . This is a song I wrote one night while breaking glass on the reservation . . . I calls it—*Fucking on Fibreglass!*

HOOVER: Give me a ball 'n beer anyday.

FREDDY: Right. Sheer shock value. No other redemptions. Oh, incidental alliteration. A simple tune. Our only aim is sensation.

HUNGRY MOTHER: That's great. Swell, and heartwarming. Here it is, fans, what you've all been waiting for! If this single don't send you, you got no place to go! Hoover and The Navajos—*Fucking—On Fibreglass!*

(*Hungry Mother puts on the 45, flicks switches: it blasts out over the PA: primitive guitar chording, hand drums, yowling and chanting, screaming, glass shattering. After two minutes of ear-splitting sound, a blues fragment snarls its way out of the maelstrom:*)

HOOVER: (*Singing, on the 45.*)
Fuckin'
On fibreglass . . .
Got that shit
Up my . . . aaaaaaaaasssss!

(*This is followed, on the 45, by a scream from Freddy that's like a baby's howl. When they hear their voices play, Hoover and Freddy trade grins. Through it all, they've been keeping the beat: Hoover drumming, Crazy Joe drinking, Freddy thrusting her pelvis in a mechanical, parodic, anti-erotic style. Fucking on Fibreglass ends with a crescendo of drumming and breaking glass. Silence.*)

HUNGRY MOTHER: (*Softly.*) So visceral . . . I can *feel* it. Uch. Where do you guys get this stuff? Monstrous. Colossal. Curdled blood, see? Destroys me. Primal.

FREDDY: (*Snickering.*) Primordial.

(*Crazy Joe gets up off the refrigerator. A hush. He goes to the turntable, takes off the 45, drops it on the floor. Pours whiskey on it. Takes a drink. Smiles. Smacks his lips.*)

CRAZY JOE: Primitive!

(*The Navajos laugh wildly. They seize piles of 45's, and begin flinging them through the air, slowly at first, then faster, to crescendo—a blizzard of black plastic. It stops. The studio floor is covered in 45s. Pause. Hoover smiles cooly behind his shades and says s o f t l y :*)

HOOVER: Aborigine.

(*Hoover and the Navajos exit. Hungry Mother stands in the debris. Streetlight snaps on. Hungry Mother walks into the light. Janis is in a shadow. He stops and stares at her. Finally:*)

HUNGRY MOTHER: Wha'choo doin' out here?

JANIS: Lurking.

HUNGRY MOTHER: Lurking. Huh. (*Slight pause.*) Hell of a place to lurk. (*Slight pause.*) Lurking long?

JANIS: Hours.

HUNGRY MOTHER: And lived to tell the tale. A-mazing. I shake my head. (*He does.*)

JANIS: So. What's the word?

HUNGRY MOTHER: *Hungry.*

JANIS: Listen, I thought maybe—you busy? I thought maybe we could get a bite.

HUNGRY MOTHER: In this neighborhood? A bite is a breeze. But will they quit after just one?

(*They both laugh.*)

JANIS: Listen. I know a place.

HUNGRY MOTHER: Yeah? Well. Okay. Alright.

JANIS: It's near here. You'll like it. Under Marauder Avenue. It floats.

HUNGRY MOTHER: A floating dive. Abso-fucking-lutely. Lezgo.

(*The streetlight flickers. The light is blue and wintery: a cold evening. Mook and Free Lance enter. Hungry Mother and Janis stop. Draw back. Unseen. Pause.*)

THE MOOK: Ho Chi Minh Trail runs through the park now.

FREE LANCE: Uptown to down.

THE MOOK: Natch. Built that way. They brought it over after the war. Reconstituted it. As it were.

FREE LANCE: What you run on it?

THE MOOK: Scag. Just like the war. Like it never ended. Them good old days. They got a replica of the war goin' on in there. Miniature. Jes' a few blocks away . . . Business as usual, babe. (*He turns his gaze on her.*) Back on the street.

FREE LANCE: Back on the streets again.

THE MOOK: I stand corrected. Back on the streets. The phrase that pays . . . I thought you were sick of the street. I been to see Mother, looking for you.

FREE LANCE: I've missed the street.

THE MOOK: I know you have. I wasn't surprised.

FREE LANCE: And the street missed me.

FREE LANCE: I miss the street. Mook. Same difference . . . I miss you. What kind of chat you say you had?

THE MOOK: Minimal. I dropped him a hint. Dammit, Free Lance, whachoo doin' out here?

FREE LANCE: Looking for you.

THE MOOK: On the street? Come on, baby. I been all over town, I come home find you *walking* my block.

FREE LANCE: (*Laughs.*) You my main squeeze, sugah. Mama want Papa-san be her first trick. Numbah one, dig?

(*Pause.*)

THE MOOK: You set me up, Free Lnace. Like a damn tar baby. Some kind of story. You fictionalizing my position. Dig? People talk. A legend in my own time. Shit. Legend in my own mind. They talkin' now. Hear 'em?

FREE LANCE: No.

THE MOOK: Erodes my credibility. People don't think I'm real. Think I'm the damn Baron Samedi or some voodoo shit. Gets tough to keep the muscle up when they put you in the same bag with Mickey the Mouse and Agent Orange. (*Hisses.*) Know what I talk, bitch?

(*She is about to respond when she hears something in the distance. They both listen.*)

FREE LANCE: Guns.

THE MOOK: Gunners.

(*He smiles. She shivers.*)

FREE LANCE: I love The Street. I go wandering on The Street. In the back of my head. Stay there forever. Stay there for good. Disappear behind my eyes. You understand?

THE MOOK: Free Lance.

FREE LANCE: I'm not going upstairs with you, Mook.

THE MOOK: Free Lance. (*Slight pause.*) I promised Mother.

FREE LANCE: No, not upstairs. I like it here. (*Slight pause.*) Leaving Mother's, I get a screamer. A rag ghost. I see him all the way down at the end of the block. He sees me. He turns. Gunfight at the Okay. I freeze. He takes a step. Takes two. Now he's running. Right at me. His mouth is open like a siren and he's screaming. He's getting closer. Closer. I can smell rot. He's got a bottle in his hand. A mickey. Like a knife. He's right on top of me. I step aside, and he goes right on by. Still screaming. Disappears into the park. Screams stop. Siren stops. *Chop.*

THE MOOK: Fags got him. Gorilla fags. They drop out of the trees like fruit.

FREE LANCE: Nothing like that happens upstairs.

THE MOOK: Damn straight. I ain't no punk. You have any other adventures since I saw you last?

FREE LANCE: Run of the mill rubble walk. Trash fire circle jerks. Rubble rabble. They try'n come on you as you walk past.

THE MOOK: It's an art. That'll teach you to run away from home. Come on in, Free Lance. Come on in, baby. Come on in with me.

FREE LANCE: Of course.

THE MOOK: Mother's worried about you. You ought to give Mother a call.

FREE LANCE: I will.

THE MOOK: I know you were close. Just tell him you okay. Set his mind. The kid's all right.

FREE LANCE: Mook. Mother's on the rag about some kids. You have anything to do with that? You boosting, hustling some kids?

THE MOOK: 'S an idea, baby. Get all my best notions from Mother.

FREE LANCE: Pimp.

(*Slight pause.*)

THE MOOK: (*Mildly.*) Don't call me that. Don't rub The Mook the wrong way. Call me monger instead.

FREE LANCE: Monger?

(*Free Lance begins to laugh, undertones of hysteria. The Mook smiles.*)

THE MOOK: Yeah. Flesh monger.

(*She stops laughing. Slight pause.*)

THE MOOK: Come on up. Come on in.

(*She is listening in the distance, again.*)

FREE LANCE: Firefight.
THE MOOK: See? Got to come with me, baby. Can't go 'way down there.

(*Pause.*)

FREE LANCE: For now. It's chilly.

(*He puts his arm around her. They start to leave.*)

FREE LANCE: (*Black.*) Watchoo tell Mothah?
THE MOOK: Heh heh heh. I tell Mothah to watch his *ass.* You blackisms gettin' bettah, baby.
FREE LANCE: (*Laughs.*) Ah, Mook. Mook. (*Strokes his face.*) You're a dizzy cunt. You know that?

(*He stares. Then laughs. Roars. Mook and Free Lance exit. Streetlight flickers. Hungry Mother steps out and stares after them. Charlie Samoa appears behind them. He's dressed as a derelict.*)

DERELICT (CHARLIE SAMOA): 'Member the cat.

(*They start. Hungry Mother doesn't recognize him.*)

HUNGRY MOTHER: Cat.
DERELICT (CHARLIE SAMOA): 'Member the cat. Curiosity and the cat. (*He starts off. Turns back.*) Jesus was not a white racist—as some people suppose. He was the only son of the living god. (*Exits.*)
JANIS: You know them?
HUNGRY MOTHER: Who?
JANIS: The . . . . . couple.
HUNGRY MOTHER: Oh yes.
JANIS: What was that? That scene.
HUNGRY MOTHER: He wants her.
JANIS: What does she want?
HUNGRY MOTHER: Out.
JANIS: What are you going to do?
HUNGRY MOTHER: What can I do?
JANIS: She wants help?
HUNGRY MOTHER: No. No. She doesn't want it.

(*Silence. Lights change. They move into the studio and undress in the half light, as Loud Speaker speaks:*)

LOUD SPEAKER: Oooeeeooo, baby, baby. Oh, oh, oh, Miss Ann. Dime-a-dance romance. No-tell Motel. Shank. Tryst. Tropics. *Tristes Tropiques.* Photo Opportunity. The House of Blue Light. Hungry . . . *and* . . . Friend!

(*Studio illuminated. Hungry Mother and Janis in the trashed studio. Janis lights a cigarette.*)

JANIS: At least we weren't on the air.
HUNGRY MOTHER: Community standards. I think I'll torch these platters. Do the whole dump in hot wax.
JANIS: I don't think it's right, quite.

(*Silence.*)

HUNGRY MOTHER: Well.
JANIS: Well.
HUNGRY MOTHER: Hope you feelin' better . . .
JANIS: Bye 'n bye.

(*Pause.*)

HUNGRY MOTHER: Yes.
JANIS: You too?
HUNGRY MOTHER: Mmmm. Bye 'n bye. 'S been a long time.
JANIS: Why? Why not?
HUNGRY MOTHER: Out of fashion. *Intimacy.* A blast from the past.
JANIS: I should talk. I haven't been, mmm, with anyone for ages. Long long time . . . Good for the blues.
HUNGRY MOTHER: Curin' or causin'?

(*Silence.*)

HUNGRY MOTHER: Walikin' blues. Talkin' blues. Stalkin' blues . . . (*He lets it go.*)
JANIS: Mother.
HUNGRY MOTHER: Yes'm.
JANIS: Mother, would you put me on the air?

(*Slight pause.*)

HUNGRY MOTHER: Sure.

(He gets up and goes to the console. Flicks switches. Blue light goes "on." She goes to the mike. Now they are both standing nearly naked in the twilight debris. Silence. She lights a cigarette. Drags. Long moment. She returns to the cot and picks up the rest of her clothes. Puts them on. They look at each other. He turns the blue light off.)

HUNGRY MOTHER: Minimal. In fact, minimal to the max. I dug it. I especially dug it when you put on your clothes. Getting dressed on the radio.
It's hot. No commercial possibilities of course. Could be cognescenti.
JANIS: I don't know what I wanted to say. I just wanted to put my voice out
there. On the radio . . . What a strange phrase. Strange thing to say. On
the air. I wanted to put it out there. On the air. Air waves. Radio waves go
on forever. To other stars.
HUNGRY MOTHER: Pulsars, baby. Will The Hungry Mother Radio Hour be
a hit on Betelgeuse six million light-years from today? Stay tuned.

(Silence.)

HUNGRY MOTHER: Let's do it again sometime.
JANIS: Let's. *(She moves to the door.)*
HUNGRY MOTHER: Absofuckinglutely.
JANIS: See you.
HUNGRY MOTHER: Abyssinia, Janis.
JANIS: Right.

(She exits. Hungry Mother retrieves his tennis shoes.)

HUNGRY MOTHER: The white man's moccasins. *(He bounds to the mike. Blue
light on.)*

LOUD SPEAKER: Rising popularity! The ratings surge! He bends their ears!
HUNGRY MOTHER: Shaddup. Hey hey hey! All systems go! This be the
Hungriest Mother alive, this be WTWI, the twilight station with the terminal blues and the twilight debris, this be a blight and bleary pre-dawn
radio debauch with the only Mother that'll *ever* love you! Coming up this
hour, Agony News Headlines, something spicy about the Pope, and the
ever-more popular Prick Hit of the Week. Plus—a bonus. A fab new soap
op: MULATTO SPLENDOR! Yes, Antebellum blues! Miscegenation,
America's favorite preoccupation! Intricate intra-ethnic color schemes!
Ancestor worship and the Daughters of the Confederacy! Something for
everyone! Impossibly overwritten! Here! On WTWI! Don't miss *Mulatto
Splendor*, the soap that's guaranteed to become a *class* struggle. In this

week's episode, Rhett discovers that Scarlett's been 'passing'—and the annual debutantes' ball is crashed by the field hands. And now—*Moan Along With Mother!* (*He sings a blues moan, minor key. First notes melodic, it quickly becomes harsh, going out of control into sobbing and retching. Subsides. Slight pause.*) There. Doesn't that feel better? (*Attacks the typewriter furiously. Newscaster:*) And now this hour's top short stories . . . Dengue Fever raging out of control across sub-Saharan Africa . . . absolutely terminal, no, I repeat, no antidote . . . Monkey Virus spreads from Germany to Georgia! If you gush black blood you've got it! And you're a goner! Isn't that something?! . . . And—the Pope is engaged! We'll be back later in the week with more on the Forty-Second Street sniper. These are this hour's top tales, brought to you by Ominous Acronyms—Ominous Acronyms, dedicated to raising the ante no matter the pot. And now a spiritual word of advice from the pastor of the First . . . Chinese Baptist . . . Church of the Deaf! (*"Chinee":*) Leveland Bluce Ree here. Lemeble! Don't wait for the hearse to take you to church! (*Cheery.*) Thank you, Leveland Bluce. Next hour, my impression of a JAP. And I don't mean Japanese. Don't miss it. But first—(*Slight pause.*) Trying to get over. (*Slight pause.*) Hauling ass. (*Slight pause. Then, shakes himself, full-speed:*) I seem to be wandering today, fans, please forgive me, bouncing off the boards like a rabid hockey puck, coming up hungry, coming up short, coming up the up and coming group destined to dethrone the once-mythical Hoover and The Navajos: Jumpin Lumpen and the Juke Savages and their new block-buster, *Idi Amin Is My Doorman!* Don't you dare miss it. But first, it's time once again for—Our Prick Hit Of The Week! Yes, every week the Mother invites you and your nominee into the studio for a little slug-*fest.* With the aid of our superbly trained staff of Swiss guerillas, we hold him down, and you let him have it! So ladies—ah, *women,* keep those nominations coming. And now—here we go again with *Mother's Prick Hit Of The Week!* (*Flicks switches. A tape goes on over the PA: it's a tape of Mother's moaning just previous. As the moaning plays, Hungry Mother rocks out, finger snaps and vocal bops. When the tape finishes he grins into the mike:*) So good. I *really* identify. The weather outlook is for unparalleled nausea—followed by protracted internal bleeding. A million-dollar weekend. (*Newscaster, ala Paul Harvey.*) Top headline . . . this . . . or any other . . . hour . . . slavery . . . on the rise . . . once again . . . in most . . . of the civilized . . . world. (*Slight pause. Low, intense.*) Consider, if you will, the following felicitous phrases . . . Jones. Slud. Double dog dare. Going down slow. Walking wounded. Hunger artist. Bane. (*Weatherman.*) Thick as slick out there, you better watch your step. (*Screaming.*) Mexican standoff! Yes! Yes! No motherfucker can touch me now! I full of the Night Train! Hear the Midnight Special call my name! I be full, so full of that damn Night Train! Nothin' I ever seen can equal the color of my i-ma-gin-ation! I am the Midnight Prerogative! (*Slight pause. Frenzied but quiet, under control, just barely: this is the emotional high of his set:*) Speaking of *jones*—I got it—for what you've all been waiting for—for those with the baddest jones of all—for those with the cold at the core of their soul—*Mother's Junk Report*! Needles are *up*. Ditto fits and kits. Rubber tubing's down. Likewise brown dreck. Something cleaner cost you more . . . here we go! Black Magic go for a dime, if you can find it, and so will Foolish Pleasure. Fifteen for Light 'n Lively, and they be gettin' a quarter for Bicentennial Gold. Hard to believe, isn't it? Topping out at a flat thirty, Death Wish! . . . Sorry, brothers and sisters, you know that's the way it goes, whiter is brighter, and less is more. Now, getting away from dreamtime and down to the street, your Mother's gonna tell you straight. All that's out there is Brown Bomber and Death Boy. A quarter, that is, seven little spoons goes for fifty, and a rip-down, half of that, jack, will cost you twenty-five. That's what's on that open market! The shit is stepped on, jack, stepped on! Worth your life to stick that shit! Cut with fucking drano, Jack! Drano! . . . (*Cooler.*) Active trading in fluff stuff around town: quarter scoops of coke scored easily on the approaches to the park, and it's snowing all over town. Storms of angel dust, methadone in ice buckets, on the rocks or with a crystal cranq chaser, and horse tranqs galore. On the sunny side up, the use of personal weapons in lethal transactions is riding a slight cooling trend—and that's got to be good news. This has been another edition of *Mother's Junk*. (*Slight pause. Upbeat.*) Ah, once that's over, I'm back on the tracks, I really am. Works like a charm. Tomorrow: *Pantheon of Scum*: a grisly scavenge through the deserted cities of the heart. You've been listening to more of the same this last half-century—brought to you by *Sayanora Thermonukes*—check us if your megatonnage droops! *Sayanora Thermonukes*—say goodbye and mean it! And now let's join, already in progress, Sugar Bear and Oz—cutting up in the Cuban Room. (*He grabs his coat and walks out, leaving the blue light "on."*)

LOUD SPEAKER: The *Casa—Cubana*!

(*Hungry Mother walks into the bar.*)

BELLY UP: Mother! Salud! How hangs it, Ma?

HUNGRY MOTHER: Somewhere else. Give me a drink. Something for the inner city man. (*He downs it and burps.*)

BELLY UP: You bet. (*He follows suit.*) Feel better?

HUNGRY MOTHER: Some.

BELLY UP: Since you're a star, have another.

HUNGRY MOTHER: Catch Hoover's act?

BELLY UP: Indelible. Crushed my head. Had to be: Hoover and The Navajos. You're getting very big, Mother. There's already a movement to save your ass.

HUNGRY MOTHER: I haven't lost it.

BELLY UP: You will. Committee to Save Hungry Mother's Ass. The Mook is getting it all together. The DA's hot and heavy on your case. He dug up a diva, and she's shrieking an aria about you to the Grand Jury right now.

HUNGRY MOTHER: What's her name?

BELLY UP: La Mook. (*He snickers. Slight pause.*)

HUNGRY MOTHER: Pays to play both ends of the street.

BELLY UP: 'S a good deal. Immunity from prosecution, all counts cept murder one, lifetime guarantee. He tags up—spray paints it on the DA's door: you The Man.

HUNGRY MOTHER: He's The Man.

BELLY UP: You The Man, Mom. Your Junk Report peddles his junk.

HUNGRY MOTHER: That's absurd.

BELLY UP: Huh huh. Scag pimps snortin' up a storm on your say so, Ma.

(*Slight pause.*)

HUNGRY MOTHER: Belly Up . . . you think they should sell smack over the counter—like aspirin?

BELLY UP: (*Laughs softly.*) C'mon, Mom. Why spoil a good thing? I'm checking on those kids for you.

HUNGRY MOTHER: Mmmmmmmm.

BELLY UP: Interesting scenario. After they go into custody of the lending institutions, poof—they disappear. I dig deeper. The big runaround. I run it down. It's easy . . . The banks sold 'em. Mook's the middle man. Commission on every kid.

HUNGRY MOTHER: Sold them.

BELLY UP: Into slavery . . . Big deal. Every two-bit banana tyrant's got a couple of Indians around the house. Right here in town I know where you can buy, no questions asked, retard kids. Cash on the barrelhead. Watch the tube?

HUNGRY MOTHER: Never.

BELLY UP: White slavery's license to print money.

(*Slight pause.*)

HUNGRY MOTHER: I made it happen. Made it all happen. Make it up—make it happen. I kept . . . talking about it . . . reporting it, you know? Fictional fact, a metaphor . . . sort of true, you know? . . . and . . . and it comes back at me. It all comes back. Drifting up from downtown . . . humming . . . the wires have picked it up . . . 'fore you know it, it's *news*, it's . . . *happened* . . . Honest, officer, it was only a fucking metaphor . . . The junk report! The junk report! Belly Up, from junk I know from nothing! The

Mook is trying to set me up . . . Last broadcast I did a slavery newsbit. Just a comedy sketch. Somebody must have picked up on it.

(*Slight pause.*)

BELLY UP: Paranoid schizophrenia. Classic case. Delusions of grandeur. Unholy power to make manifest The Word. Unable to distinguish between cause and effect. Egocentric cosmology . . . Pull yourself together. You just water, Mother. Glass. You just show it back. Artists count for nothing, Mom. Don't take it so tough.

HUNGRY MOTHER: (*Mumbles.*) Bui doi.

BELLY UP: You don't say.

HUNGRY MOTHER: Bui doi.

BELLY UP: Bui doi. Dust of life. Street urchins. Half-breed Honda banditos. (*Slight pause.*) Shit. I had you lamped, Mom. I knew you been there. The 'Nam. Moo goo gai pan, my ass. (*Slight pause. Softer:*) Whadjoo take the fall for? Over *there.*

HUNGRY MOTHER: (*Winks, smiles wanly.*) Fragged the fucker. Fragged him.

(*He gets up and leaves the bar. After he's gone:*)

BELLY UP: See you 'round, Mom.

(*On the street, Hungry Mother turns his collar up against the cold. A Prostitute (Johnnie Sucrose) and A Pimp (Jimmy Shillelagh) loiter on the edges of the light. A Derelict (Charlie Samoa) stutter dances up to Hungry Mother.*)

DERELICT (CHARLIE SAMOA): Ladies and gentlemen! For your listening entertainment—the Latin from Manhattan! Hey! Hey, man, it's cold! Cold! Thirty cents for some apricot brandy, man. That's it. That's all we need.

HUNGRY MOTHER: Sorry.

DERELICT (CHARLIE SAMOA): It's cold, man. Anything. Come on, we just shot some junk, man, we need that brandy, come *on!*

HUNGRY MOTHER: I don't have anything.

DERELICT (CHARLIE SAMOA): Man, your heart's so hard you wouldn't give God a break. Shit. Hey, brothers, c'mon . . .

(*They fade. Hungry Mother enters the studio; the blue light is "on."*)

HUNGRY MOTHER: Hungry Mother here, it's a fine fine super fine pre-dawn funk—smoke blankets the greater metropolitan area, they continue to machine-gun survivors outside our studio, rap rap rap rap rap and the *hits* just keep on comin'—and all told it looks like another fine fine super fine day in this fine fine city of ours! Before we descend into a welter of obscure pronouns, here's the plot—(*Lickety-split lung-screech.*) SUNDAY! Beautiful Sunday at U.S. Dragstrip Thirty just south of the tarpits! Thrill to the unholy smells and sounds and sight-gags as Captain O-blivion two-time cracked vertebrae champion heading for a head-on collision in his plutonium charged heavy-water under glass thresher goes against Free Bubba Free B. in his multi-national banana consortium funny car! PLUS! Demolition derby! You'll want to be there when the lights go out! PLUS! Hundreds of prize doors! PLUS! Chapped lips! PLUS! Blood-mad brahma bulls released every few seconds in the seating areas to stampede crazily through the stands! DON'T YOU DARE BE THERE! MISS IT! MISS IT! SUNDAY! SUNDAY! SUNDAY! (*Pause. Cool, calm, very liberal underground FM.*) And now, this week's interview with a Woman in the streets . . . Screaming Annie, dressed in ribbons. (*Phone rings, rings again. Flicks switches. Hungry Mother jumps at it.*) Free Lance?

(*Janis's voice live over PA—thick and drowsy.*)

JANIS: Mother, this is me.

HUNGRY MOTHER: How are you?

JANIS: Alright . . . I wanted to say thank you . . .

HUNGRY MOTHER: For what? You sound sort of—

JANIS: Mother . . . ah . . . I just . . . just wanted, just want you—I just, Mother—we on the air?

HUNGRY MOTHER: Yeah, you want me to take us off?

JANIS: Won't be necessary . . . Mother, I'm sorry.

(*Perhaps there is a sound, something falling, a hard surface. Perhaps not. We no longer hear Janis's drowsy breathing over the PA, but the line is still open.*)

HUNGRY MOTHER: For what? (*He freezes.*)

(*Lights change.*)

LOUD SPEAKER: Live Flashback! Live! From the Hotel Abyss! The Flophouse of Stalinism! The Very First Broadcast! Hungry Mother—In The Beginning!

(*Studio illuminated. A tres haute couture Free Lance strikes a pose. Hungry Mother's taped voice comes over the PA:*)

HUNGRY MOTHER: (*On tape.*) A warm warm welcome to WTWI call letters, and to the station for which they stand.

(Hungry Mother breaks freeze and goes to mike. They are both younger, fresher.)

HUNGRY MOTHER: Dressed to kill. To a T. To the teeth. As she parades up and down in front of our microphone—*(She does, flashing a barracuda grin on every turn.)* isn't she lovely? Isn't she wonderful, ladies and gentlemen? Wrapped from head to toe in a delicious apricot leather.

FREE LANCE: *(Laughs.)* Bastard.

HUNGRY MOTHER: Yes, just a vision of fruit loveliness. This is the Hungry Mother, at WTWI, a nouveau station with a nouveau view, on what we hope to be the first of many many twilight broadcasts with you. And on our maiden broadcast we have a maiden broad—

FREE LANCE: Vaudeville's dead, sweetie.

HUNGRY MOTHER: Here in our fruit lovely studios. With us today—Polish Vodka! One of the highest-paid, uh, what exactly is it you do, dear?

FREE LANCE: Make it up, baby.

HUNGRY MOTHER: Right. And for our inaugural broadcast we're going to feature something that's uniquely suited to the very special medium of radio: a fashion show. That's right. Ought to give you some idea of what you're up against here at WTWI. So, let's shove off. The First Annual WTWI Twilight Fashions Show. Isn't she lovely? A vision. Simply a vision. Pol Vod is so—well, slender—no, thin . . . cadaverous, really . . . poking ribs, hollow cheeks . . . a dream, really—slight potbelly, haunted eyes, leather boots, and all the rest of it. Wearing a lovely barbed wire pendant, and modelling for us that sensational new black lip glass. So positively sado-masch, wouldn't you say? Deco-deco, innit? If I were to coin it, I'd call it—*Dachau Chic.* How's that strike you, darling?

FREE LANCE: Perf, Mother. Just perf.

HUNGRY MOTHER: Dachau Chic, indeed. Absolutely stunning. And now Polish Vodka is going to do something very *kinetic*, demonstrating the amazing glide and flow, warp and woof woof of apricot leather, aren't you darling? Yes, she's sweeping up and down in front of our microphone—*(In fact, she is standing very still now, watching him.)* whew. What a woman. Sheer Poetry, pretty as a picture. What a woman, lovely, lovely. What? What's she doing now? Ladies and gentle—*(Hushed.)* Oh, I wish you could see this. She's—dare I describe it? Who dat who say who dat? She's—taking *off* that scrumptious apricot leather—*strip* by scrumptious *strip.* She's—*peeling off!* Oh, my, oh God, oh gracious! Oh so fine! Backfield in motion! Peel me, baby, peel me off! Oh, my, oh . . . what . . . breasts, what—what *dugs!* . . . and—and now . . . she's doing something perfectly . . . *indescribable* . . . with a silk handkerchief . . . oh . . . my . . . I ONLY WISH I COULD DESCRIBE IT TO YOU FULLY! WORDS FAIL ME! OH! OH! OH! . . . oh. *(Pause.)* Whew. Oh my. Thank you, ducks. Worked me into a veritable lather. Thanks so much.

FREE LANCE: (*Dryly.*) Not at all.

HUNGRY MOTHER: Really . . . stunning. No other word will do. State of the art striptease.

FREE LANCE: My pleasure. Avec plaisir.

HUNGRY MOTHER: No, no mine. How d'you feel?

FREE LANCE: A bit chilly.

HUNGRY MOTHER: I don't wonder. Feel free to cover up. I hope that was as good for you as it was for me. Do you have something beautiful for us? Song and dance? A bit of the old soft foot? Why don't you just *whip* something up?

FREE LANCE: Oh, yes, I've got something for you. I've come prepared. I'd like to do for you now at this time—my impresion of a JAP.

(*Slight pause.*)

HUNGRY MOTHER: I beg your pardon.

FREE LANCE: Jewish American Princess.

HUNGRY MOTHER: Oh . . . sounds *fun.*

FREE LANCE: Well . . . here goes. (*As she speaks—nasal Long Island accent—she sinuously removes her clothes. Her speech, harsh and sharp, absolutely counterpoint to her sexy elegant movement. Hungry Mother watches the strip, amazed.*) I just you know been hanging out, you know? You know what I mean? I got these like you know *problems* on my head, you know—I mean it's so off-putting. And if I could just iron 'em out you know, don't you know, it would be *smooth sailing*, no problem, I'm telling you. But it's anything but easy. It has to do with this relationship, and it's so heavy. It's like, you know, such a *hassle.* Who am I to know where it's going? I swear to God I just don't understand men for the rest of my natural life. I mean, it is so *shitty.* It's shitty being with him. It's shitty being without him. I mean, he is such a fuck. You know? I tell him, I say to him, you are such a fuck. I mean, it is trauma time again . . . Am I making sense? (*She finishes the strip perfectly timed on the last word, dressed only in long leather boots.*)

HUNGRY MOTHER: Very convincing.

FREE LANCE: Felt good.

HUNGRY MOTHER: I'm not a Jewish American Princess, but I found it as offensive as the next person.

FREE LANCE: I thought you'd like it. (*Slight pause.*) Kiss my vagina.

(*Slight pause.*)

HUNGRY MOTHER: Meshuga. I don't think I can do that on the air.

FREE LANCE: Why not? You're such a fuck. Oh, Mother, kiss my vagina.

(*Slight pause.*)

HUNGRY MOTHER: Extend my metaphor . . . Kiss my vagina, extend my metaphor. . . . Listening audience, the next sound you will hear—will be—me and Pol Vod—playing chess.

(*Lights change. Free Lance fades. Studio illuminated. Hungry Mother stares at the phone in his hand. A loud, empty drone . . . He drops it. Grabs his coat, walks into the street. It's dark and cold. The Derelict approaches.*)

DERELICT (CHARLIE SAMOA): Hey, man. I almost made my trap. Just about got it, just about got it made. Just four cents short. I know you got a nickle. It's cold. Come on, man, I ast you before. *Nice.*
HUNGRY MOTHER: Okay.

(*Hungry Mother hands the Derelict a coin; he gives Hungry Mother one in return.*)

DERELICT (CHARLIE SAMOA): Here, man. Change.
HUNGRY MOTHER: Honest man.
DERELICT (CHARLIE SAMOA): Apricot brandy. Jesus in a bottle.

(*The Derelict scuttles off into the dark. The Pimp and The Prostitute appear on the edges of the light.*)

PROSTITUTE (JOHNNIE SUCROSE): Hey, John. Looking for something?
HUNGRY MOTHER: Pay phone.
PIMP (JIMMY SHILLELAGH): Not on this block.
PROSTITUTE (JOHNNIE SUCROSE): Lonely, honey? Party?

(*The Derelict (Charlie Samoa) comes back around the corner, a bottle in a paper bag.*)

DERELICT (CHARLIE SAMOA): Care for a choke?
HUNGRY MOTHER: No thanks.

(*The Derelict hits Hungry Mother across the face with the bottle. He falls to his knees. Blood.*)

DERELICT (CHARLIE SAMOA): How 'bout now?
HUNGRY MOTHER: Stuff it.

(*The Derelict walks around Hungry Mother, stops, sighs.*)

DERELICT (CHARLIE SAMOA): Hungry Momma. Hungry Momma. The real item.
HUNGRY MOTHER: Charlie Samoa.

(Slight pause.)

CHARLIE SAMOA: Acute.

HUNGRY MOTHER: Cholly. Watchoo doin' on the street, Cholly?

CHARLIE SAMOA: I beat the rap, Mom.

HUNGRY MOTHER: Congratulations.

CHARLIE SAMOA: I knew you'd be happy for me.

HUNGRY MOTHER: Nobody loves you like your Mother, Cholly. Where's your pals. Johnnie Suc. Jimmy Shill.

CHARLIE SAMOA: At home.

(Jimmy Shillelagh strikes a match, illuminating the darkness. Charlie laughs.)

CHARLIE SAMOA: Tuning up their fingers.

(Hungry Mother glances at Johnnie and Jimmy.)

HUNGRY MOTHER: Okay, Cholly Sam, I'm mugged. Consider me mugged. Take it all. Spectacles, testicles, wallet, and wings.

CHARLIE SAMOA: *(Half grins.)* Sssssssssss.

HUNGRY MOTHER: C'mon, Cholly Sam! Do your number! Run it down! Dissemble!

(Slight pause.)

CHARLIE SAMOA: Dissemble. Shit . . . Big Ma-moo, ain't you something? Talk about barbarians, shit like that. You sound just like a boo-jwa-zee. You know that?

HUNGRY MOTHER: Where'd you learn that word?

CHARLIE SAMOA: What word? Bar-barian?

HUNGRY MOTHER: Bourgeoisie.

CHARLIE SAMOA: CC. C'mon, Mom, lighten up. Get rid of that boojwa snide. I been to CC. We all been to CC. All God's chillun been to City College . . . *(Laughs.)* Which accounts for dem rising expectations. *(He begins to stalk Hungry Mother.)* Expectations which can in no way be satisfied. Now or ever.

(Hungry Mother begins speaking very rapidly, as if to fend him off with words.)

HUNGRY MOTHER: Tell me, as a member of the affected class, do you believe there is a deliberate, that is to say conscious effort on the part of the authorities, if you will, the powers that be, or if you prefer the money men, the movers and shakers, the high rolling high rise boys, the fat cats, the leopard-coat ladies—(*Jimmy and Johnnie join in the stalk, snarling; Hungry Mother falters, but goes on:*)—to, uh, u, cut back, uh, basic social services, restrict access to education, lower the already abysmal standard of living and further degrade the quality of life for the poor, in a cynical calculated attempt to discourage democratic tendencies, stifle aspirations, slay rising expectations, and narcoticize anger, in order to escape culpability and social conflagration?

CHARLIE SAMOA: Yeah. In a word.

HUNGRY MOTHER: Fat lot of good it did you, learning that word.

CHARLIE SAMOA: (*Laughs.*) Barbarian? No, Mother, it did not do me no good at all. I shoulda known better. Waste of time. Coulda been out on the street. Fulfilling my destiny as a social predator. My folks, you know?

HUNGRY MOTHER: Is there a pay phone around here?

CHARLIE SAMOA: Old folks, you know? They get sappy. All the resins harden up. They didn't cop to the dead end.

HUNGRY MOTHER: (*Cheery radio.*) They never apprehended the dynamics of racial interaction.

CHARLIE SAMOA: Yeah. They never apprehended the *dynamic*. Anybody can talk like you, Mother. You know that? Anybody. Who you wanna call this hour?

HUNGRY MOTHER: Emergency. 911.

CHARLIE SAMOA: Number's been changed. Unlisted. That l'il girl snuffed herself on your show tonight. That your idea?

HUNGRY MOTHER: Fuck off.

CHARLIE SAMOA: Way too late for the SOS. Is that a first?

HUNGRY MOTHER: What do you think?

CHARLIE SAMOA: I think so . . . I think it is. Now, *that's* a record, Mother. Your best show. So far.

HUNGRY MOTHER: My fan club. You guys must be the new bulge in my demographics.

JOHNNY SUCROSE: I told you. We never miss a show.

CHARLIE SAMOA: Bastard. I be all over you like ugly on a gorilla.

JOHNNIE SUCROSE: Like *white* on rice.

(*They laugh. Charlie Samoa is winding a chain around his fist.*)

HUNGRY MOTHER: Is this any way for a fan club to act?

JOHNNIE SUCROSE: I wouldn't give you the sweat off my balls.

JIMMY SHILLELAGH: Mistah Kurtz, Motha, he dead.

(*They mug him, ferociously. As they do, studio lights up: Hoover & The Navajos enter, in their dark glasses, and trash the studio; blue broadcast light in the studio goes out; mugging ends; Charlie, Johnnie, and Jimmy exit, exhilarated; trashing stops, Crazy Joe and*

Freddy exit; Hoover, with great ceremony and delicacy, pulls a white feather from his vest and floats it down upon the wreckage; Hoover smiles cooly and strolls out. Bloodied and shaken, Hungry Mother staggers into the ruined studio.)

HUNGRY MOTHER: Oh, sweet Christ. (*He picks up the feather.*) Got to be— Hoover and the—(*He pulls the dead blue bulb out of the socket and smashes it on the floor.*) Navajos! (*Roots around, finds another blue bulb.*) All right. (*Carefully replaces it. Nothing. He starts to laugh. Flicks switches. Strikes the console, tearing his hands. Laughter becomes sobs, then screams on each blow. Stops, exhausted. The Mook enters. Hungry Mother turns to The Mook and raises his bloody hands.*) My impersonation of Screaming Annie.

THE MOOK: With ribbons.

HUNGRY MOTHER: Agaga.

THE MOOK: I come to get you out, Mother.

HUNGRY MOTHER: Can't.

THE MOOK: Why?

HUNGRY MOTHER: I'm . . . *estranged.*

THE MOOK: Anomie?

HUNGRY MOTHER: (*Looks up at him.*) You been to CC too. Cholly Sam's right. Anybody can talk like me. Yeah. Anomie. It's *rude* out there.

THE MOOK: Rude.

HUNGRY MOTHER: The weather today, Mook, very rude with streaks of mean. Never underestimate the effects of rudeness on a disintegrating personality.

THE MOOK: A little rude, maybe. Somewhat abrupt. Always a little rude this time of year. Gulf stream. Me, I call it brisk. Crisp collars, sharp lapels.

HUNGRY MOTHER: I lead a life of rudeness.

THE MOOK: Genteel. Always.

HUNGRY MOTHER: Rudeness. Covered with dogshit. Tell you something. Shit doesn't increase arithmetically. It increases geometrically. So, instead of twice as much shit, you got shit squared and shit cubed.

THE MOOK: (*Laughing softly.*) I can dig it. Come on, Mother. Come with me.

HUNGRY MOTHER: Why?

THE MOOK: They gonna bust you.

HUNGRY MOTHER: How you know that?

THE MOOK: I set you up.

(*Pause. Hungry Mother gets to his feet, stumbles around, finds the bean can.*)

HUNGRY MOTHER: Bean?

THE MOOK: Le's go.

HUNGRY MOTHER: Lemme alone. It's been a tough day.

THE MOOK: Le's go baby! I can . . . finesse it for you.

HUNGRY MOTHER: Forget it. No big deal. Been busted before.

THE MOOK: But whatchoo gonna do with yo'mouthpiece shut down? Whatchoo gonna do when you can't run yo' mouth?

HUNGRY MOTHER: Tell you what you can do for me, Mook. Tell you what.
(*Formally.*) Why don't you loan me a dollar or two . . .

THE MOOK: So the dogs won't piss on you?

(*They both laugh.*)

HUNGRY MOTHER: Outstanding. You know the phrase.

THE MOOK: (*Doing a little dance of inspiration.*) C'mon big Mom. Snap back,
baby, snap back! You my second string. The Mook lookin' for you to
follow in his steps. Bounce back, Mom. You can do it. Bounce back!

(*Hungry Mother lies down.*)

THE MOOK: Charp. (*He flips a coin on Hungry Mother's chest.*) There you go,
boy. Knock yo'se'f out.

(*Hungry Mother leaps up and grabs the bowie knife.*)

HUNGRY MOTHER: (*Very quietly.*) What do you say we engage in a little inter-
necine behavior?

THE MOOK: Stay cool, baby. You can hack it.

HUNGRY MOTHER: Let's go to the mat. Just you and me.

THE MOOK: Don't act the honkey. I found Free Lance.

(*This stops Hungry Mother cold. He stares at The Mook for a moment, then throws the
knife into the floor.*)

HUNGRY MOTHER: Where?

THE MOOK: She came in. I took her back.

HUNGRY MOTHER: That's *white* of you.

THE MOOK: Easy. Easy. Don't press your luck.

HUNGRY MOTHER: Sorry . . . She alright?

THE MOOK: Well, you know, Mother, excess sentiment has always been my
tragic flaw. My tragic flaw. She had made a monkey out of me, Mother.
Set a deadly precedent. She had burned the goddamn church. To see the
church burn, Mother, is to realize you *can* burn the church. Powerful
realization. It was incumbent upon me—as a businessman—to provide a
metaphor. An antidote. Powerful one. I cannot abide no more fires . . . Of
course, I realize I was in danger—danger of fulfilling the cliche Free Lance
had constructed for me. So I struggled. I love Free Lance. You know that.

But what could I do? There was just no way home. She had put herself in the box. Deep. So I said to my pretty little self—piss on it. Ever cut yourself on a piece of paper? (*The Mook draws a hand across his throat.*) Linen stationery. Slit. Gush. *Sharp.* Bled blue, bled blue. Black gash. Mouth to mouth. My hands were cold. What bothered me most was fulfilling the cliche. Predestination jive. 'Course, she could have been rescued. By you. Violins up, violins out. Perfect. And let me off the hook. Muffed it, Mother.

HUNGRY MOTHER: I could call you names.

THE MOOK: Charlie Samoa works for me.

(*Hungry Mother stares.*)

HUNGRY MOTHER: Why'd they mug me? Give me a plot point. Something to hang on to.

THE MOOK: Reason? Let go, baby. (*Laughs.*) What if I told you that l'il slit who checked out over your air—that was Charlie's sister. I had to let him have you.

HUNGRY MOTHER: No relation.

THE MOOK: No reason. No reason at all. 'Cause he *felt* like it . . . I *made* you, Mother. Don't you dare forget it. Was The Mook who turned yo' volume up, and nobody else. So's you could be *heard.* So's you could run yo' mouth. Put it out there. On de air. You done good by me. I 'preciate that. Made me a lot of scratch. The bust be here soon. I got to bust my Mother now—but I sure as shit can still save yo' ass.

HUNGRY MOTHER: Pimp. Scag scum. Smack ghoul.

THE MOOK: Tsk. Tsk. Tsk. Feeble. Mighty lame. You shoulda held on to that knife, boy. You ignorant, Mama. Got to teach you all the rules to you own game. (*Tenderly.*) Come with me, Mother. Don't be bitter.

HUNGRY MOTHER: (*Shaking his head.*) The exigencies change.

(*A beat, and then The Mook roars, raucous falsetto laughter.*)

THE MOOK: Keep after them blackisms, boy! You keep after them blackisms, boy! You get there yet! . . . You know, you right, Mom. I be feelin' pimpish to-day! Be feeling pimpish. (*At the door, he turns back.*) Momma—I thought you'd like to know—I got a terrific price for them kids. (*Roars again. Stops.*) Keep after it, boy. You get to be a nigger yet. (*Exits.*)

(*Hungry Mother makes his way to the mike. Flicks switches.* The blue light stays ''off.'' *He doesn't seem to notice.*)

HUNGRY MOTHER: (*Into the mike.*) Test if it dead . . . Give me a try before you pass me by . . . Close enough for ground zero . . . I've got some good phrases from romantic literature in my head. It's too bad . . . This is The Hungry Mother. The Universal Disk Jockey. God's own deejay. Goin' down slow. (*Black.*) Cat's pajamas . . . This is your Hungry Mother talkin' to you! I cannot be slow—that's why I'm so fast! (*Sings an offhand blues.*) Goin' down slow—oh goin' down slow—but at least I am—goin' down—on yoouuu. (*Laid back Top 40*) One of our very very large numbers, I just know you're gonna love this one— an old old stand-bye, a super-monster in its time—an antediluvian smash—Sweet Gash! Oh so sweet! Play it for me just one more time! (*Frenzied Top 40*) Get down! As your audio agitator I strongly advise you to get down! Get Down! Work yourselves into a frenzy with—Screaming Annie! (*A series of gagging screams. Then in the grand manner.*) When men were men and rock and roll was king. Never the twain shall meet. Send a salami to your boy in the army. (*Slight pause.*) Talking heads. Runs on lethargy. Human freedom diminishing, even vanishing. Ruination. (*Mellifluous.*) We'll have the latest up-to-date quotations on—human wreckage futures in a moment—This is your favorite Hungry Mother, illuminating the dark contours of native speech. (*Pause. From this point on, the various radio voices drop away.*) Fuck. Fuck it. Fucked up. Hit you across your fucking mouth. Fuck with me and I'll really fuck you up . . . I try to watch my language, but I'm a victim of history. Or is it eschatology? Verbal inflation is at an all-time high. (*Slight pause.*) First Chinese Baptist Church of the Deaf. (*Slight pause.*) Social engineering. Upward mobility. *Stiletto.* (*Slight pause. A travel agent.*) Vacation in—*steamy*—South Africa! (*Slight pause.*) Say *hungry.* (*Slight pause. Cheery salesman.*) Death Boy, Brown Bomber, White Death, Stallion Stick, Casa Boom, Snow Storm, Allah Supreme, White Noise, Sweet Surrender, Death Wish, Turkish Delight! Any size lot, any cut ratio, buy in bulk and saaaave! If we don't have it, it ain't worth having! If our sauce don't send you, you got no place to go! (*Laughs, then screaming.*) That junk is shit! Shit! Stay 'way. Mother advises you to stay a-way—lay off it all 'cept for Death Wish Smoking Mixture Number 3. After all—why stick when you can blow? (*Slight pause.*) Stick with us. (*Laughs.*) Stick *with* us. Stick with *us.* Stick it. (*Beat.*) Twenty-four hour shooting galleries! (*Slight pause.*) The American Meat Institute presents. Our Lady Of The Cage. A new barbed-wire ballet. With automatic weapons. (*Slight pause.*) Say hungry . . . I'm interested in abused forms. (*Black.*) She not only willing, she *able.* Bevy. Doctor Feelgood. (*Sportscaster.*) Playing hurt. Photo finish. Cut to ribbons . . . That goes without saying. (*Beat.*) Dead on my feet. Dead on my feet. (*Slight pause.*) I pay lip service every chance I get. Flophouse of Stalinism. Two mules and a colored boy. Better a cocksucker than a Communist. (*Pause.*) Down avenues of blue exhaust. (*Pause.*) Voodoo kit. Razor ribbon. Front me 'til Friday. A day late and a dollar short. Tryin' to get over. (*Pause.*)

Spike that beautiful black vein! Spike it! (*Pause.*) Say *hungry*! . . . Born to shoot junk. Strafe me, baby. Strafe me. Up against it. *Aphasia*. All the rage. Hungry. Riff. On the rag. In the name of the father, and of the son, and of the holocaust. World without end. Shit from shortcake. Ecstatic suffering. (*He falters.*) I disremember. (*Slight pause. Trembling:*) Brush fire wars. Bane of my existence. Blue sky *ventures*! (*Top 40 outburst.*) The watchword for today—*hydrogenize slumism*! Bear that in mind. (*Pause.*) Under the gun. (*Pause.*) Under the gun. (*Pause.*) Under the gun. (*Pause.*) When I get back . . . When I get back to The World—(*Lightly.*) I ain't gonna do nothin' . . . but stay black—an' *die*. (*Slight pause.*) I'm *serious*. (*Laughs. Freezes.*)
LOUD SPEAKER: Hungry Mother . . . The Final Image.

(*The blue broadcast light pops "on." After a moment the lights dim and slowly fade. Out. The blue light glows a moment, then extinguishes. Blackout.*)

END

Playwrights' Biographies

Murray Mednick first saw his plays produced in the mid-sixties at Theatre Genesis, one of the best known early off-off Broadway theatres. His many plays, including *The Hawk, The Hunter, The Deer Kill*, have been produced mainly in New York and California theatres. A director as well as writer, Mednick has in the last few years begun a cycle of "Coyote" plays. He is a founder and artistic director of the Padua Hills Playwrights Workshop.

Adrienne Kennedy began her career in the theatre with the powerful *Funnyhouse of a Negro*, which opened in 1964. Since then she has continued to write plays that challenge dramatic form. Her plays include *The Owl Answers, A Lesson in Dead Language, An Evening with Dead Essex*, which have been premiered in several off-Broadway theatres. She teaches at the University of California, Berkeley.

Richard Lees is an award-winning playwright whose work has been produced at the Yale Repertory Theatre, Mark Taper Forum Lab, South Coast Repertory, the Guthrie Theatre, the Empty Space and the Old Globe. His plays include *Out of Synch, Land's End, Ophelia*, and *Murders Rising*. He has also written one novel and several screenplays.

Lee Breuer has been an important figure in the American theatre for at least the last dozen years. A founder of the innovative Mabou Mines, he wrote and directed several of the company's major works, including his own "Animations" series. His *Gospel at Colonus*, a reworking of Sophocles's classic in black gospel version, opened in 1983 to great acclaim at the Brooklyn Academy of Music. *Hajj* marks his first excursion into video and live performance.

Jane Martin is a Louisvillian and a member of the Actors Theatre of Louisville staff. *Talking With . . .* , a collection of several monologues for women, which includes *Rodeo* and *Clear Glass Marbles*, is her first work for the stage.

Eric Overmyer is Literary Manager of Playwrights Horizons and playwright-in-residence at Center Stage, Baltimore. He is the author of several plays.